CREATING THE CULTURE OF REFORM

IN ANTEBELLUM AMERICA

Creating the Culture of Reform in Antebellum America

T. GREGORY GARVEY

The University of Georgia Press

Athens and London

Paperback edition, 2010

© 2006 by The University of Georgia Press

Athens, Georgia 30602

All rights reserved

Designed by Mindy Basinger Hill

Set in Monotype Centaur by BookComp, Inc.

Most University of Georgia Press titles

are available from popular e-book vendors.

Printed digitally

The Library of Congress has cataloged the

hardcover edition of this book as follows:

Garvey, T. Gregory, 1962–

Creating the culture of reform in antebellum America / T. Gregory Garvey.

xii, 263 p. ; 24 cm.

Includes bibliographical references (p. [223]–235) and index.

ISBN-13: 978-0-8203-2685-6 (hardcover : alk. paper)

ISBN-10: 0-8203-2685-2 (hardcover : alk. paper)

1. United States—History—1815–1861.   2. Social reformers—

United States—History—19th century.   3. United

States—Social conditions—To 1865.   I. Title.

E415.7.G26 2006

303.48'4'097309034—dc22   2005014069

Paperback ISBN 978-0-8203-3519-3

British Library Cataloging-in-Publication Data available

FOR KATHLEEN

CONTENTS

ACKNOWLEDGMENTS

Quite a few people made important contributions to this book. The content of individual chapters has been strongly influenced by feedback I received from the members of the Rochester University Social Historian (RUSH) draft group. The members of this group gave careful and thoughtful comments on the introduction and the chapter on Garrison and Douglass. I presented a version of the Grimké-Beecher chapter at a conference of the Society for the History of the Early American Republic (SHEAR) and initiated correspondences that helped me contextualize the chapter. Most important in this regard is the help I received from members of the Emerson Society: Ron Bosco, David Robinson, Barbara Packer, and Len Gougeon, who have been in running dialogue with this project for several years.

Colleagues at SUNY–Brockport have also been instrumental. I am particularly indebted to our former Dean of Letters and Sciences Michael Maggiotto, who helped me arrange a semester leave to work out the relationships of discursive democracy to the extragovernmental organizations that created a culture of reform in antebellum America. Colleen Donaldson was important in enabling me to get funding for research assistance. I am also grateful to colleagues in the Department of English: Mark Anderson, Bob Gemmet, Yuko Matsukawa, and especially Roger Kurtz; and to two chairs, Earl Ingersoll and Elizabeth Hinds. Through their help with the research, Sarah Bendschneider and Zabrina Packard expanded the range of the book and helped me back out of many dead ends. I also want to thank Bernice Graham, Ken Jones, Matt Kilmer, Rob Seguin, and Allison Parker. My friends Olga Zinovieva and Vadim Ptitsyn at the SUNY Center on Russia and the United States in Moscow also generously allowed me to disappear for days at a time to work on revising the manuscript.

This is the second book I have done with the University of Georgia Press, and I want to thank the press for the time they have taken with the process and for recruiting careful and thoughtful readers for both projects. The two readers of this text did much to help me figure out, among other things, important continuity issues in the argument. I am also grateful to Nancy Grayson, Jon Davies, Barbara Wojhoski, and Heather Dubnick, who turned the manuscript into a book.

ABBREVIATIONS

ALB   Lyman Beecher, *Autobiography of Lyman Beecher*, edited by Barbara Cross, 2 vols. Cambridge, Mass.: Harvard University Press, 1961.

AW   Ralph Waldo Emerson, *Emerson's Antislavery Writings*, edited by Len Gougeon and Joel Myerson. New Haven, Conn.: Yale University Press, 1995.

CW   Ralph Waldo Emerson, *Collected Works of Ralph Waldo Emerson*, edited by Alfred R. Ferguson, Jean Ferguson Carr et al., 5 vols. to date. Cambridge, Mass.: Harvard University Press, 1971–.

EE   Catharine E. Beecher, *An Essay on the Education of Female Teachers*. New York: Van Nostrand & Dwight, 1835.

ES   Catharine E. Beecher, *An Essay on Slavery and Abolitionism with Reference to the Duty of American Females*. Philadelphia: Henry Perkins, 1837.

FDP   Frederick Douglass, *The Frederick Douglass Papers*, edited by John Blassingame and John R. McGivigan, 6 vols. New Haven, Conn.: Yale University Press: 1979–92.

JMN   Ralph Waldo Emerson, *The Journals and Miscellaneous Notebooks of Ralph Waldo Emerson*, edited by William H. Gilman et al., 16 vols. Cambridge, Mass.: Harvard University Press, 1960–82.

L   Ralph Waldo Emerson, *The Letters of Ralph Waldo Emerson*, edited by Ralph Rusk and Eleanor Tilton, 10 vols. New York: Columbia University Press, 1939–95.

LCB   Angelina Grimké, *Letters to Catherine E. Beecher, in Reply to an Essay on Slavery and Abolitionism*. Boston: I. Knapp, 1838.

Lib.   William Lloyd Garrison, *The Liberator* (1831–61).

LWFD   Frederick Douglass, *The Life and Writings of Frederick Douglass*, edited by Philip S. Foner, 5 vols. New York: International Publishers, 1950–75.

LWLG   William Lloyd Garrison, *The Letters of William Lloyd Garrison*, edited by Walter M. Merrill and Louis Ruchames, 6 vols. Cambridge, Mass.: Harvard University Press, 1971–81.

MBMF   Frederick Douglass, *My Bondage and My Freedom*, edited by William L. Andrews. 1855; Urbana: University of Illinois Press, 1987.

N   Frederick Douglass, *Narrative of the Life of Frederick Douglass, An American Slave*. 1845; Boston: Bedford Books, 1993.

PY   *Public Years of Sarah and Angelina Grimké, Selected Writings, 1835–1839*, edited by Larry Ceplair. New York: Columbia University Press, 1989.

W   Ralph Waldo Emerson, *The Complete Works of Ralph Waldo Emerson*, edited by E. W. Emerson, Centenary Edition, 12 vols. Boston: Houghton Mifflin, 1903–4.

WEC William Ellery Channing, *The Works of William Ellery Channing, D.D.*, 6 vols. Boston: James Monroe, 1843.

WGL *Letters of Theodore Dwight Weld, Angelina Grimké Weld, and Sarah Grimké, 1822–1844*, edited by Gilbert H. Barnes and Dwight L. Dumond, 2 vols. New York: D. Appleton–Century, 1938.

WLB Lyman Beecher, *The Works of Lyman Beecher*, 2 vols. Boston: John P. Jewett.

WSDW Daniel Webster, *The Writings and Speeches of Daniel Webster*, 18 vols. Boston: Little Brown, 1903.

CREATING THE CULTURE OF REFORM

IN ANTEBELLUM AMERICA

Discursive Democracy
and the Culture of Reform

Antebellum social reform movements, especially antislavery and women's rights, shaped public discourse in ways that still define the manner in which Americans deal with divisive issues. The relationships that these reform movements created not only redefined Americans' understanding of citizenship and equality; they also created a culture of reform through which people debated moral and ethical questions. Paradoxically, as American politics slowly polarized into the regional blocs that signaled secession and civil war, reformers of all ideological persuasions were constructing instruments of public dialogue that would become vital means for addressing the most threatening and divisive questions to face the nation.

The original founders of the culture of reform emerged out of the doctrinal debate that fractured an increasingly pluralistic Protestant church in the late eighteenth century. Just as religious reformers do today, the evangelicals who fostered antebellum revivals responded to what they saw as a fragmented, disordered, and morally bankrupt society by hearkening back to a world of metaphysical order and religious cohesiveness through the rhetoric of "traditional values" grounded in the paternalistic patterns of religious obedience. In the ebb and flow of religious fervor that they represent, revivals in the nineteenth century dramatize the ideological instability of a diverse people struggling to synthesize Protestant religious traditions with the Enlightenment epistemologies that were central to the American Revolution. As the contemporary debate between advocates of creationism and evolutionary science indicates, this tension still runs strong through the culture wars that are one legacy of this first blossoming of the culture of reform. As they mediated tension, conservative and liberal ministers of the antebellum period popularized modes of publicity that were appropriated by advocates outside the boundaries of their churches and served as models for a wide variety of secular reform movements. The antislavery and women's rights movements, though they owe much to the debates of the sectarians, coalesced as discrete movements partly to address tensions within the society that were not being effectively addressed by churches or the state. In terms of the role that the culture of reform has come to play in American democracy, it is important that the procedures and instruments of publicity that defined it were developed outside the boundaries of the government. Indeed, although the reform movements that grew out of this period often seek legislation, their primary goal is to shape and influence public opinion. Legislative action is almost a denouement, the formal institutionalization of a critical change that has already taken place in the society.

The religious debates that stand at the origin of the culture of reform were themselves part of a broad structural change in American society. The growth of religious pluralism as a permanent feature of the American cultural landscape signaled an expansion of the role that free public debate organized by voluntary associations would play in mediating social conflict. During the Unitarian controversy that wracked the standing orders of New England churches, rather than standing as a cohesive body and resolving tension through traditional instruments such as the synod or ecclesiastical trial, clergy in all theological camps developed propaganda campaigns that mimicked the norms of the marketplace and the political realm. This move into the public sphere to mediate a dispute over the interpretation of the Bible was the first step toward the creation of a freestanding culture of reform that would become a permanent feature of American society. It indicates the creation of a forum for public debate outside politics or the market, but one that nonetheless follows the norms of political or commercial advocacy.

Early in his career, for example, Ralph Waldo Emerson complained that reform movements and religious creeds had become indistinguishable parts of an emerging marketplace of religious and moral ideas. In "The Transcendentalist," he writes that "each 'cause,' as it is called—say Abolition, or Temperance, say Calvinism, or Unitarianism—becomes speedily a little shop, where the article . . . is now made up into portable and convenient cakes, and retailed in small quantities to suit purchasers" (*CW* 1:12). What is most revealing here is not Emerson's sense that religion shares traits with lesser institutions, but that he sees abolitionism, temperance, Calvinism, and Unitarianism as relative equals in a single discursive structure that stands in a propagandistic relationship to the general population. It is also less important that Emerson uses an economic metaphor to describe the expansion of the Jacksonian marketplace than that this metaphor describes politically important debates taking place broadly in the public realm, among a heterogeneous community, rather than narrowly, in a traditional institution, among an exclusive group of elite citizens. Emerson is responding to changes that redefined relationships between authoritative and other institutions, and above all, between institutions and the publics that sustain them.

Through chapters on religious reform, the women's rights movement, and the antislavery movement, which comprise the core of this book, I map the emergence of a culture of public debate that has not only enabled Americans continually to mediate deep divisions in the society but also profoundly influenced their understanding of equality and citizenship. In the process, I also describe a set of norms that continue to define the way discussions about reform occur in American society. In that the book is structured around a group of interconnected debates rather than the logical progression of an ideological tradition, *Creating the Culture of Reform in Antebellum America* describes a culture of reform that comprises conservative or reactionary as well as progressive voices. This emphasis on debate is important not only because it represents the context in which women's rights and antislavery emerged as movements but also because conservative activists unquestionably understood themselves as reformers seeking to influence broad trends in American society.

I have chosen to focus on the debates that have left the most lasting structural impact on American civil society. The Unitarian controversy, in my view, is paradigmatic because it articulates the core discursive structure of the culture of reform. The debates between Angelina Grimké and Catharine Beecher over the implications of women seeking civil equality and between William Lloyd Garrison and Frederick Douglass over relationships between race, moral authority, and political participation are central episodes in the emergence of a pluralistic sphere of reform discourse. These two debates did more than give voice to suppressed identities. They demanded a type of public recognition and reciprocity that fundamentally redefined American definitions of equality and citizenship. In the chapter on Emerson's self-reliance, I highlight the issue of public sincerity as a vital symbol of the movement of social mediation into a realm of public discourse. I argue that Emerson, by undertaking self-reliance as a theory of community, extrapolates a model of democratic citizenship grounded not in the procedures of politics but in the culture of reform.

For a variety of reasons, I do not address temperance or communitarian reform, both very influential in the antebellum period and of recurring importance since then. Neither of these movements, however, redefined the structure of public discourse in the way that women's rights or antislavery did. Indeed, Ronald Walters concludes that temperance "was far less threatening to the social order than antislavery, women's rights, and most other antebellum reforms. If anything, it promised to defend that status quo against the forces of dissipation." Steven Mintz reiterates Walters's conclusion, arguing that temperance was the "unifying reform" that linked evangelism to a larger "politics of virtue" but that it did not challenge the structure of the public sphere.[1] Also, though communitarianism is vitally important to understanding antebellum society, it does not represent the most important traditions of modeling utopia. In this book I analyze church communities and Garrison's perfectionist society, which consciously sought to embody earthly utopias even as they actively propagandized. This model of representing utopia, in my view, has made a deeper, more lasting, and more easily recognizable impact on American society than the communitarian experiments of the antebellum period.

Toward the goal of describing the culture of reform as a mode of debate, each of the three central chapters of this book describes a critical conversation in which diverse public intellectuals argued substantive issues and in the process developed new models of public selfhood and terms of democratic dialogue. In addition to describing contests for control over key ideas, these conversations also mark the emergence of a cadre of professional activists and reformers. Even though many of the secular reformers emerged out of religious contexts, they created a set of independent reform associations that were distinct from churches and political parties. Among the reformers, intense personal commitment combined with equally intense ideological difference to create crucible-like sites of public debate in which reformers contested social norms with opponents and colleagues alike. As the inventors of an emerging culture of reform, this founding generation also had to define standards, norms, and conventions to structure the new mode of public dialogue that they were constructing. In debates about the rhetorical conventions that should characterize an ideal public realm, reformers raised vital ethical questions about public sincerity and the legitimization of social norms. Analyzing these questions, especially the question of public sincerity, which in important respects is *the* issue that distinguishes reform rhetoric from the conventions of partisan politics, is also a central task of this book.

The public sphere in which these critical conversations took place was char-acterized by contrasting expectations of sincerity. On one level, in both the emergence of women's rights reform and the early rhetoric of racial equality, publicity implied an honest, progressive process through which civic-minded citizens expressed their interests in order to mediate differences. But on another level, the public sphere implied a realm of verbal coercion and manipulation where private interests and identity groups appropriated the rhetoric of civic idealism as a mode of manipulation rather than conversation.[2] From its very beginnings, the culture of reform has been characterized by conflicting assump-tions about sincerity and insincerity. Regardless of their agendas, the founders of reform movements had to deal with the accusation that they were motivated by partisan self-interest rather than by sincere moral or civic commitment. This tension between sincerity and duplicity functioned more as a condition in which reform discourse was conducted than as a problem that reformers had to over-come. In theoretical terms, sincere communication is a hallmark of recognition, as Charles Taylor calls it, or of reciprocity in John Rawls's variant, and thus is a vital element in the mediation of a pluralistic public discourse.[3]

One way to imagine the emergence of debates about social reform as a culture with identifiable norms is by emphasizing the role of sincerity in motivating activists to create and promote secular reform associations. In this book I look especially at Angelina Grimké, William Lloyd Garrison, and Ralph Waldo Emer-son to exemplify this issue. Grimké and Garrison were people of deep religious faith, but they were also alienated by the unwillingness of churches to place moral integrity over institutional harmony, especially on the issue of slavery. Ironically, as Garrison concluded that the gradualist position of Lyman Beecher and the Congregationalists was not just immoral but was publicized in bad faith, he repudiated Beecherism in order to construct a voice that could represent sincere morality in the public realm. While churches and political parties struggled to maintain credibility as sites of sincere public dialogue, the Garrisonian model of antislavery gained stature as an exemplar of public commitment to moral principle. As the legitimacy of this model of reform through public sincerity grew, it gained converts ranging from Angelina Grimké in the 1830s to Ralph Waldo Emerson in the 1850s.

The question of public sincerity is thus also central to the culture of reform because the debates that nurtured reform permitted a simulation of civil equality for committed individuals who were outside the official public sphere. In addition to the emergence of a permanent culture of reform, the antebellum period saw the first serious challenges to a homogeneously white male public sphere. As Robyn Wiegman, Robert Fanuzzi, and Nancy Isenberg have argued, the homogeneity of citizenship in antebellum America facilitated stability in some respects but also provoked action by disenfranchised groups.[4] As the groups, especially African Americans and women, made self-conscious claims for access to civil discourse, they forced a second restructuring of the public sphere. Though the official public sphere of the citizen remained relatively homogeneous until after the Civil War, the informal public arena, where norms are debated and legitimized, began to change from a homogeneous to a pluralistic structure during the antebellum period. Thus, one of the most important debates in the formation of the culture of reform involved the constellation of issues that mediate access to the public sphere. This constellation was shaped not only by factors such as race and gender but also by tensions among traditional institutions of authority, especially institutions of religious and civil authority. Access to public discourse was also mediated by another set of issues involving the psychological relationship of marginal people to the public sphere. For political outsiders such as white women and black slaves, internalized feelings of inferiority or fear of reprisal for claiming a public presence influenced the way they integrated themselves into public debate. The positionalities that either define a self-reflexive sense of authority or an internalized lack of authority pervade the writing of the people who made the culture of reform a site open to the representation of a plurality of ideologies and identities.

The rhetorical project of facilitating pluralism by claiming equality on the public stage was very different for Angelina Grimké and Frederick Douglass, and this dimension of their lives as reformers reveals much about the subtleties of public authority and the grounds on which noncitizens imagined themselves as equal participants in public discourse. In the debate between Angelina Grimké and Catharine Beecher, for example, the central issue was the implications for femininity of women participating as partisans in divisive political struggles. In their debate, Grimké and Beecher made arguments grounded in religious faith, liberal human rights doctrine, and antebellum domesticity in order to analyze the merits of women's participation in reform associations. While the Grimké-Beecher debate focused on the gender politics of publicity and partisanship, Frederick Douglass's break from William Lloyd Garrison underscores the role that the intersubjective recognition of rhetorical authority played in legitimizing the presence of African American voices in public discourse. In contrast to the ideal of republican citizenship that Garrison largely embraced, an ideal in which status as an independent private citizen gives one birthright access to public discourse, Douglass grounded his claim to equality in the structure of public discourse itself. By Douglass's reasoning, since the legitimization of social norms was rapidly moving into a sphere of public debate, gaining access to that realm of civil mediation represented a means of claiming equality in a reformed, pluralistic public sphere.

Although women's rights emerged most forcefully after the schism over the "woman question" in the antislavery movement, I have chosen to put analysis of the Garrison-Douglass relationship after my analysis of the Grimké-Beecher debate because, of all the reformers I deal with, Douglass most explicitly addressed the relationship between the culture of reform and the political system. In his shift from Christian perfectionism to pro-Constitution political abolitionism, Douglass most fully articulated the ways in which the antebellum culture of reform anticipates later transformations of equality and citizenship. While Angelina Grimké offered a strong justification for recognizing women's right of access to the partisan structures of public discourse, Douglass brought this justification to bear directly on Americans' construction of political citizenship. In his strategic decision to recognize the Constitution, Douglass articulated a model of equality grounded not so much in liberal assumptions about the autonomy and inherent equality of all people as in the relationship between equality and participation in the debates that define public norms.

Though my perspective is probably more Rawlsian than Habermasian, I agree that there is a utopian strain in the emergence of the culture of reform as a discursive structure. This strain runs through the efforts of a wide variety of reformers to imagine a realm of sincere public discourse that functions not just as a site of political mediation but also as a space in which authentic selfhood can be discovered, articulated, and affirmed through reciprocal recognition. Angelina Grimké believed it urgent to claim for women a place in partisan debate because she felt that repressing her impulses represented a kind of personal failure. For Grimké, political speech verified both selfhood and the authenticity of her convictions. As I will argue, William Lloyd Garrison made the public confession of sincerely held convictions essential to his own sense of moral integrity. Even Frederick Douglass could embrace the Constitution and the structure of political coercion that had defined him as a slave because the realm of critical public discourse also allowed him to redefine the nature of civil equality. Despite the framers' unquestionable desire to protect slavery, Douglass saw in the Constitution a coercive power with which to both overcome slavery and instantiate equality by making the Constitution itself the subject of debate in a pluralistic public discourse. In each of these cases, moral commitment and its attendant sense of identity is authenticated not in the private realm of intimate relations but on the public stage through participation in ideological debate.

Publicity, public sincerity, and the moral nature of reform movements were also, of course, vital topics of interest to Ralph Waldo Emerson. In the closing chapter of this book, I bring Emerson's emphasis on sincerity as a necessary element of self-reliance to bear on his argument that the rampant hypocrisy of politicians' rhetoric about slavery threatened the viability of the nation. In doing so, I hope to dramatize the contrast between the conventions of the culture of reform and the political discourse it reacted against. Despite serious reservations about the new class of reformers that had sprung up during his lifetime, Emerson tended to admire reform discourse over political discourse because despite its sensationalism, it was direct, sincere, and honest. By contrast, in the political venues where discussion of slavery was not actively suppressed, it was euphemistic, veiled, or simply dishonest. In *The Impending Crisis*, David M. Potter describes the implications of legislators' displacement of serious discussion of slavery from the institution itself to questions about the problem of the expansion of slavery into the territories. Doctrines created to expand or stifle slavery in the West became "so many converters to be used by men who needed to discuss the slavery question in terms of something other than slavery. In their legal subtleties and constitutional refinements, the doctrines appear today as political circumlocutions, exercises in a kind of constitutional scholasticism designed to concentrate attention upon slavery where it did not exist and to avoid contact with the real issue of slavery in the states." But despite the sleight of hand that suppressed sincere discussion of slavery in the official political realm, Potter paraphrases Thomas Hart Benton to explain the stakes: "Benton characterized two of the doctrines in a figure of speech that illuminated their functional reality and their historical importance: Wilmot's [antislavery] doctrine and Calhoun's [proslavery] doctrine, he said, were like the two blades of a pair of shears: neither blade, by itself, would cut very effectively; but the two together could sever the bonds of Union" (61–62).

As I emphasize in the epilogue, the problem of constructing a dialogue in which all participants not only speak sincerely but also believe that their antagonists are doing so too affects each critical conversation and connects them all to fundamental questions about the conditions of legitimacy for democratic authority. Indeed, the assumption that the political realm was a site of strategic manipulation rather than a locus of sincere dialogue about issues of common concern is a central motivation of transcendentalist social criticism and accounts for much of Emerson's and Thoreau's contempt for politics. The critical voice that Emerson constructed out of the relationship between religion, secular re-form discourse, and his own sense of self as a public intellectual underscores the problem of public sincerity in the 1850s.

By the logic of politicians like Calhoun and Webster, open discussion of slavery would cause the nation to collapse. Hence, they suppressed it whenever possible and obfuscated it when discussion was unavoidable. By their reasoning, the salvation of the Union was contingent on a strategic distortion of the realities of American slavery. But by Emerson's logic such intentional distortion of the public discourse represented a form of suicide both for the nation and for each citizen. It corrupted honest speaking and listening, which he viewed as the lifeblood of self-reliance and the force that permits mutual affirmation of self and community. In the mid 1850s, as the nation increasingly lived at the place where dialogue turned to force with the fugitive slave law and guerilla war on the frontier, Emerson saw the arena of public sincerity becoming smaller and smaller. The disunionist tropes and bitter condemnation of politics that characterize his writing of the late 1850s indicate his shift toward the culture of reform as the last steward of an authentic critical public discourse. Emerson's response to the emergence of the culture of reform thus underscores the relationship of sincere dialogue to the strategic action that pervaded antebellum public discourse. The reputation of the major transcendentalists as figures hostile to social reform is an ironic legacy of their efforts to describe a realm of critical conversation that could avoid the alienating conventions they saw in the political and religious discourses of their day.[5] For Emerson in particular, sincere public discourse, be it in religious, reform, or political settings, was the indispensable ingredient that binds selves and communities into an organic relationship.

Critical Conversations

As a partly theoretical project, my effort to explain the emergence of antebellum reform discourse is grounded in an ambivalent dialogue with the liberal consensus theory that continues to provide many of the metaphors of American public life.

Though now largely eclipsed by pluralist, multicultural, and discursive models of American culture, this tradition of cultural theory remains a vital force, at least in the popular imagination. For the purposes of this book, the idea of a liberal consensus describes an imagined rather than a literal context. For my purpose, the idea of consensus as a form of universal agreement is probably more important than the often contradictory meanings that are attributed to liberalism. Though it works in a paradoxical fashion, the idea of a preexisting liberal consensus influenced and in some ways determined the pluralistic discursive and institutional structures that grew up within it. The assumption that the United States was a progressive nation destined to work its way to a utopian combination of individualism and equality has underpinned a wide variety of contradictory movements. At the end of his book *Moralists and Modernizers*, Steven Mintz integrates the broad scope of antebellum reformers into a single "liberal" tradition. "In the American context," Mintz concludes, "liberal reformers have been those people who believed in universal moral standards, who sought to remove arbitrary barriers that stifled individual responsibility and fulfillment, and who refused to acquiesce to social injustices in the name of laissez-faire economics and the free market" (155). The men and women who organized toward this end "were not merely social critics," Mintz goes on; they were also "modernizers, consolidators, and systematizers" who designed "such social institutions as the modern criminal justice system, the public school system, and the mental health system" (155). Rather than understanding antebellum reform as part of an identifiably liberal tradition, I present it as a structure of debate. Though the idea of liberal progress is important, I hope to underscore the extent to which these reformers created a new sphere of public activism that remains central to the means through which Americans mediate social conflicts. Toward this end, distinctly illiberal forces must stand alongside the modernizers. In the antebellum period, this group of reformers included evangelicals, advocates of domesticity, nativists, colonizationists, even those who sought to expand slavery. In the argument of *Creating the Culture of Reform in Antebellum America*, the liberal consensus model represents both an antagonist and a context in that, on the one hand, it tends to collapse oppositions into a single tradition, and, on the other hand, it enables a broad plurality of reformers to see themselves working toward a millennial consensus. I have kept the consensus theory in the peripheral vision of the following case studies, while focusing more rigorously on the implications of contemporary theories of discursive democracy and the politics of recognition for antebellum reform culture.

In a passage from *The Social Contract* that will remind Americanists of Thomas Jefferson's ideal of agrarian republicanism, Rousseau describes a mythic transition in public discourse that makes vivid the tension between sincerity and distorted self-expression that has characterized theories of democratic public discourse since the eighteenth century. Rousseau imagines a consensus society that consists of independent citizens meeting in the shade of an oak tree: "When we see among the happiest people in the world bands of peasants regulating the affairs of state under an oak tree, and always acting wisely, can we help feeling a certain contempt for the refinements of other nations, which employ so much skill and mastery to make themselves at once illustrious and wretched?" (149). This civility rests on an underlying consensus of values. The oak tree is a site for the articulation of the "general will" in the form of transparent self-expression. Under it, the words of individual "peasants" perfectly express what "everyone already feels." Speakers propose norms that neither need debate nor require reciprocal recognition of competing world-views. The laws "give voice" to a general will that in its universality obviates the value of "intrigues or of eloquence" to mediate the competing interests of ideological pluralism. This example of civil dialogue under the oak tree represents a democracy-in-consensus, a society in which individuality and equality are perfectly harmonized because the society is ideologically homogeneous. In Rousseau's imagination, it marks the mythic origin of the social contract, a prelapsarian place of authenticity and freedom that stands in opposition to a constrained, compromised, and corrupt world of experience.

But in Rousseau's imagination, this mythic utopia lasts only as long as the society is perfectly homogeneous. The fall occurs when a "particular interest" introduces opaque relationships of communication. According to Rousseau, "When particular interests begin to make themselves felt and [factions] begin to exert an influence over the greater society, the common interest becomes corrupted and meets opposition; voting is no longer unanimous; the general will is no longer the will of all; contradictions and disputes arise; and even the best opinion is not allowed to prevail unchallenged."[6] In its original state, the oak tree represents a consensus society, but it does not represent a dialogic society or even a rational society. It only functions because of its absolute transparency. Every member of the society shares the same subconscious desires, so there is no discontinuity between private desire and self-expression. Equally, since there is no difference between personal and communal desire, there is also no difference between self-expression and the general will. With no need to mediate conflicting perceptions of the public good, there is no call for dialogic reason or for mediating the complexities of a pluralistic society. Rousseau's oak tree is a place of perfect transparency, where desire is continuous from unconsciousness to consciousness, and from consciousness to utterance, where it receives unanimous public affirmation.

But in its fallen state, the oak tree begins to represent the complexities and contradictions of actual democratic dialogue. Rousseau presents this fall from consensus in terms not just of selfishness but also of intentional duplicity and public deception: "When the meanest interest impudently flaunts the sacred name of the public good, then the general will is silenced: everyone, animated by secret motives, ceases to speak as a citizen any more than if the state had never existed; and the people enacts in the guise of laws iniquitous decrees which have private interest as their only end."[7] The ideal of transparency that Rousseau imagines bypasses dialogue among diverse value systems because it assumes an underlying consensus among all members of the society. In antebellum America, if any such consensus existed at all, it was disrupted on many levels and grew increasingly strained as the Union began to fray. Nonetheless, the lack of an actual underlying consensus does not negate the mythic ideal that consensus was the destiny of American democracy, a destiny that had to be either constructed as a future utopia or reclaimed by a mythic return to the Rousseauvian oak tree.

On a more practical level, the problem of defining legitimate civil authority in pluralistic or dissensus societies has become central to theories of discursive democracy and to theories of public discourse more generally.[8] In important respects, the long-running debate between liberal and communitarian political philosophers is focused on the implications of pluralism for democratic dialogue. In literary theory, analysis of intersubjective dialogue and plural value orientations has largely displaced the priority of ideas such as authorial intent and direct referentiality. One way in which I intend to contribute to this line of analysis is by arguing that the reform movements of the antebellum period changed the meaning of equality by institutionalizing access to public dialogue as a necessary condition in American definitions of equality. This redefinition of equality shifted the structure of the public sphere away from homogeneity and toward structural pluralism.

The reform organizations that emerged to advocate the justice and practical necessity of a pluralistic public sphere established the structure of nongovernmental voluntary organizations struggling to define public opinion that still exists today. They also made the case that in a liberal society access to public debate is a human right rather than a privilege of citizenship. Along the same line, antebellum models of citizenship—and Emersonian selfhood as a paradigmatic example of it—are best understood as products of immanent dialogues about the structure of public discourse rather than as deracinated philosophical constructs. Ultimately, even though the context for the debates that I analyze is the public sphere, my interest in this study is not the public sphere as a phenomenon but the way publicity, public presence, and public recognition influenced ideals of legitimate authority, equality, and selfhood. By reconstructing critical conversations at the origin of the culture of reform, I have sought to track instabilities in the construction of authority—the terms of its brief and unstable coalescence, its constant momentum toward diffusion, and the implications for selfhood of such instability.

Two analyses of antebellum American culture have helped me bridge the theory-history divide and integrate philosophical models of discursive democracy into the patterns of dissent within liberal consensus that run so strongly in American society. Both Sacvan Bercovitch's 1993 book, *Rites of Assent*, and Nancy Ruttenburg's 1997 work, *Democratic Personality*, situate acts of public self-representation as indispensable rituals that simultaneously define selfhood and make statements in ongoing dialogues about authority and value. On a historical level, Bercovitch's reconstruction of the antebellum American imagination presents consensus as a crucial imaginative force within a specific national history. On a theoretical level, Bercovitchian "rites of assent" anticipate consensus in much the same way that Habermasian communicative acts rely on the consensual assumptions of the ideal speech situation.[9]

In the context of social reform, the quasi-Platonic connection between the assumption that civil society is grounded in consensual assent and actual public acts of radical dissent enabled reformers to sustain a progressive rhetoric that had broad implications for conventions governing public discourse. Nancy Ruttenburg, in case studies as diverse as the Salem witch trials and Herman Melville's *Billy Budd*, describes transgressive public self-representation as an indispensable element of democratic self-consciousness. For my purposes, what is important about Ruttenburg's model of "democratic personality" is that the culture in which it emerged recognized transgression as a legitimate and even necessary mode of democratic self-empowerment. In Ruttenburg's construction, the individual demonstrates autonomy by violating accepted social conventions; these

violations then become topics of public debate in which the ethics and legitimacy of specific transgressions are mediated. In this process, just as transgression
affirms the autonomy of the individual, public tolerance of civil disobedience
continually reaffirms the society's self-recognition as democratic. This ethical
dimension of dissent and its link to a pluralistic public sphere are central to
the ability of early reform movements to organize and remain viable on the
public stage. For Ruttenburg, as for Bercovitch, the transgressive public self-
representations that characterized early reform movements drew on an underlying
faith in utopian consensus that simultaneously affirmed and allowed reform in
the institutions that characterized American society. These two books complicate
Rousseau's simpler model of prerational consensus because they define dissent
not as a corruption of the general will but as a complex affirmation of shared
assumptions about autonomy, publicity, and the type of dialogue that sustains
democratic civil society. In effect, Bercovitch and Ruttenburg redeem acts of dissent by linking them to a utopian consciousness that makes civil disobedience
necessary. In this dialectic, acts of civil disobedience represent statements in a
critical conversation about norms and values that either are or are not oriented
toward the common good.

The intersection of private conviction and public expression in the arguments
that Bercovitch and Ruttenburg make reflects many of the concerns of contemporary theorists of discursive democracy. The most important aspect of this
body of thought for my argument is that it asks us to treat reason as a result
of communicative action.[10] Theories of discursive democracy shift the site of
the intellectual evolution of culture away from the individual consciousness and
resituate it in a realm of intersubjective dialogue. In this context, "reason" ceases
to signify a faculty like sight or hearing that individuals bring to bear on problems
and begins to describe an intersubjective process that unfolds through pluralistic
dialogue. Looking at antebellum reform as a series of debates or dialogues about
the good life rather than as a period of dramatically clashing personalities or
material interests emphasizes the role that norms of communication play in
defining the reform strategies of activists and reformers. Beyond their vanities
and fascinating idiosyncrasies, the diverse reformers who created the culture
of reform were the representative voices of a people debating the necessary
conditions of a rational and humane society.

My effort to analyze the conventions of antebellum reform is significantly
influenced by John Rawls, Jürgen Habermas, and critics of their analyses of

public discourse.[11] Much of my analysis is rooted in Georgia Warnke's idea of "hermeneutic conversation," which integrates Rawlsian and Habermasian thought.[12] The conflict between deeply held assumptions about social order and equality, and the challenges these assumptions faced from reformers' ideals, reflects many of the concerns of contemporary theorists of discursive democracy. In recent thought in this field, four issues are paramount: defining criteria of access to public discourse; theorizing the role of rational public dialogue in legitimizing democratic authority; explaining the ambiguities of integrating equality and pluralism; and situating the image of uncoerced consensus as the ideal of democratic authority.

Jürgen Habermas's formulation of these issues in his early work on the bourgeois public sphere has, of course, produced a vast body of commentary. As a means of sidestepping debate on the merits of Habermasian theory, let me note that the tension Habermas defines between public sincerity as a model of critical discourse and the forces that work to distort it is important to the theoretical framework of this book. This dialectic is dramatized by the contrast between two Habermasian ideals: the ideal speech situation and strategic action. The ideal speech situation represents a model of public reason in which free and equal subjects represent their own interests and debate the merits of interests that other sincere speakers present. In it, dialogue is motivated not by a desire to achieve a specific goal but by the desire to achieve authentic understanding in a conversation free of coercion by forces such as social position or wealth. The ideal speech situation represents Rousseau's oak tree revised to allow for dialogue among a plurality of interests. Further, Habermas treats the ideal speech situation as an assumption rather than as an actual experience. It represents a Platonic ideal that Habermas contends is implicit in every utterance. The ideal of transparent mutual understanding always functions as the assumed ideal of any dialogue. Thus, as Habermas contends, actual conversations "anticipate," "tend toward," or desire to achieve the transparency of the ideal speech situation. This Platonic dimension of Habermas's formulations—the idea that actual communication coexists with a Platonic ideal of perfect mutual understanding—links his theory to the myth of the liberal consensus in American cultural history. Both posit that an imagined utopian end-state is an assumed context for communication and social change. Just as Habermas would argue that every communicative act implicitly expresses a utopian ideal speech situation, every act of reform implicitly articulates some model of utopia or another.

However, the image of perfect "truthfulness," as Habermas tends to call it, co-exists with a form of communication in which the goal of mutual understanding is intentionally subverted to achieve selfish objectives. "Strategic action," the evil twin of the ideal speech situation, describes communicative situations in which one speaker strives to advance a hidden agenda by disguising it as authentic self-representation and sincere communication.[13] This intentional distortion of transparency is important for my effort to analyze the culture of reform because strategic action is a form of hiding within public argumentation. As strategic action disguises practical objectives, it seeks to avoid discursive analysis and authentic legitimization by creating the illusion that practical goals have been evaluated in rational debate.[14] This mode of communication, as Habermas defines it, is an intentional distortion of the presuppositions of the ideal speech situation. Strategic action is a public confidence game in which a speaker relies on his auditors' assumption that conversation is sincere in order to manipulate communication and advance an unstated objective, a hidden agenda. This form of insincere communication, which Rousseau describes as a force that destroys both legitimate authority and the very idea of citizenship, represents a model of dystopia that has always shadowed the progressive goals of discursive democracy. Fear of strategic action as a fundamental and constant threat to the legitimacy of actual democratic dialogue is at the root of the anxieties that James Madison addresses in his discussion of factions in *The Federalist*, number 10, and that Richard Hofstadter describes in *The Paranoid Style in American Politics*. Also, the tradition of seeking conspiracies to explain major political events perfectly exemplifies tension between the assumptions underpinning sincere and strategic paradigms of public speech.

In my use of these two concepts to analyze transformations in reform discourse, sincerity and strategic action coexist in the public arena in which people debate issues of general concern. This is where John Rawls's idea of "overlapping consensus" affects my argument. In *Political Liberalism*, Rawls refines his theory of justice as fairness to accept new complexities of an irreducible but reasonable pluralism. In doing so, Rawls shifts his thought toward the problem of dialogue between speakers with insurmountable ideological differences. As he frames the problem, "political liberalism takes for granted not simply pluralism, but the fact of reasonable pluralism; and beyond this, it supposes that of the main existing reasonable comprehensive doctrines, some are religious." In this environment "the problem of political liberalism is to work out a conception of political justice for a constitutional democratic regime that the plurality of reasonable doctrines—always a feature of the culture of a free democratic regime—might endorse" (xx).

The heart of Rawls's effort to integrate a permanent pluralism into discursive democracy is in the connection between a "reasonable pluralism" that still leaves room for "overlapping consensus." Rawls concludes that a multiplicity of value systems is "itself the outcome of the free exercise of human reason under conditions of liberty," so that pluralism rather than consensus is the end-state of liberal democracy.[15] But this reasonable pluralism still has a foundation in the principle of justice as fairness, and this requires recognition and reciprocity across intellectual boundaries. As an example, Rawls situates the dialogues intended to establish reasonable pluralism among issues central to antebellum reform: "The criterion of reciprocity is normally violated whenever basic liberties are denied. For what reasons can both satisfy the criterion of reciprocity and justify holding some [people] as slaves, or imposing property qualifications on the right to vote, or denying the suffrage to women?"[16] These failures of reciprocal recognition Rawls considers irrational or simply violent and thus outside the boundaries of reasonable pluralism and overlapping consensus.

Despite the mutability of overlapping consensus and the multiplicity of rational pluralism, Rawlsian liberalism remains a perfectionist and even utopian construction of political dialogue. Rather than seeking simply to answer questions of order such as "How is it possible that there may exist over time a stable and just society of free and equal citizens profoundly divided by reasonable religious, philosophical, and moral doctrines?" Rawls develops a theory of progressive pluralism. In his construction of public reason, he imagines a process of evolution that avoids resolving pluralism into utopian consensus in favor of a dialectic of perpetual pluralistic dialogue that incrementally purges forms of inequality and oppression.[17] In this model, the utopian impulse is linked to ongoing pluralistic dialogue rather than to the resolution of pluralism into consensus.

The perfectionist impulses of Rawlsian pluralism work forward through sites of rational and progressive public discourse.[18] The critical public realm in which this dialogue occurs is both the incubator of ideological change and the discursive site where conventional wisdom is tested in order to be reaffirmed or reformed. The extragovernmental character and legitimizing function of critical discourse that both Habermas and Rawls describe in theoretical terms also characterizes the context in which American reformers developed institutions and organs of propaganda. Critical discourse, Habermas argues, originated as a form of aesthetic criticism in which an elite class of intellectuals evaluated the merits of cultural artifacts such as literature and music. This mode of evaluative or critical discourse incrementally colonized politics and economics to create the "bourgeois public sphere."[19] In Habermas's early model, the "critical public" thus defined an exclusive and largely homogeneous group of people who, because of property or tradition, were empowered to participate in the discourse that legitimizes political authority. This definition, of course, also closely resembles the qualifications for enfranchisement and citizenship in the early republic. Yet even in its early exclusiveness, an elite and homogeneous republican citizenship reflects the connection between the context of civic-minded rationality and the dialogic process of legitimizing norms that is the function of critical discourse. Ironically, the very exclusivity of the public sphere in the early republic represented a kind of cockeyed assurance of a rational critical public, even if its exclusivity undermined its claims to democratic legitimacy.

Ideally, studying the process of debate within the narrow and exclusive critical public sphere of the early national period should reveal a kind of golden age of American civil society, a time when disinterested reason and public spirit motivated political correspondence, speeches, and newspaper reportage. As Michael Warner explains in describing the public sphere of Revolutionary America, anonymous political polemics became the definitive form of critical discourse in eighteenth-century America.[20] Anonymity reflected the rationality of critical dialogue because it separated reason from personality and thus, though it still reflected class and education, implied the priority of rational debate over deference to station.

Though Warner at times comes close to discussing Revolutionary-era print culture in ideal terms, other efforts to find examples of discursive reason have led historians such as Michael Schudson and Mary Ryan to conclude that disinterested reason has always been a rare commodity in American civil society. Schudson and Ryan both argue that factional strife and partisan motives characterized political discourse throughout the eighteenth and nineteenth centuries. After analyzing voting patterns in the period leading up to the Lincoln-Douglass debates, Schudson concludes that "mid-nineteenth-century Americans were devoutly attached to political parties" and that "ethnic and religious communities provided the basis for political allegiances and very often were closely connected to the ideological content of political parties."[21] Ryan, in exploring the conditions of women's access to the public realm, comes to a similar conclusion. She writes that the emerging urban public of the mid-nineteenth century "found its social base in amorphous groupings of citizens aggregated according to ethnicity, class, race, pet cause, and party affiliation."[22] In both cases, critical public discourse in America was structured around the advocacy of particular interests rather than around a disinterested desire to promote the common good.

Most recently, Robert Fanuzzi has brought this process full circle by directly connecting the public sphere of Garrisonian antislavery to the ideals of publicity that Warner extrapolates from Habermas and applies to the early republic. "Even as they sought to 'abolitionize' a socially diverse reading public," Fanuzzi argues, "the New England abolitionists hoped to create a deliberately anachronistic public sphere that would be home to unlimited exercise of free speech, the disinterested consideration of the public good, and above all, the resistance [to slavery] of a liberty-loving people." The Garrisonian community, in Fanuzzi's view, consciously modeled itself on an already mythic revolutionary past in order to "mediate between distinct historical eras so that successive visions of the American republic could be brought to bear on each other."[23] Fanuzzi defines the abolitionist public sphere narrowly, largely as the *Liberator*, the black press, and Frederick Douglass's newspapers. He situates the Garrisonian model as an effort to deploy a mythic discursive structure as both a vehicle of social change and an image of utopia in its own right. I agree that Garrison presented his community as a model for utopia, but I also see its roots more in Christian perfectionism than in an Enlightenment progressive narrative. The perfectionist impulse was more important to Garrison than the Enlightenment tradition of rational public dialogue. This distinction is relevant because it shaped Garrison's come-outer philosophy, which, in turn, represented a profound problem in Frederick Douglass's relation to the public sphere.

In the discussions that comprised critical public dialogue in antebellum America, reformers pitted their reasons for reform against the inertia of tradition and the conservatism of entrenched interests. As Nancy Fraser and others have explained, there is an inherent conservatism even in utopian constructions of discursive democracy.[24] But there is also a synchronic dimension to critical public dialogue that facilitates dissident projects. Authoritative institutions almost always work to silence, stigmatize, and suppress supporters of reform and petitions for access by disenfranchised groups. When a radical voice actually

attains publication, however, traditional voices of authority must meet it on
the ground of reason and defend their legitimacy on rational bases. Even if, as
Rawls and Richard Rorty argue, rationality is rooted in actual social practices
and the institutions that facilitate them, critical public dialogue is always a debate
about reasons for accepting one norm or value over another. As Rorty especially
emphasizes, self-interest and disinterested reason are extraordinarily difficult to
separate in these discussions.

In the theoretical models that Habermas and Rawls describe, critical public
discourse excludes strategic action as a distortion of a philosophically valuable
mode of discussion. But the conventions of antebellum reform make it difficult
to use such a narrow definition. In actual debate among reformers, sincerity was
an idealistic goal more than a practical condition. For my purposes, the critical
public realm will have flexible boundaries so that I can describe how sincerity,
institutional contexts, and intentional manipulation intersect in antebellum reform discourse. It is important that I loosen the terms because the strategies of
emerging voices and their impact on norms for participating in critical public
discourse are themselves objects of central interest in this study. Indeed, as they
still are today, charges of insincerity, hypocrisy, or self-interest are inextricable
parts of reform culture. Hence, the following case studies are focused on the
borders of the critical public sphere so that I can analyze arguments for inclusion
that required Americans to revise consensual understandings of publicity and
equality.

Pluralism and the Borders of Legitimacy

Despite growing ethnic and religious pluralism and intensifying sectional identities, antebellum Americans often assumed that the United States would evolve
into a society that was both harmonious and homogeneous. In the discourse of
politicians, ministers, and reformers, it was conventional to represent the will of
the people as a unified and even a quasi-divine force. This sense of a potential
consensus not only helped legitimize civil authority but also emphasized Americans' sense of themselves as a chosen people. Three examples illustrate a variety
of ways in which images of consensus characterized the political imagination
of the antebellum period. George Bancroft, in his 1835 essay "The Office of
the People in Art, Government and Religion," defines a parallel between the
individual's and the society's duty to work toward perfection: "If it is the duty of

the individual to strive after a perfection like the perfection of God, how much more ought a nation to be the image of deity. The common mind is the true Parian marble, fit to be wrought into likeness to a God" (422–23). According to Bancroft, the common mind represents both a national mean, a kind of statistical average, and a collective condition representative of the demos. In this passage, Bancroft extends the ideal of representative selfhood to the nation as a whole. He anticipates its investment with the transcendent authority that will define perfect continuity between the individual and the society. As he describes it, this "duty" is a shared national obligation that represents both a spiritual apotheosis and the perfection of political authority. In drawing these links, he both assumes the presence of a single "common mind" and asserts a social obligation to sculpt this mind into an image of divinity. The singular and plural connotations of "the common mind" create an ambiguity that harmonizes the multiplicities of society into an image of a single individual striving for self-perfection.

The impulse to imagine a consensus society through the metaphor of a single organic self connected to the godhead also pervades Ralph Waldo Emerson's writing. He opens one of his most famous essays, "The American Scholar," with images that represent his attitude toward consensual and pluralistic social structures. "The old fable," Emerson begins, "covers a doctrine ever new and sublime, that there is One Man—present to all particular men only partially or through one faculty; and that you must take the whole society to find the whole man." In contrast to the "fable," where society is represented in an organic, masculine metaphor, the world of experience appears to Emerson like something out of a nightmare. "The state of society," Emerson laments, "is one in which the members have suffered amputation from the trunk, and strut about so many walking monsters—a good finger, a neck, a stomach, an elbow, but never a man" (*CW* 1:53). The images of the "One Man" and of the "walking monsters" are Emerson's contrasting metaphors for the consensual society that he hoped to see America become and the increasingly pluralistic society that he saw around him. Emerson feared that his society was becoming increasingly disconnected from a shared spiritual center that all people could recognize as an expression of their innermost senses of self. At the end of "The American Scholar," Emerson explicitly connects the integration that defines a consensus society to a spiritual apotheosis similar to that which Bancroft asks Americans to sculpt in the common mind. If individuals can achieve autonomy, Emerson concludes, "the dread of man and the love of man shall be a wall of defence and a wreath of joy around all. A nation of men will for the first time exist, because each believes himself inspired by the Divine Soul which also inspires all men" (*CW* 1:70).

In what is likely the most emphatic articulation of the anticipated convergence of consensus with divine authority, Senator (later President) Andrew Johnson spoke of a literal convergence between democracy and divinity. About midway through his 1858 speech advocating passage of the Homestead Bill, Johnson claimed: "I believe man can be elevated; man can become more and more endowed with divinity; and as he does he becomes more God-like in his character and capable of governing himself. Let us go on elevating our people, perfecting our institutions, until democracy shall reach such a point of perfection that we can acclaim with truth that the voice of the people is the voice of God."[25] Even Johnson's use of the singular definite article, "the," to identify the unified aggregate of all voices underscores his assumption that a consensual will underpinned the deepening differences that characterized political discourse on the cusp of the Civil War. After one more presidential election, the very institutions to which he referred in this speech would divide rather than unify the nation. Like Bancroft and Emerson, Johnson envisioned the perfected demos in singular rather than pluralistic terms. Equally important, he defined the perfection of democratic authority through the symbolic emergence of a voice that articulates a consensually unified popular will: *the* voice of *the* people.

Although the debates I analyze in this book describe the pluralization of the public sphere, they occurred within the rhetoric of deeply rooted assumptions about the consensual ends of American democracy. Even Frederick Douglass's bitter speech "What to the Slave Is the Fourth of July?" begins with a hagiographic tribute to the "saving principles" of the founding fathers and ends with a defense of the U.S. Constitution. The reform movements themselves drew strength from these assumptions even as reformers disrupted efforts to argue for an already-existing consensus. During the antebellum period, reformers successfully expanded the franchise to include white males of all economic classes. They also organized movements seeking human rights for slaves and civil rights for women and free blacks.

Though this generation of reformers laid the foundations of a pluralistic public discourse, psychologically they usually understood their work in terms of the myth of consensus. However, in the cases that Frederick Douglass and Angelina Grimké made for enfranchisement and that Catharine Beecher made against it, we can see the beginnings of the identity politics that is central to contemporary pluralism. In their efforts to redefine civil equality to recognize the differences embedded in gender and race, Grimké and Douglass introduced themes that over time would become central to pluralist models of equality. Beyond recognition of an abstract right to civil equality, Grimké and Douglass asked for recognition of particularities of their identities that were not universally valued. Though they vacillated between an abstract model of universal citizenship and a pluralistic model that insisted on the recognition of blackness and femininity, both Grimké and Douglass ultimately insisted not on the elision of difference as a condition of citizenship but on the reciprocal recognition of difference as a structural element of public discourse.[26]

The ideal of a nation moving toward consensus and the unpredictable agendas of the reformers also reflect Americans' anxiety about the legitimization of democratic authority. The presence of dissent in a democratic system not only affirms the autonomy of individuals but also challenges the legitimacy of social norms and institutional sources of authority. Dissent, in effect, reveals not just the contingent but the incomplete nature of majoritarian authority, and it underscores the social boundaries within which democratically established norms can claim to be legitimate.[27] Jacques Lacan's concept of the "lack" is useful in explaining the relationship between dissenters such as abolitionists and women's rights activists and the voice of the majority. In Lacanian terms, the lack of the universal assent that defines Rousseauvian consensus marks an absence that both calls into being desire for a "more perfect union" of diverse value systems and demonstrates the limitations of majoritarian legitimacy.[28] The lack of universal assent in democratic society is related to the idea of consensus in the same way that the desire for meaning in language is related to the idea of the transcendental signified. Each concept defines the theoretical perfection of authority, either political or rhetorical. Each concept also defines a condition that cannot be achieved in practice but is assumed or anticipated by practice. Just as a word in Lacanian theory projects a trace of transcendental significance, the will of the majority in the public discourse of a democracy always projects a trace of the authority of consensus. In American culture, what might be called the legitimacy gap between the will of the majority and its mythic perfection through universal assent is filled by the rhetoric of consensus represented by the quotations from Bancroft, Emerson, and Johnson.

In addition to obfuscating the gap between majority and consensus, however, the rhetoric of consensus actually legitimizes the culture of reform. In his theory of the moral distinctiveness of representative democracy, George Kateb argues that the permanent lack of consensus creates an ethics of political authority rooted in the pluralistic and dialogic process of democratic legitimization. Defining political legitimacy in representative democracies as a "chastened"— in the sense of both purified and humbled—form of authority, Kateb posits that "in a representative democracy, political authority is in essence partial. . . . A part—a party or faction or coalition—is temporarily allowed to stand for the whole. Parts take turns standing for the whole, giving it a temporary moral emphasis or coloration. The very association of authority and partisanship promotes a sense of moral indeterminacy."[29] Since electoral victory represents only the temporary ascendance of one voice among a plurality of representative points of view, any victor's authority is contextualized both by general recognition of his or her ideological bias and by the fact that the people as a whole are factionally divided. Kateb alludes to this diffusion of authority by contrasting it with systems grounded in nondiscursive modes of legitimization: "From the perspective of societies that do not constitute political authority by means of the electoral system, it might seem that political authority does not exist in representative democracies. Or, at the least, that political authority is in a constant state of crisis or always on the verge of dissolution."[30] The apparent instability of partisan authority marks its ebb and flow between officeholders and the sovereign citizens. As elections come and go, the process of legitimizing political authority follows a routine of diffusion and centralization as it is placed in representative voices.

Antebellum Americans lived in a world where a rhetoric of consensus had both religious and civil connotations. This rhetoric allowed leaders of emergent reform movements to see themselves not just as dissenting voices of conscience, but as the spokespeople of the consensus society that was destined to emerge. Ironically, even as it moved the models of equality and citizenship away from homogeneity and toward the reciprocities of pluralism, the culture of reform embodied the lack that distinguished the world of experience from the imagined ideal of consensus. Despite its orientation toward consensus, this millennial rhetoric created metaphors of communal progress that fostered the growth of reform culture and laid the foundations of a public sphere committed to integrating equality and pluralism.

On the other hand, as much as the myth of consensus enabled people of all ideological orientations to understand reform as a progressive mode of critical

conversation, in its appropriation by religious sectarians and political and reform partisans, it also represented the problem of public discourse as strategic
action. In this regard the most important threat that sincere critical discourse
faced during the antebellum period was the appropriation of the rhetoric of
utopian liberty as part of the effort to sustain slavery. Abraham Lincoln, thinking about similarities and contradictions between midcentury antislavery and
anti-immigrant movements, contextualized them in relation to the forces driving toward pluralism: "How can anyone who abhors the oppression of negroes
be in favor of degrading classes of white people? . . . As a nation, we began by
declaring that 'all men are created equal.' Now we practically read it as 'all men
are created equal, except negroes.' When the Know-Nothings get control, it will
read 'all men are created equal, except negroes, foreigners, and Catholics.'"[31]
The danger that Americans would choose to preserve a homogeneous critical
public by instituting a strategic discourse of liberty influenced efforts both to
expand and to curtail organized dissent. Most dramatically, the 1835 gag rule in
the House of Representatives and the tabling of women's rights and antislavery
petitions acknowledged the inability of existing institutions to provide discursive
platforms for the honest discussion of vitally important but divisive issues.

Expanding the Critical Public

If not inherently, then at least in the evolution of the public sphere in the United
States, the legitimacy of norms has been connected to the inclusiveness of the
processes that construct them. Disenfranchised people, by calling attention to the
difference between the egalitarian language of the Declaration of Independence
and the exclusionary practices of the United States, can and have challenged
the legitimacy of a system authorized by the consent of the governed. This
type of challenge, which was leveled in the antebellum period by a variety of
interests, requires that the official public realm either expand to include those
who claim the right to self-representation or reconstitute its legitimacy on a new
foundation.[32] Over time, a pattern of challenge and debate at the borders of the
critical public realm has tended—after long and often brutal struggle—to make
the official public sphere broader and more heterogeneous.

   In this book, the chapters on the Grimké-Beecher debate and on Frederick
Douglass's break from William Lloyd Garrison analyze efforts to expand critical public dialogue by recognizing not only the right of women and African

Americans to speak in public on issues of general concern but also the broader structural changes that allowed the culture of reform to emerge. The history of the expansion of access to public discourse in the United States is the story of repeated efforts to claim a legitimate presence in a critical public sphere that defined universal accessibility as one of its foundational principles. Nonetheless, reform culture constantly abutted this principle against discursive conventions and historical traditions that limited access to public self-representation. These struggles for access have been the source of significant praise as well as important criticism of democratic culture. On the one hand, democracies have been responsive to the calls of marginal groups and minorities for some measure of representation and social power. On the other hand, however, authoritative institutions have also deployed powerful rhetorics that create illusions of equality and permit glib reproduction of patterns of domination. The nuances of combinations of public power, legal protection, and continued discrimination and disempowerment have added important layers to the developing theory of public discourse and the public sphere. Among the most relevant to the project of defining pluralist structures of public discourse is the distinction between "strong" and "weak" publics, or between those whose power is recognized within critical discourse and those whose public self-representations are still focused on the process of self-legitimization as participants in public discourse.[33] Harriet Martineau, writing from England after touring the United States, explains the principle of accessibility in relation to Jacksonian America. "In that self-governing nation," Martineau points out, "all are held to have an equal interest in the principles of its institutions and to be bound in equal duty to watch their workings. Politics are a universal duty. None are exempted from obligation but the unrepresented; and they, in theory, are none."[34] The principle of accessibility is the acid test of democratic critical publicity—if anyone, no matter how lowly, is rebuffed in his or her attempt to participate in public debate, the public sphere is spontaneously privatized. As an unofficial site of dialogue about issues of broad public interest, the realm of critical public discourse is always characterized by openness even if, as is the case in the United States, a rhetoric of consensus and modes of strategic action simultaneously facilitate and distort the integrity of its dialogues and people's freedom to participate in them.

The debates that resulted in universal white male suffrage during the 1820s illustrate the pattern through which the boundaries of the critical public sphere were challenged and redefined. James P. Young summarizes the transition from an elite to a democratic public sphere by noting that "liberalism in its origins is primarily a theory of limited government. If government can be limited by democratic means, well and good, but democracy, in the liberal tradition is often seen as a problem for defenders of constitutional liberties and sometimes as an open threat. Not until the nineteenth century can one find a fully developed democratic theory of liberal politics."[35] The state constitutions that were ratified during the early Federal period mark a transitional phase in this process of integrating liberalism, as a set of philosophical assumptions, and democracy, as a mode of political legitimization. Politicians sought to establish a limited government in which political power would remain in the hands of a small and homogeneous group of property-owning white males. At the same time that the founders sought to ensure political stability by requiring hefty property ownership in order to vote for the upper houses of state legislatures, they also sought to establish democratic legitimacy by making the lower houses of state legislatures representative of the people. Further, during the antebellum period, elections for the U.S. Senate were usually conducted through these exclusive upper houses, using a mode of indirect election that remained legal until passage of the Seventeenth Amendment in 1917. As the nuts-and-bolts institutions of representative democracy were being assembled, the nation's political leaders sought to balance the stability they associated with liberal republicanism against the political legitimacy offered by democracy. One of the key elements in the founders' ideal for a stable republic is embodied in their efforts to restrict the franchise to a homogeneous group of white, property-owning men. The first major popular reform movement aimed to expand the franchise to include white males of all economic classes.

By the end of the 1820s, agitation for an expanded franchise had forced several states to revise their constitutions and extend voting rights to white males who did not own property. At these conventions, Americans as prominent as Daniel Webster continued to favor the restricted franchise of the Federalist constitutions. Supporters of the limited franchise based their position on the long-standing argument that the ownership of property made the citizen economically independent and therefore able to form opinions and cast votes based exclusively on his desire to promote the public good.[36] Speaking at the Massachusetts Constitutional Convention of 1821, Webster drew the connection between the ownership of property and political stability:

The true principle of a free and popular government would seem to be so to construct it as to give all, or at least the great majority, an interest in its preservation. . . . Universal suffrage, for example, could not long exist in a community, where there was great inequality of property. . . . When this class [of propertyless voter] becomes numerous, it grows clamorous. It looks on property as its prey and plunder, and is naturally ready, at all times, for violence and revolution. It would seem, then, the part of political wisdom to found government on property.[37]

The core of Webster's argument is not that universal suffrage could not exist with a great "inequality of property," but that "inequality of property" could not exist long under universal suffrage. Webster's underlying fear was that extending the franchise would lead to class war and allow the base desires of the poor to destabilize the society.

In contrast to the slippery-slope-to-chaos arguments of those who favored property requirements for the franchise, the proponents of universal white male suffrage went right to the problem of legitimacy. Advocates of an expanded franchise extended the principle of universality from the quasi-official realm of verbal dissent—a realm protected by traditions of free speech and often by explicit provisions of the existing state constitutions—to the realm of official public enfranchisement, symbolized by the right to vote. At the Virginia franchise-reform convention, no less a figure than John Marshall declared, on behalf of the nonfreeholders of Richmond, that Americans had always been taught "that all power is vested in, and derived from the people; not the freeholders: that the majority of the community [have] . . . the political right of creating and remoulding at will, their civil institutions."[38] An even more eloquent argument for the extension of the suffrage came from P. R. Livingston of New York, who directly rebutted the position of Webster and like-minded defenders of the privilege of property. Livingston asserted that reason and good sense depend neither on economic independence nor on property: "If the title to land contributed to the elevation of the mind, or if it gave stability to independence, or added wisdom to virtue, there might be good reason for proportioning the right of suffrage to the acres of soil. But experience has shown that property forms not the scale of worth, and that character does not spring from the ground."[39] This statement eloquently and somehow poignantly casts a theoretical argument in pragmatic terms. The implication is that a restricted franchise, though a violation of democratic principles, might be sufferable if it produced fair and just government. But since it does not, the "right of suffrage" should at least be true to the principles of democratic legitimacy.

By the time Andrew Jackson became president in 1829, this debate was largely finished, and most states had instituted universal white-male suffrage. The reform of franchise laws in the early nineteenth century resulted in a redefinition of the requirements for stature as an "official" member of the public sphere. But as the tone of Marshall's statement indicates, the extension of the franchise had occurred not as a uniform march toward greater inclusivity but as an arduous progression from a classically republican to a liberal democratic model of political culture. Such expansions of the public sphere would continue to move, as they had prior to the emergence of Jacksonian democracy, haltingly and unevenly. The effort to restrict the franchise represents an attempt to keep political power vested in a distinct and homogeneous set of voices. Against these efforts to maintain homogeneity at the expense of democratic legitimacy, the campaign to expand the franchise represents the principle of universality in action. By redefining the economics of enfranchisement, this early reform movement made the public sphere more pluralistic and anticipated a pattern in which African American men, women of all races, and citizens between the ages of eighteen and twenty-one years would conduct their own campaigns to reshape the ranks of the fully enfranchised citizenry.

Even though debates over the franchise were central to the political values of antebellum culture, the move toward universal white male suffrage is somewhat unusual because it sought explicitly to transform the political structure. The expansion of the franchise demonstrates both the activity of a critical public and the impact of the principle of universality on the boundaries of the official public realm. By contrast, the development of the culture of reform that it accompanied occurred largely in informal public realms where self-selected groups worked to influence public opinion.[40]

This focus on changing values reflects the roots that the culture of reform has in religious thought. The basic tactics of reform culture were popularized by ministers who were trying to sustain the hegemony of the Protestant church in a context where a broader set of interests, both religious and secular, were claiming the loyalty of their congregations. The culture of reform took its strongest imprint from the ministers who mediated between longstanding models of authority and new forms of publicity that were redefining relationships between ministers and congregations. The seemingly arcane debates between

orthodox and liberal ministers that are the focus of the first chapter are important partly because they reveal foundational assumptions about authority that
are still apparent in contemporary society, especially in the ways that evangelicals
understand the demands of their faith. But for my purpose, the debates within
the New England clergy are most important because they are paradigmatic.
In these debates ministers not only invented and honed the media that other
reformers would make central to freestanding secular reform movements; they
also faced the ethical and rhetorical problems that went hand in hand with the
expansion of a pluralistic society and the growth of a pluralistic critical public
sphere.

CHAPTER ONE

Religious Pluralism and the Origins of the Culture of Reform

During the three decades between Henry Ware's election to the Hollis Chair of Divinity at Harvard in 1805 and the disestablishment of Congregationalism in Massachusetts, the New England ministry underwent a transformation metaphoric of broader trends toward pluralism in antebellum society. Movements that would restructure the role of the church in American society were pressed forward by theological liberals within the church as well as by members of external religious and secular institutions. Though the New England clergy had a tradition of internal debate dating back to the antinomian controversy of the 1630s, the first third of the nineteenth century is distinctive because it marks the struggles of an increasingly fractured clergy to adapt to a society in which the nature of religious authority was in flux. Unlike their Puritan forebears, the ministers of the early nineteenth century lived in a society where their voices represented one position among a plurality of religious voices and where religion represented a voluntary rather than an official locus of authority. More acutely than any other single group of people, the ministers of New England felt the structural transformation that was redefining public discourse in the nation as a whole.

As Ann Douglas observes in *The Feminization of American Culture*, the disestablishment of New England's Protestant churches serves as an apt symbol for the redefinition of religious authority between the Revolution and the blossoming of secular reform culture in the 1830s (22–28). Arguing that the process that culminated in disestablishment reflects the inability of the Congregationalist Church to maintain its preeminence as a moral authority, Douglas underscores the effect of the shift away from state support on the type of influence that ministers could enforce. In a politically and commercially robust land where the conduits of power could bypass the church and run directly from the warehouses of merchants and manufacturers to the offices of government, Americans, as Douglas puts it, viewed their clergymen as "hesitant promulgators of feminine virtues in an era of militant masculinity, strangers in the promised land" (22). As ministers adjusted to the decentralization of political authority and the disestablishment of religion, they became either conciliatory figures who mediated debate among diverse discourses of authority or illocutionary powerhouses who called the errant back to the faith at evangelical revivals. In either case, the clergy was authorized by its status as a homogenous link to the divine, a connection that allowed it to serve as a legitimizing counterpart to the state.

However, in light of recent analyses of publicity in the United States, especially those by Michael Warner and Nancy Isenberg, the metaphor of privatization/feminization at the heart of Douglas's theory of feminization can be inverted by emphasizing the ministry's new position in critical discourse.[1] Even as disestablishment seemed to make ministers "promulgators of feminine virtues," the process that led to disestablishment also forced the church to fend for itself in the critical public sphere. The privatization of the church resembles commercialization as much as it does feminization; perhaps even more than a marketplace for material goods, it resembles the emergence of a partisan, masculine culture of mass political parties. Disestablishment made religious creeds equal in the eyes of the state, and by severing the connection between the government and religious institutions, New Englanders placed their churches on the same legal and discursive footing as political parties, workingmen's organizations, merchant associations, and reform societies. Though the liberal theological movement that eventually became Unitarianism was in part a manifestation of the feminization of clerical power, "liberal Christianity," by casting the minister in a new role, was also a mode of adapting to tectonic social change. As the shapers of Unitarian thought drifted away from the Congregationalist tradition, they still wished to sustain the moral authority, responsibility, and privilege of their class. But in the course of their endeavor to harmonize competing interests both inside and outside the church, the Unitarians changed the basic principles that justified the authority of the minister. They transformed the minister from the earthly representative of the ultimate authoritative discourse—the word of God as revealed in the Bible—into a kind of philosophical diplomat who mediated between competing epistemological traditions. Liberal clergymen from Ebeneezer Gay through Joseph Stevens Buckminster and Andrews Norton drove the process of integrating theology with secular intellectual disciplines by attempting to reconcile scripture with the scientific and other empirical discourses that had emerged to compete with theology for epistemological authority.[2]

This response on the part of the Unitarians indicates that disestablishment represents more than a dissipation of ministerial authority. It also marks a transition away from a public sphere grounded in the assumption that consensual recognition of a single religious creed will promote social harmony. Disestablishment reflects a personalization and democratization of spirituality, a movement away from institutional contexts toward acts of recognition and consent freely given by the individual.[3] Jürgen Habermas, in his analysis of the origins of modern procedures for legitimizing authority, argues that with the growth of religious pluralism, the individual's freedom to choose a denominational affiliation represents "the first sphere of private autonomy" and thus defines a key moment in the structural transformation of the public sphere.[4] John Rawls identifies the emergence of religious pluralism in the Reformation as the origin of political liberalism.[5] The freedom to choose religious affiliation thus reflects not just a transfer of authority away from the church but also puts the individual in a position of power over the church. Yet rather than seeking to define the theological nuances of, or account for the results of, the long-running debate between conservative and liberal ministers in post-Revolution America, I hope to present this critical conversation as a process of vocational and epistemological adaptation to changing assumptions about legitimate authority. In addition to everything else it discloses, the schism within the standing orders of New England churches reveals the ministry adapting to the fact that their congregations were laying claim to a form of autonomy that forced the ministry to change as a public institution.

One element of the restructuring of the public sphere that both factions of ministers found especially threatening was the ability of political and other secular institutions to restructure the relationship between ministers and congregations. As David Robinson notes, the long critique of Calvinism that followed the Great Awakening set the context for the emergence of a public sphere in which "religion and religious institutions" did not have "complete dominance over the intellectual world."[6] Nathan Hatch, in *The Democratization of American Religion*, emphasizes the importance of broad popular dialogue in redefining the role of the minister and the function of the church. Hatch concludes that "abstractions and generalities about the Second Great Awakening as a conservative force have obscured the egalitarianism powerfully at work in the new nation. As common people became significant actors on the religious scene, there was increasing confusion and angry debate over the purpose and function of the church" (5). As Hatch and Robinson both explain, the Awakening revitalized religious institutions of all sorts and thus betokened a period of rapidly expanding denominational pluralism.

The growth of religious newspapers designed to shape public opinion was central to this process. Mark Noll emphasizes the importance of religious journalism not just in religious debate but in the diversification and transformation of American print culture as a whole. As he notes, it was "evangelical Protestants who drove the great development of popular communication between the Revolution and the Civil War. In that period, evangelicals, whether as individuals or in voluntary societies, literally transformed the ground rules of print."[7] In a broader context, divisions within Congregationalism can be understood partly as competing modes of adapting to a more comprehensive diffusion of religious authority. In the background of debates between orthodox and liberal ministers such as Jedidiah Morse and Joseph Steven Buckminster or Moses Stuart and William Ellery Channing, the heirs of Puritan spirituality were struggling to adapt to the growth of Methodism, Baptism, and Catholicism. This growing pluralism created a sense of urgency that made mass publication a necessary accessory of any religious movement that hoped to prosper in the newly competitive sphere of voluntary religious association. Lyman Beecher met Charles Grandison Finney and sought to temper the "new measures" he had introduced into orthodox evangelism. The American Bible Society and the American Tract Society emerged to carry religious discourse through the same instruments that would carry mass political discourse and expand consumer culture in Jacksonian America. We might adjust Noll's conclusion that evangelicals transformed the ground rules of print to emphasize the importance of *debate* between liberal and orthodox ministers as the engine of transformation. In this transformation, the legitimizing site of religious authority shifted from the sacred sphere, where ministers propounded the comprehensive and seamless will of God, to a realm of public debate, where sects and ministers competed for the loyalty of the faithful.

In an interesting parallel, just as the expansion of the critical public sphere occurred through debate at its margins, a debate between Protestants and Catholics on the nation's geographical margin illustrates the crisis that religious pluralism was creating within New England's mainstream Protestant churches. In 1829 the

Jesuit order of the Catholic Church took over what is now St. Louis University. Partly in response to this event on the frontier, the Congregationalists founded Lane Seminary in Cincinnati and lured Lyman Beecher from his work against the Unitarians in Boston to take up this new challenge on the border between the United States and its territories. Yet, as so often happened, this move not only fueled religious pluralism but also promoted critical conversation and created an incubator for reform culture. When Lyman Beecher and the faculty of Lane Seminary sought to intervene in a debate between gradual and immediate abolitionists in 1834, they divided the college, helped the more liberal Oberlin College develop a constituency, and drove some Lane students to become activists in Garrison's and other immediatist movements.

The inability of the New England clergy to adapt to changing circumstances by closing ranks as they had in earlier conflicts reflects the seriousness of the forces that were reshaping the philosophical assumptions that underpinned faith. Far from presenting a united front, the New England clergy fractured into competing institutions, each of which developed mass media to promote its theology. Equally, the growth of the religious press was important not only because it created an apparatus of publicity that previously did not exist but also because during the Unitarian controversy instruments of mass publicity emerged as an indispensable vehicle of debate among members of a once-cohesive elite.

Both liberal and orthodox ministers recognized that as a dialogic public sphere became increasingly important to the legitimization of authority, a vital source of the minister's authority had become unstable and was vacillating between the pulpit and the pew. The minister's power to define moral values was contingent on the authority of the voice that he projected into the public realm. But the status of that voice hinged on the minister's ability to maintain popular confidence in the validity of the legitimizing assumptions that gave him a claim on people's loyalty.[8] Although the minister of a disestablished church could argue that he represented the unmediated voice of God, as a practical matter he had to compete for individuals' confidence in the same pluralistic context as the representatives of secular institutions. Like secular institutions, churches had to function as self-interested organizations competing for a share in the marketplace of religious faith.[9] The ministry was thus pushed into the masculine and partisan public sphere, where it had to sustain and reproduce itself without even nominal structural support from the state. In his autobiography, Lyman Beecher expresses the sense of panic followed by tough-love gratitude that disestablishment caused in his ministry. He laments disestablishment in Connecticut as "the worst attack [he had] ever met in [his] life," but in retrospect, he reverses himself and reinterprets it as a sort of masculine liberation:

> The injury done to the cause of Christ, as we then supposed, was irreparable. For several days I suffered what no tongue can tell *for the best thing that ever happened to the state of Connecticut.* It cut the churches loose from dependence on state support. It threw them wholly on their own resources and on God.
>
> They say ministers have lost their influence; the fact is, they have gained. By voluntary efforts, societies, missions, and revivals, they exert a deeper influence than they could by queues, and shoe-buckles, and cocked hats, and gold-headed canes. (*ALB* 1:344)

By losing the emblems of traditional authority and being forced into the realm of grassroots organizing, evangelical Christianity became free to participate in critical dialogue with unrestrained zeal. Beecher even identifies core institutions that the evangelicals popularized in the critical public sphere. As Mark Noll and Nathan Hatch explain, the growth of outsider denominations such as the Baptists and the Methodists, along with the expansion of the religious press within Congregationalism, represents the means through which orthodox ministers adapted to the combative realm of critical publicity.[10] Of course, parallel claims can be made for the liberals' adaptation to changing circumstances. By adopting rational religion, theological liberals lost the Calvinist rigor necessary to preach jeremiads as their evangelical counterparts still could do, but by converting the political, economic, and intellectual leaders of Massachusetts to Unitarianism, they achieved a level of public influence that was out of proportion to their small numbers.

The different methods that orthodox and liberal ministers developed between the 1790s and the mid-1830s dramatize different means of adapting to the erosion of assumptions that had underpinned standing orders of churches in American states. While theological liberals incrementally embraced the philosophical assumptions on which the liberal public sphere rested, orthodox ministers worked to sustain a model of authority that remained grounded in conscious submission to God's power as it is represented in the revealed truths of the Bible. As these alternative strategies developed, both factions participated in defining the structure of critical public dialogue and did much to shape the conventions of the culture of reform. In its emphasis on reason and its willingness to accept the authority of scientific and philosophical inquiry, the liberals' dialogic spirituality embodied the structure of reasonable pluralism mediated through critical discourse. Though orthodox ministers rejected the movement toward toleration as a degradation of God's legitimate authority, they shaped critical public discourse by embracing the combative and partisan structure of the public sphere as a means of promoting their own vision of faith.

As the unity of the Congregationalist Church weakened, the formal dissolution of the Standing Order of Massachusetts Churches was not far behind; it came in 1833, when the legislature voted to disestablish Congregationalism as the state's official religion. From that point on, the Congregationalist Church had to compete for members on the same terms as the Baptist, Catholic, Episcopal, Methodist, and other churches that sprang up to challenge the preeminence of Congregationalism in New England. The disestablishment of the church marks the growing pluralism of the public realm, an expansion compounded by the variety of political and economic institutions that were driving the legitimization of authority away from the rituals of tradition and toward debate in the critical public sphere. The emergence of a plurality of competing voices of authority, both religious and secular, forced ministers to change the foundations of their legitimization. In the same way that Max Horkheimer and Theodor W. Adorno describe the emergence of a "culture industry" that undermined the critical function of art, the recruitment and conversion practices of "religious entrepreneurs" mark the emergence of a religion industry that blurred the lines between commerce and faith. This flattening of a previously hierarchical discursive structure, the transition from a public sphere where the minister could assume a superordinate position into one where churches, political parties, and commercial interests all spoke as equals in an integrated forum, underscores the changing structure of the public realm.

In their efforts to deal with the symptoms of transformation, liberal and orthodox Congregationalists were in the forefront of conducting ideological debate through print culture. The conservatives founded the *Connecticut Evangelical Magazine* in 1800 and then the *Missionary Magazine*. These permuted into Jedidiah Morse and Jeremiah Evarts's *Panoplist* in 1805, which merged with the *Missionary Magazine* three years later. In the next generation, major evangelicals founded their own newspapers. Nathaniel Taylor established the *Christian Spectator*. Lyman Beecher founded the *Spirit of the Pilgrims* in Boston in 1828 as a specific effort to provoke theological debate in the stronghold of liberal Christianity. The liberals, despite their anti-evangelical culture, were equally industrious in the realm of print. Between 1800 and 1830, they founded the *Literary Miscellany*, the *Monthly Anthology*, the *Christian Monitor*, the *General Repository and Review*, the *Christian Disciple*, and the *Christian Examiner*. With the *Dial*, Margaret Fuller and Ralph Waldo Emerson sought to extend this dialogue beyond the boundaries of Christian spirituality.

The changing structure of legitimacy that caused disestablishment and pushed the church into critical dialogue also produced these journals as a new vehicle of legitimization. The rapid permutation and combination of the journals express the displacements and tensions, the intellectual risks and hesitations, the zeal of evangelism, and the fear of chaos that accompanied the incorporation of critical discourse as the definitive procedure of legitimization in the Jefferson-Jackson period. The growth of religious journalism represents a print culture "bubble" that set the stage for the antislavery and reform press that grew after 1830. More important, though, this bubble shows the movement of a profound philosophical debate into the realm of critical public dialogue. As Henry May has shown in his study of the Enlightenment in America, Enlightenment rationalism always remained in dialectical tension with a Puritan world-view that related all phenomena to the working of a single, active, determinative God.[11] The debate between the orthodox and the liberal faction, more than the transition from the one to the other, is the vital heuristic for the origin of reform discourse in the antebellum United States. Indeed, one can see the pull-and-tug of the forces at play in the Unitarian controversy even in the dialectical tension that Ralph Waldo Emerson established between a liberalism that draws authority from the rational powers of the self and his more conservative impulse to believe in a single universal spirit that requires perfect submission and obedience.

The Orthodox Imagination and the Problem of Critical Conversation

After the death of Samuel Hopkins's brother Daniel, the erudite liberal minister William Bentley, who presided at the wedding of Nathaniel Hawthorne's parents, remarked in his diary that he thought he had heard Hopkins "boast that he read only the Bible."[12] Bentley went on to criticize Hopkins for a kind of anti-intellectual fastidiousness, noting that "he had no library, no relish for literature, & but little acquaintance with literary men."[13] Ironically, by remaining rigorously biblical, Hopkins asserted an epistemology that dramatizes one of two orthodox responses to the growth of religious pluralism. By closing his mind to all sources of authority other than the Bible, Hopkins retained spiritual purity. He linked his thought as tightly as possible to the text that orthodox divines regarded as the only legitimate source of truth and knowledge. In effect, he asserted a personal discipline that mirrored an ideal of church discipline.

In his narrowness, Reverend Hopkins modeled an imagination that harks back to his Puritan forbears. As Sacvan Bercovitch explains in *Puritan Origins of the American Self*, since truth is revealed in the Bible, and since revelation is immutable and unchanging, the adventure of Christian faith is not to explain the phenomena of the world by inventing scientific or philosophical theories but to reconcile real-world experience and phenomena with the unchanging truths of revelation.[14] In part, this required Hopkins to avoid the temptations of worldly philosophy. The same challenge of reconciling and maintaining the faith that compelled the Puritans to interpret the invisible world through Providence still obtained in Jeffersonian America. But in the post-Revolutionary world, the orthodox imagination was forced to maintain this tradition in a nation that had embraced a model of civil authority rooted in the legitimizing force of public debate and in the idea that autonomous individuals were capable of ordering a just society.

Compounding this philosophical dissonance between civil and religious assumptions, the democratization of religious discourse and its move from a realm of superordinate status into the critical public sphere intensified the challenge of defining orthodoxy as the locus of salvific faith. In an ordination sermon given at Concord in 1828, Rev. James Thompson almost plaintively revealed the dialogic forces against which orthodox ministers had to contend in their effort to maintain their status. Thompson began his sermon by describing the relative authority of religious and secular voices: "What is done here [in the pulpit] transcends in importance and dignity all other concerns of life; that no exchange, no legislature, no cabinet on earth is entrusted with duties that bear the least conceivable proportion in the depth and compass of their interest to those which claim our attention here."[15] Thompson implicitly acknowledged that religious discourse is in competition with the discourses of authority represented by merchants and politicians. Although he did not trivialize the discourses that characterize these other arenas, he unequivocally asserted the superordinate "depth and compass" of the minister's authority. The distinction between divine and secular voices that Thompson made implies a social structure that, while it admits the presence of a plurality of institutions of authority, assumes that the guiding principles of secular institutions should emanate from the pulpit. In structural terms, Thompson sought to place the minister's voice above the critical public sphere as a voice of prescription and judgment.

The way that such a prescriptive model of authority affected the rhetoric of orthodox ministers is apparent in another 1828 ordination sermon, delivered by Horace Chapin at the ordination of Charles Molson. Chapin began with a typical justification of revealed religion: "God has revealed the Gospel, . . . hence it is evident [that] the Gospel can be defined—its meaning is fixed."[16] Ironically, Chapin began his sermon by using the language of rational analysis to pass from the realm of reasoned understanding to that of irrational faith. Though his rhetoric creates the illusion that he is moving through a series of logical deductions, his explanation actually hinges on statements such as "God has revealed the Gospel" or "Christ, its author, is the light of the world." These tropes work their way toward statements that reinforce the hermetic nature of the Gospels: "This brief statement is a proof, that the Gospel is a definite system, or does interpret and define itself." Chapin underscored this unitary mode of interpretation to avoid any hint that the gospel authorizes religious pluralism: "Ministers are not to preach a gospel as being one of many, but the gospel in distinction from all other systems of belief." The minister should "reason out of the scriptures, and not from the feelings, views, and false philosophy of man."[17]

Given the fixed meaning of the Gospels, the minister's purpose was to teach revealed truths in a way that his congregation could understand. The supernatural realities, the realities that are paradoxically the most imminent and the least accessible, deal with a realm that could only be apprehended through the imagination. Thus, the orthodox rhetorician must teach the gospel both as a "revelation of simple facts," as Chapin put it, and as the script of a cosmic struggle between invisible supernatural forces.[18] In a kind of metaphysical paradox, the orthodox rhetorician should give his hearer a sense of the cosmic struggle that can trigger the conversion experience by making the overarching reality of a metaphysical duel between Christ and Satan comprehensible through the senses. Chapin parsed the supernatural struggle, modeling the type of division and subordination that structures his model of spirituality: "This gospel reveals a future world; shows us man as he is, and where he will be in eternity; spreads before us the day 'for which all other days are made,' the decision of the final Judge, and the eternal separation, that takes place between the righteous and the wicked. Thus what is of vast interest to three worlds, and to the sovereign of all, Father, Son, and Holy Ghost, is committed to the herald of salvation."[19] The "herald of salvation," as Chapin described the minister, continually reasserts the worlds of God, Satan, and mortal man for a society where even the terms of this struggle were losing their mystical immanence.

By the 1820s the elements of orthodox faith that served as pathways to the providential realm—miracles, the divinity of Jesus, the mystery of the tripartite God—connoted sectarian debate in a pluralistic religious context as much as they marked divine magnificence and human paltriness. As Chapin and other orthodox ministers saw it, their lapsed colleagues among the Unitarians had humanized religion by minimizing the role that "irrational" faith played in the acceptance of scriptural authority. In literary terms, the liberals undermined religion by turning a fundamentally imaginative experience into a rational one.

The fate of John Codman, which Conrad Wright details in his essay "Institutional Reconstruction in the Unitarian Controversy," dramatizes the problems orthodox ministers faced by treating their pulpits as models of consensus that required submission to orthodox interpretations of scripture.[20] In the Codman case, a minister's insistence on strict doctrinal orthodoxy came into conflict with the doctrinal pluralism of his congregation. In 1808—the year that Andover Seminary was founded to compete with liberal Harvard—the Second Church of Dorchester, Massachusetts, hired a newly ordained minister, John Codman, to replace the minister who had served them since before the Revolutionary War. As Wright explains, in the ordination process the church officers were careful to verify Codman's orthodoxy. The young minister assured the committee: "I think it my duty in the presence of a heart searching God, and of this Church, to declare my firm, unshaken faith in those doctrines, that are sometimes called the doctrines of the reformation, the doctrines of the cross," and, using the accepted euphemism with which orthodox ministers referred to doctrines that the liberals were challenging, in "the peculiar doctrines of the Gospel."[21]

This statement reassured the committee. But to his parishioners' surprise, Codman's ethics caused him to resist exchanging pulpits with liberal ministers on the ground that it would implicitly sanction religious pluralism and even promote the liberal theology that he opposed. In effect, opening his pulpit would make it a cipher of exactly the kind of pluralistic dialogue that threatened the orthodox minister's position as the moral authority for his flock.[22] In a supportive letter that Codman received from Samuel Miller, a professor of theology at Princeton, the ethical stakes of orthodox pastoral philosophy are stated rather neatly. The liberals, Miller asserted, "are not only betrayed by their omissions, but also, by their phraseology and by their theological language; so that, in fact, they seldom enter our pulpits without holding out to our people false grounds of hope."[23] Miller's support for Codman was rooted in the sense of a metaphysical obligation that orthodox ministers speak with one voice and articulate a single coherent doctrine within which the faithful must live. Codman's rigor was not simply bullheadedness; his position was compelled by a philosophical rejection of the idea that a dialogic pulpit has religious legitimacy or spiritual value. Yet despite his principled position, Codman's refusal to exchange with liberals provoked a controversy in which church members attempted to oust him as minister. Two councils were held to arbitrate the conflict. After extended deliberation, neither council was willing to dissolve the connection between Codman and the Second Church of Dorchester. They did, however, admonish him to give liberal ministers access to his pulpit. Codman remained intransigent. In an assertion of traditional relations of power between minister and congregation, he construed his role to be that of a shepherd who is responsible for steering his flock away from potential moral hazards by maintaining church discipline. This meant keeping liberal theological voices out of his pulpit.

In significant respects, Codman's position was supported by the laws of the Commonwealth. Until the Standing Order was dissolved in 1833, ministers received tax revenues as compensation for their service as "public teacher[s] of piety, religion, and morality." Though Codman's actions did not transgress his constitutionally defined role, his reluctance to let liberals preach in his church divided his congregation and actually undermined the kind of submission to authority that he represented. In order to remain cohesive, the community expected its pulpit to represent the plurality of theological views that prevailed in the parish. But to Codman such pluralism was anathema because his role was not to promote social cohesion by reflecting the ideological diversity of his flock and thereby reinforce the autonomous spiritualities of various congregants. On the contrary, it was to define a godly social order by explaining the implications of revealed religion.

The problem, as Codman saw it, was not just that wrong doctrines might be taught from his pulpit but also that his pulpit might be the source of a *multiplicity* of doctrines. Indeed, that members of his congregation could embrace any of a variety of doctrines amplified the danger of facilitating theological pluralism by implicitly recognizing a dialogic pulpit as a legitimate form of Christian ministry. In the end, when the ecclesiastical councils failed to force Codman to change his policy, the liberals had exhausted all means that the church offered them in their quest to gain access to liberal preaching. They then left the church and resolved the conflict according to the more liberal norms of secular institutions. The liberals literally sold their pews to orthodox church members and formed a liberal Third Church of Dorchester.

The outcome of this conflict illustrates the problem that emerged when ministers attempted to enforce consensus even within the boundaries of a single congregation. Codman, of course, could not stem religious liberalism or the expansion of religious pluralism. But he hoped, at least, to sustain his own pulpit as a haven of orthodoxy. Ironically, Codman was victorious, but his victory was pyrrhic. He maintained the integrity of his church, but he preached to a smaller congregation, and his actions divided rather than unified the community. In the end, the crisis was resolved neither by a revalidation of orthodox doctrine nor by a suppression of liberal views, but by moving the conflict from a traditional institutional structure that sought to enforce consensus under the minister's authority to a parallel one that facilitated pluralism. Codman's strategy of maintaining the faith as a haven, as an alternative godly community in a world where religious authority had diffused from a homogeneous center into a cacophonous debate, represents a model of spirituality that stands in opposition to both the movement of legitimization into critical dialogue and to the norms of tolerance that underpin reciprocal recognition.

John Rawls finds it extremely difficult to harmonize the type of compulsory unanimity that Codman enforced with the underlying assumptions of public reason. In his final book, *The Law of Peoples*, Rawls concludes that "a feature of public reasoning, then, is that it proceeds entirely within a political conception of justice." Even though public discussions allow people to introduce "at any time our comprehensive doctrine, religious or nonreligious," it also requires that "we give properly public reasons to support the principles and policies our comprehensive doctrine is said to support" (144). The model of legitimate authority that Codman represents stands in a kind of schizophrenic relationship to the expansion of critical public discourse. At least by Rawls's logic, the desire for hegemony that Codman asserted within his church is incompatible with liberal society. He goes so far as to say that "while no one is expected to put his or her religious or nonreligious doctrine in danger, we must each give up forever the hope of changing the constitution so as to establish our religion's hegemony" (150).

The problem with the pluralism of Rawlsian public reason, as the orthodox faction would have seen it, is exactly the same problem that they saw in Unitarianism. By arguing that a religious doctrine must be legitimized discursively through "properly public reasons," Rawls and the Unitarians submit doctrine to a test other than faith. Rawls can harmonize the orthodox religious and discursive models of authority only by treating tolerance as a test of faith. In endorsing a pluralistic society ordered by discursive democracy rather than by faith, the believers in "a religious doctrine may say that such are the limits God sets to our liberty."[24] By "limits" Rawls means "liberty of conscience and toleration," which would permit evangelism but not the religious control of civil society. In most respects, the evangelical ministers who developed the media of reform culture accepted Rawls's terms. They saw their country as a place in need of missionaries who could save a misguided people and lead them back to the true church.

Orthodoxy and Publicity

While the models of orthodoxy represented by Daniel Hopkins and John Codman exemplify modes of remaining pure in a world that was falling away from the true faith, a group of ministers who would ultimately be more influential in shaping the culture of reform went to the vanguard of theological dispute. As they did so, their efforts to reinvigorate orthodox Christianity made structural contributions to the process of liberalization that they were actually working to counteract. By bringing the debate to the bar of public opinion, propagandists such as Jedidiah Morse and revivalists such as Lyman Beecher implicitly recognized the authority of lay people to arbitrate disputes among ministers. However, orthodox Congregationalists were stuck in a dilemma: they could strive to remain above the fray and embody an uncompromising, Codman-like orthodoxy, or, by becoming propagandists and aggressively defending their faith, they could integrate themselves into the very structure of publicity that was undermining orthodox hegemony and promoting discursive democracy. The roles that Jedidiah Morse and Lyman Beecher played in provoking the formation of the American Unitarian Association in 1825 is a macrocosmic version of the role Codman played in founding the Third Church of Dorchester.

Though the spiritual come-outerism that Daniel Hopkins described contrasts sharply with the propaganda machines developed by Jedidiah Morse and Lyman Beecher, the epistemological assumptions behind these two responses to changing norms are very similar. In attempting to organize a "society for the suppression of vice and the promotion of good morals" in 1812, Beecher wrote to Asahel Hooker: "The time has come when it becomes every friend of this state to wake up and exert his whole influence to save it from innovation and democracy"; Beecher warned, "If we stand idle, we lose our habits and institutions piecemeal, as fast as innovation and ambition shall dare to urge on the work" (*ALB* 1:257–58). For Beecher "innovation" denoted the influence of rationalism on church doctrine and "democracy" denoted the shifting of authority away from ministers and toward congregations. Both Codman's orthodoxy and Beecher's evangelism were motivated by the desire to sustain a model of truth that was inherently at odds with the pluralistic assumptions and egalitarian impulses of democratic political debate and the dialogic procedures of modern epistemology.

Jedidiah Morse and Lyman Beecher thus represent an important irony in the religious history of the United States. In contrast to Codman, Morse and Beecher threw themselves wholeheartedly into the debates between orthodox and liberal ministers. In the emergence of the culture of reform, their methods are more important than their theological positions because they created the media infrastructure that made theological debate the template for the secular reform movements that grew out of them. In the first phase of the Unitarian controversy, Jedidiah Morse developed a propaganda machine extensive enough for one historian to define him as the first "evangelical commercialist."[25]

Though Morse is probably best known for his role in opposing the growth of liberal Christianity at Harvard, for him that transition represented only the most insidious manifestation of trends that were threatening to undermine the virtue of the society as a whole. In a 1798 sermon titled "The Present Dangers, and Consequent Duties of the Citizens of the United States of America," Morse articulated the dynamics of anxiety that accompanied the democratization of public discourse. This sermon, part of the backlash against Thomas Paine's *Age of Reason* (1794), personifies rationalism as a conspiracy of the Bavarian Illuminati that was intent on infiltrating the United States.[26] Morse's most recent biographer, Richard J. Moss, connects the fears that motivated the sermon directly to the rise of the Jeffersonian Democrats. Moss argues that "Morse simply could not deal with the idea of a political party challenging the party in power, [so] . . .

he transformed the political faction led by Jefferson into 'Jacobins.'"[27] For the scriptural text of "The Present Dangers," Morse took a passage from the ninth psalm that enabled him both to argue that the foundation of American society was threatened and to sound a call to arms: "If the foundations be destroyed, what can the righteous do?" In his view, the founding principles of the republic were being sapped by a "new philosophy" that was threatening to undermine the Federalist structures of authority. The challenges Morse described define a series of threats to order and an incremental movement toward chaos. He summarized the likely outcome of liberal philosophical principles. Among their fruits could be reckoned:

> our unhappy and threatening political divisions; the unceasing abuse of our wise and faithful rulers; the virulent opposition to some of the laws of our country, and the measures of the Supreme Executive; the Pennsylvania insurrection; the industrious circulation of baneful and corrupting books, and the consequent wonderful spread of infidelity, impiety and immorality; the arts made use of to revive ancient prejudices and cherish party spirit by concealing or disguising the truth and propagating falsehoods; and lastly, the apparently systematic endeavours made to destroy, not only the influence and support, but the official existence of the Clergy.[28]

Though for Morse all these factors indicated a threat to the foundations of the society, he was especially anxious about challenges to the minister's authority. Ministers, as the guardians of legitimate truth and authentic knowledge, represented an authority that required obedience. In their submission to divine guidance and the revealed truths of the Bible, orthodox ministers modeled legitimate relations for the society as a whole. Just as ministers submitted to divine authority, in a godly world congregations would submit to ministerial authority.

To respond to the threat, though, Morse did not encourage his fellow citizens to ferret out the conspirators and reaffirm traditional relations between state, church, and people; rather, he stressed the importance of counteracting humanist and rationalist thought. At times, Morse echoed Cotton Mather: "Our pious ancestors saw the hand of GOD in everything, more especially in all signal events, such as pestilence, famine, earthquakes, war, and other calamities. But it has become fashionable of late, to ascribe these things to the uncontrolled operations of *natural* causes, and to keep out of view the Divine agency." By shifting the locus of intellectual explanation for the phenomenal world from a providential to a rationalist context, liberal philosophy not only emphasized human rational power but also disrupted the communal recognition of an omnipotence that commands submission. This original disruption in the fabric of legitimate authority threatened to cause chaos in the United States: "These same principles, my brethren, which *have produced incalculable mischief and misery in other countries*, are deeply rooted and widely spreading through our own; and are preparing the way for the armies which have desolated Europe."[29]

The path of influence that Morse charted for the new philosophy leads from newspapers through misguided members of the clergy to dominion over public opinion. "In some of our news-papers," Morse lamented, "which are read by too many with more avidity, and more faith than the Holy Bible, [ministers] are continually reproached and vilified; and every low artifice is used to lessen their influence and usefulness." This evil influence had expanded to infect the clergy and seduced some ministers to work against the faith. Morse thus castigated liberal ministers: "Little are these good people aware . . . that, blinded by their prejudices, they are in fact aiding with all their influence, the adversaries of religion in subverting its foundation." The spread of irreligion had progressed so far that it had even brought the issue of clerical disestablishment into the foreground: "So numerous indeed and bold have the adversaries of the clergy become, so confident of their strength, that even in our legislature, they have lately ventured to bring forward and strenuously to advocate measures and publicly avow opinions, tending directly and almost infallibly to deprive a great part of the present Clergy of regular support."[30] The disestablishment of the church, for Morse, would symbolize the final victory of false philosophy and herald the perfect corruption of American society.

The metaphor of conspiracy that runs throughout "The Present Dangers" illustrates Morse's psychology. Morse feared that liberalism would transfer the legitimation of social authority from a visible to an invisible realm. As a site of authoritative discourse, the orthodox pulpit was distinctly visible, and it functioned as the legitimizing site of other discourses. On an aesthetic level, the central act of the minister's life was preaching revealed religion from a pulpit physically raised above the congregation that gathered to hear him. The minister even preached on a day specifically designated for communal worship. The pulpit represented a centralized, hierarchical structure of authoritative discourse that was continually reproduced through ritual and tradition. By contrast, sites of critical discourse are decentralized and diffused throughout the society. They consist of newspaper reports and editorial dialogues. They flow back and forth from official to unofficial sites of dialogue. Rather than being fixed in time and place, or in rituals that reaffirm a comprehensive social order, sites of critical discourse bring political discussion into direct contact with spiritual and scientific study. In the process of public reason that is at the heart of discursive democracy, participants can even speak or publish anonymously, projecting only their voices without becoming embodied at all.

Morse saw the struggle between these two models of constructing authority as a guerilla war in which the visible saints of the church stood opposed to the veiled Jacobin societies that manipulated public opinion. He concluded his sermon by exhorting his readers to steer away from the vanity of liberal rationalism: "Let us not then become enamored of this vain and insidious philosophy, nor imagine that infidelity is any mark of profound thinking, or of acute penetration." In an apocalyptic closing exhortation, he framed the struggle fully as a critical debate for dominion over public opinion. "If ever the time shall come," Morse warned, "when the new philosophy shall attain ascendancy over public opinion, and men who have embraced its principles, shall be able to control our state and national counsels, 'America must drink the cup of Babylon. Then she will become a limb of the beast, whose body God hath said shall be given to the burning flame.'"[31] Morse's comparison of Enlightenment thought to Babylon underscores the paradigm shift that he was working to counteract. In Morse's view, the pluralism inherent in discursive democracy and public reason threatened the foundations of truth and knowledge. To interpret Morse's opposition to liberal Christianity purely in political terms would discount the stakes he saw in the struggle. Though orthodox opposition definitely reflected the interests of an elite trying to maintain its authority, discursive democracy in religion and in epistemology more generally represented a Babylonian collapse of social order.

Rather than adopting Codman's strategy, though, Morse carried his faith into the struggle to dominate public opinion and became an important pioneer of religious popular culture. Borrowing from an English example, he developed the first tract society in the United States. In 1803 he founded the Massachusetts Society for Promoting Christian Knowledge and began publishing the *Panoplist* in 1805. In 1816 he convinced his son to establish the nation's first religious newspaper, the *Boston Recorder*, which two of his sons later developed into the *New York Observer*.[32] In his campaign to contain the spread of liberal Christianity and to sustain orthodox Congregationalism against the growth of other evangelical denominations, Morse's work was remarkably successful.[33] But it was also an unwitting capitulation to the very model of public reasoning that he rejected. In effect, Morse appropriated the instruments of critical conversation to argue against the value of critical conversation. Ironically, even though Morse connected the legitimizing procedures of discursive democracy with chaos, he not only embraced but also became a central architect of the critical public sphere that has made a pluralistic culture of reform a permanent feature of American civil society.

While Morse's development of tract societies, missions to western territories, and periodicals illustrates the dilemma facing the orthodox faction, the revivalism of his successor, Lyman Beecher, represents the intensity of the imaginative challenge they faced. Nancy Ruttenburg, in analyzing Beecher's predecessor, George Whitfield, characterizes Whitfield's revivals as the first mature embodiment of democratic personality. Ruttenburg defines this identity both in terms of public utterance and in terms of antiauthoritarian public action.[34] But Beecher's revivalism was also fundamentally different from that which Whitfield offered because it invited an experience of religious self-recognition that might sustain an identity under siege by processes of democratization in politics and religion.

Beecher parallels Morse in his criticism of liberal rationalism. In his 1817 sermon "The Bible a Code of Laws," Beecher exhorted his auditors to push their religious lives into the realm of sentiment as a means of provoking the imaginative leap that sustains evangelical faith. Some ministers, Beecher argued, "assert that to love the Lord our God does not imply any *sensible affection*, . . . but the rational religion of perception and intellectual admiration; and [they imply] that by the *heart* is intended not the heart, but the head" (*WLB* 2:179). By granting reason, science, and philosophy the status of authoritative discourses in a rational pluralistic dialogue—a paradoxically rational spirituality—liberal theology challenged orthodox Congregationalism at the point of transition between a Puritan imagination focused on the gap between human and divine power and an Enlightenment epistemology focused on human powers to understand and explain phenomena. Even in ordination sermons, orthodox divines felt compelled to remind themselves of the relationship between reason and faith. Beecher explained:

> Remember that yours is the office of an expositor of that divine book, and not of a legislator, to revise and modify its sacred pages. Be not wise in your own conceit;

and dare not to be wise above what is written. Bring to your aid, for the exposition of the Scriptures, the resources of human learning; but bring with these a heart humbled with a sense of its own deceitfulness and depravity, and filled with strong desires, and groanings that cannot be uttered, for the illumination and guidance of the Spirit; remembering that ignorance and unsanctified knowledge alike puff up, and subject to condemnation. (*WLB* 2:196)

Like the Edward Taylor of the *Preparatory Meditations*, Beecher's faithful minister would seek divine illumination through an ever-growing recognition of his own "deceitfulness and depravity." Even as behavior should be restrained by an overriding consciousness of mortal weakness, the intellectual liberty implicit in theological pluralism would resolve itself by reconfirming orthodox doctrine. Beecher continued:

Dare to think for yourself; but do not imagine that independence can compensate for indolence, or ignorance, or heresy, or hatred of the truth; or that, to be independent, you must, of course, despise antiquity, and differ from the vast majority of the wise, and great, and good.

Dare to think for yourself. Let no creed bind you because it is reputed orthodox, until you perceive its agreement with the Scriptures. But, then, though everywhere spoken against, adopt it; remembering that the Bible may be epitomized and its meaning retained, and your reverence for creeds be only reverence for the Bible. (*WLB* 2:196–97)

Beecher encouraged his colleagues to live as free agents, but he also prescribed the path that such freedom should take. Intellectual liberty created the opportunity to reaffirm orthodoxy. Though the orthodox imagination might stray from the straight and narrow path, it did so mainly to create the opportunity for self-recognition as depraved. Thus, the wandering feet of the orthodox imagination also must inevitably return home to orthodoxy humbled by an overwhelming sense of sinfulness, fear of damnation, and desire for forgiveness.

This pattern of lapse and reaffirmation is reflected in the revivals that characterized the 1830s and 1840s. The movement that created the burned-over district in New York and the Finneyite "new measures" in the west embodies this pattern in early nineteenth-century evangelical Christianity.[35] Through the Jefferson-Jackson period, orthodox evangelicals lived in a world that was increasingly invested in ideals of masculine autonomy and material individualism. The revivals of ministers who still had imaginative roots in the world of established religion, who preached mortal weakness over liberal autonomy, depravity over the power of good works, and dependence on God's grace over self-reliance, represent the apparatus of Calvinist faith as it clashed with the emerging assumptions and tenets of Jacksonian liberalism. The evangelical minister faced the constant necessity of reviving orthodoxy in a world that was gravitating away from the imaginative structures of authentic orthodox Congregationalism.

The price that John Codman paid in social cohesion and the sectarian environment that Morse and Beecher promoted are symptomatic of the simultaneous expansion of religious pluralism and the intensification of orthodox efforts to sustain not just orthodox faith but the array of social relationships that went with it. In a remarkable reminiscence, Harriet Beecher Stowe evocatively renders their sense of displacement from an orderly and godly world. As she recalls her father's arrival in Boston in 1826, Stowe laments:

> When Mr. Beecher came to Boston, Calvinism or orthodoxy was the despised and persecuted form of faith. It was the dethroned royal family wandering like a permitted mendicant in the city where once it had held court, and Unitarianism reigned in its stead.
>
> All the literary men of Massachusetts were Unitarian. All the trustees and professors of Harvard College were Unitarians. All the elite of wealth and fashion crowded Unitarian churches. The judges on the bench were Unitarian, giving decisions by which the peculiar features of church organization, so carefully ordained by the pilgrim fathers, had been nullified. The Church, as consisting, according to their belief, in regenerate people, had been ignored, and all the power had passed into the hands of the congregation. (*ALB* 2:81)

Stowe strikes several revealing chords in this passage. She characterizes orthodoxy as a form of traditional, centralized authority that had been forced from the "court," with all its connotations of regal authority, to the street, with its connotations of anonymity, liminality, and powerlessness. Especially telling in her description of shifting power relations between ministers and congregations, Stowe characterizes the orthodox minister as a "mendicant" who is permitted to speak but who appeals to the hearer from a position of weakness rather than strength. In contrast to outcast orthodoxy, the Unitarians appear as a kind of religio-social cabal made up of the rich and the cultured. After drawing her sketches of the contending parties, Stowe describes the shift as a transition from religious to democratic authority. The church of "regenerate people" that was "ordained" by the Pilgrim fathers had been dismantled. The result was that "all power had passed into the hands of the congregation," and the regal Congregationalist minister had metamorphosed into the worldly Unitarian minister. In Stowe's eyes the dismantling of orthodoxy seems to transform the church into a social movement rather than a religious institution.

Stowe's sketch of a traditional form of authority being disempowered by an unholy alliance between secular and religious institutions functions as a parable of the orthodox view of Christianity in the critical public realm. It illustrates both the imaginative relationships that orthodoxy required and the combination of forces that subverted its hegemony. The orthodox had once reigned like a royal family, drawing their strength from "belief" in the "peculiar features" of church doctrine that the Pilgrim fathers had passed down to them. As the influence of other voices began to impinge on ministerial authority, the "peculiar features" that gave orthodoxy its superordinate status were either nullified—as in Codman's case—or compartmentalized as the idiosyncratic beliefs of a discreet and homogeneous community contained within an increasingly pluralistic society.[36]

Ultimately, the orthodox faction was in a no-win situation, at least in regard to reestablishing Congregationalist hegemony. Without the power to suppress other faiths and discourses of authority, they were inexorably drawn into popular debate with their rivals. As such, they became one of several voices in a critical conversation about religion. Although they successfully maintained the integrity of their church, even enhanced it through disestablishment, they also contributed much of the media for the secular culture of reform. The newspapers, circuit riders, and revivals they pioneered in the effort to sustain orthodoxy were all adapted for use by the antislavery movement. The closest link in this regard is, of course, that between William Lloyd Garrison and Lyman Beecher. Garrison attended Beecher's church in the late 1820s, and the model of moral suasion that immediatist abolitionism promoted is a direct adaptation of evangelical exhortation and conversion. But the orthodox faction's focus on shaping public opinion through instruments of mass media was its most important contribution to the emergence of the culture of reform. The growth of religious pluralism and the propaganda wars that were central to it made congregations the audience of publications and the juries of public debates. However reluctantly, and contrary to their own theocentric world-view, the ministers who led the fight were compelled to accept the practical autonomy of each individual who joined their churches. The orthodox Congregationalists' "mission" to their changing nation thus defined basic methods of grassroots organizing that are still vital to reform culture. By contrast, the Unitarians sought to harmonize their theology with the changing structure of publicity by incorporating discursive democracy into the very core of their spirituality. While the adherents of orthodoxy provided the tactics, the liberals worked out the epistemological theory that allowed reform culture to become a permanent feature of American civil society.

The Dialogue of Faith in Unitarian Spirituality

In 1892 one of Unitarianism's first historians, Joseph Henry Allen, tried to explain the outcome of the Unitarians' effort to integrate faith and reason. Allen concluded that by the end of the nineteenth century, while Unitarianism had been "the liberal side of the old Congregational body, so [now] it must know itself as the Christian side of the broader scientific movement of [the] time."[37] Liberal Christianity, as Allen's Unitarian forbears understood it, marked an effort to use Enlightenment rationalism to demystify Christianity and thereby revive the faith of the early Christian era. Sydney Ahlstrom and Jonathan Carey underscore this image of eighteenth- and early nineteenth-century liberalism by titling their anthology of Unitarian writings *An American Reformation*. Just as the early Protestants sought to purify Christianity by rejecting Catholic mysticism and ritual, the liberal Congregationalists sought to purge their faith of the irrational elements they saw in Protestant doctrine.

Unitarian minister and historian James Freeman Clarke, for example, interprets church history in relation to reclaiming an appropriate relationship between spiritual and formal dimensions of Christianity. "The Roman Catholics [have] made the visible church, or outward Christian community, the central idea of Christianity, and have changed this into a close[d] corporation of priests, it was natural, perhaps, that Protestants should go too far in another direction. Accordingly, the central idea in Protestantism is not the Church, but the salvation of the soul; not social, but personal religion."[38] This project of turning faith back to its origins, the liberals held, authorized them to undertake a thorough revaluation of orthodox practice because, as Clarke notes: "We find also that as the apostolic Church had no creed and no bishop, neither had it any fixed or settled forms."[39] In the process of reclaiming an early Christian ideal, however, the liberals embraced two principles that decentered orthodox spirituality. First, they challenged the uniform inspiration of the Bible, arguing that the Bible is a multivocal text that includes both God's voice and those of the texts' mortal authors. Second, they embraced the principle that reason—understood as a capacity to discover truth by combining faith with secular modes of analysis—represents a divine capacity that makes humans like God.[40] The liberals thus both read multivocal pluralism into the Bible itself and integrated theology into a pluralistic epistemology.

In their efforts to reconcile Christian doctrine with Enlightenment epistemology, the Unitarians actually occupied a middle ground. More radical figures such as Robert Dale Owen, Frances Wright, and George Henry Evans articulated a mode of utopian reform that sought to transform the society through purely secular means. Both through the communitarian movement and through organizations such as the Workingmen's Party founded in Philadelphia in 1828, these reformers represent secular and materialist approaches to social progress. Like the religious reformers, they were aggressive participants in print culture, establishing journals such as the *Mechanics Free Press* and the *Working Man's Advocate*. Also, these organizations established lyceum-like libraries and lecture series grounded in scientific inquiry. Owen and Wright founded the Hall of Science in New York, at which, Louis Masur writes, "for the price of three cents for men and no charge for women, visitors heard talks on astronomy, anatomy, and perspectival drawing as well as debates on questions such as whether 'the light of reason is a trustworthy and sufficient guide to happiness.'" While the working-class movement viewed the Unitarians as elitist and representative less of social reform than of the interests of capital, they saw the orthodox evangelicals as a potential source of religious tyranny. Masur quotes the *Working Man's Advocate* denouncing evangelical revivals as "a gigantic effort" by "a certain class of theologians . . . to get power into their hands, to be used for the destruction of our . . . republican institutions."[41]

Institutions such as the Hall of Science and other working-men's educational associations were indispensable to Emerson's career and are part of the context of events such as the Amory Hall lecture series and the Chardon Street conventions, on which Emerson and Garrison worked together as organizers. Owen and Wright's Hall of Science, however, proved unable to compete with the revival movement and the forces driving religious sectarianism. In the fall of 1833, Owen sold the hall to a Methodist congregation.[42]

Though William Ellery Channing's 1819 sermon "Unitarian Christianity" is the best statement of liberal Christian doctrine, his 1828 sermon "Likeness to God" is the most important expression of antebellum Unitarian spirituality because it places the human mind in continuity with, rather than alienation from, the mind of God. The Unitarians' commitment to intellectual pluralism shifted the central idea of spirituality from what Beecher described as the need for submission to what William Ellery Channing described as the recognition of human "likeness to God." The key idea of Unitarian epistemology is that the individual has the potential to embody godlike goodness and transcendent truth. Orthodox faith is motivated by the imaginative effort to internalize the need for perfect submission to the Spirit, whereas Unitarian faith is motivated by a full-hearted effort to emulate divine wisdom. Knowledge for the orthodox Congregationalists meant understanding the boundaries of human power and the consequent need for obedience to time-honored traditions that link the present to the biblical age; in Unitarian eyes knowledge meant an ethical progressivism that measured the reform of church doctrine as growth rather than infidelity. Instead of resisting pluralism in religious and epistemological discourse more generally, liberal faith required an ecumenical openness to the possible truth value of all discourses of knowledge. Rawls treats Unitarian-style epistemological pluralism as one of the fundamental elements of his political conception of justice. He writes that the "conception of justice" in a liberal society "should be, as far as possible, independent of the opposing and conflicting philosophical doctrines that citizens affirm. In formulating such a conception, political liberalism applies the principle of toleration to philosophy itself."[43]

The Unitarian point of view represents the integration of rationalist and pluralist elements of Enlightenment epistemology into Protestant spirituality. This point of view gave Unitarians a fundamentally different attitude toward critical dialogue and the critical public realm as a site for the legitimation of authority. While the orthodox Congregationalists used the media of critical discourse to fight critical discourse, the Unitarians appropriated the sphere of critical discourse as the locus of spiritual inquiry and came close to equating participation in critical dialogue with prayer. Unitarian worship represents the confluence of several streams of thought: Christian doctrine, the quest for knowledge, and a liberal form of moral perfectionism. As such, it is a structure that permits the type of mediation characteristic of overlapping consensus in a plural society. As the presence of religious pluralism places strains on a society, Rawls continues: "The religious doctrines that in a previous century were the professed basis of society have gradually given way to principles of constitutional government that all citizens, whatever their religious view, can endorse." In the shift from a comprehensive to a constitutional view, the society also moves toward a structure of authority grounded in discursive procedures that mediate between opposed or contradictory world-views. In Rawls's terms, the Unitarians represented a shift toward a political conception of religion because the procedures of discursive democracy are central to Unitarian faith and are part of a broad discussion of the good life. Equally, this distinction between comprehensive and procedural models is important in understanding Frederick Douglass's change of opinion on the Constitution. In the evolution of his thought, the Garrisonian Christian perfectionist reading of the Constitution stands in for the orthodox monovocal reading of the Bible. Moving away from the Garrisonian reading, Douglass rejected the Constitution as a sacred text and treated it as a site of political mediation that required the broadest kind of pluralist reciprocity. This shift from a comprehensive to a procedural perspective on the Constitution enabled Douglass to imagine himself as an equal in the discursive process of legitimizing the authority of the Constitution.

Perhaps the difference between the orthodox and the liberal imagination can be seen most vividly in the disparity between John Codman's effort to sustain an exclusive, monovocal discourse and William Ellery Channing's defense of the atheist freethinker Abner Kneeland. In 1834 Kneeland published three articles in a journal he edited for the Society of Free Inquirers. Accused of blasphemy, he was arrested, tried, convicted, and sentenced to three months in jail. In the process of appealing this conviction, Channing joined Ellis Gray Loring in petitioning the governor to pardon Kneeland. Though Channing rejected the substance of Kneeland's position, he ultimately held the right to free discussion to be more important than the dogmatic reaffirmation of doctrine. He understood the episode in a way that dramatizes the Unitarians' investment in critical dialogue as a form of religious inquiry. At the beginning of their petition, Loring, Channing, and others frame their case with a summary statement of liberal confidence in the value of critical public dialogue. Channing and the liberals opposed the imprisonment of Kneeland for the following reasons: "Because the punishment proposed to be inflicted is believed to be at variance with the spirit of our institutions and our age, and with the soundest expositions of those civil and religious rights which are at once founded in our nature, and guaranteed by the constitutions of the United States and of this Commonwealth; because the freedom of speech and the press is the chief instrument of the progress of truth and of social improvements and is never to be restrained by legislation."[44] As this passage indicates, the spirit of moral generosity and toleration for honest processes of inquiry is at the very core of Unitarian spirituality. Oddly echoing Lyman Beecher's remarks on disestablishment, Channing and his cosigners also argued that the state should not intervene against Kneeland because it should leave churches to fight their own battles in the realm of public debate.

The petitioners sought a pardon for Kneeland "because religion needs no support from penal law, and is grossly dishonored by interpositions for its defense, which imply that it cannot be trusted to its own strength and to the weapons of reason and persuasion in the hands of its friends." The liberals implicitly argued that government interference feminizes the church by assuming that it needs protection through an official vehicle of censorship. Far from requiring official sanctions that prop up state support for Christianity, the interests of the church were best served by "the weapons of reason and persuasion," which would support the stronger argument in critical conversation. The petition also repeats this position in less defensive terms, explaining that the state erred because "by punishing infidel opinions, we shake one of the strongest foundations of faith, namely, the evidence which arises to religion from the fact that it stands firm and gathers strength amidst the severest and most unfettered investigation of its claims."[45] By the petitioners' logic, it was the state, rather than Abner Kneeland, that had attacked Christianity.

After the petition drive failed and the controversy surrounding his support for it abated, Channing mused to the Unitarian social worker Joseph Tuckerman: "As I know Christianity, it is so at war with the present condition of society, that it cannot be spoken and acted out without great offense. The want of Christian spirit, of Christ's spirit towards our fallen fellow-creatures is most mournful. I would drink of it more freely."[46] In these remarks, Channing responded not only to the Congregationalists' effort to position him as a public defender of atheism but also to the strategic discourse that characterized sectarian partisanship in the Kneeland controversy. The orthodox evangelicals did not see Abner Kneeland as a significant threat, but they could not pass up the opportunity to attack the Unitarians. Nonetheless, with the supernaturalism of the orthodox imagination in mind, the Unitarians' dialogic approach to the Bible did skirt the margins of atheism. By rejecting the idea of the uniform inspiration of the Gospels, the Unitarians rejected one of the definitive tenets of orthodox Christianity. Whereas

Codman had allowed his church to fracture rather than preside over a pluralist pulpit, Channing not only defended the most radically pluralist discussion of religious ideas; he also defined spirituality and the strength of the church in relation to critical debate rather than in relation to the rigorous adherence to a comprehensive doctrine.

In "Unitarian Christianity," a sermon that synthesizes the most important elements of liberal faith into a single statement, Channing justified the Unitarians' pluralistic approach to biblical interpretation. According to Channing, "The Bible treats of subjects on which we receive ideas from other sources besides itself; such subjects as the nature, passions, relations, and duties of man; and it expects us to restrain and modify its language by the known truths which observation and experience furnish on these topics" (*WEC* 3:62). Even though Channing was arguing here for ongoing reinterpretation of biblical "language," he rhetorically justified his position through an implied yearning within the Bible itself. It "expects" to be restrained and modified when "known truths" that are established by secular disciplines contradict traditional understandings of scripture.

Rather than treating the gospel as a "code of laws" that furnishes Christians with rules for "their entire direction in all things," as Lyman Beecher did, the liberals treated the Bible as a source of moral principles that includes both the word of God and those of his fallible prophets and apostles (*WLB* 2:280). In reading the Bible, the minister had an obligation to distinguish between the universal voice of the Godhead and the idiosyncratic voices of his interlocutors. Channing argued: "The different portions of this book, instead of being confined to general truths, refer perpetually to the times when they were written, to states of society, to modes of thinking, to controversies in the church, to feelings and usages which have passed away, and [to] . . . what was of temporary and local application" (*WEC* 3:63). As he separated relevant from irrelevant material within the Bible, Channing did not confine his argument to outdated customs; he also claimed the authority to rethink the values and judgments of the Bible's authors: "We find, too that some of these books are strongly marked by the genius and character of their respective writers, that the Holy Spirit did not so guide the Apostles as to suspend the peculiarities of their minds and that a knowledge of their feelings, and of the influences under which they were placed, is one of the preparations for understanding their writings" (*WEC* 3:63).

This attitude toward the authority of biblical authors, as Channing admitted, caused conservatives to claim that Unitarians "exalt reason above revelation" and that they prefer their "own wisdom to God's" (*WEC* 3:62). In what the orthodox faction saw as an epistemological power grab, liberals changed the relationship between the Bible and the reader by placing the reader's intelligence in an evaluative position over sacred writ. This method of interpretation both democratized biblical discourses by making its truth status contingent on verification by other discourses and situated the minister as a mediator in a critical conversation among authoritative discourses. "With these views of the bible," Channing concluded, "we feel it our bound duty to exercise our reason upon it perpetually, to compare, to infer, to look beyond the letter to the spirit, to seek in the nature of the subject, and the aim of the writer, his true meaning; and, in general, to make use of what is known, for explaining what is difficult, and for discovering new truths" (*WEC* 3:63). In Unitarian spirituality, the minister was less the "herald of justice" who explains God's will to the masses than he was a mediator who orchestrates the conflicting claims of biblical, historical, and scientific discourses.

In sum, the spiritual mission of the minister was different for the Unitarians than it was for the orthodox Congregationalists. The orthodox faction claimed responsibility for reminding the faithful of their place in the invisible supernatural battle between Christ and Satan. The Unitarians, on the other hand, claimed responsibility for facilitating an ethical and rational quest for the true and the good. In this reformation of pastoral responsibility, the center of gravity shifted from the orthodox emphasis on the ubiquity of sin to the Unitarians' emphasis on the power to be good. In the Unitarians' dialogue of faith, the minister's task was to produce a sense of yearning for and motion toward divine wisdom rather than submission to transcendent power.

As Channing put it in his sermon "Likeness to God," "The idea of God, sublime and awful as it is, is the idea of our own spiritual nature purified and enlarged to infinity" (*WEC* 3:233–34). In the place of innate depravity, Channing asserted a moral will that gravitates toward perfect goodness. "In truth," Channing continued, "the soul is always bursting its limits. It thirsts continually for wider knowledge. It pushes forward to untried happiness. It has deep wants which nothing limited can appease. Its true element and end is an unbounded good. Thus, God's infinity has its image in the soul." Further, this likeness "rejoices to diffuse itself" and is apparent throughout creation, from the "structure of a single leaf" to the "great deeds of history" and "the discoveries of philosophy" (*WEC* 3:238–39). The Unitarians' faith thus found spirituality and authentic religion through intense dialogic encounters among diverse discourses of knowledge. The faith itself was in the belief that these encounters are a form of prayer. Indeed, the most important contribution the Unitarians made to the conceptual architecture of the culture of reform is the importance they attributed to public sincerity in their spirituality. When, in his review of the Abner Kneeland affair, Channing complained of "the want of Christian spirit," he was lamenting that the debate over Kneeland was driven by sectarian and partisan interests rather than by spiritual or ethical considerations. The debate, in Channing's view, was insincere, "political," not oriented toward honest understanding, and thus it failed to embody the tolerance of "Christian spirit." The Unitarian dialogue of faith required an effort at sincere self-expression and called for equally sincere responses. As a form of critical conversation, the Unitarians' pluralist spirituality thus invested the procedures of discursive democracy with a utopian religious dimension. It simultaneously sought the perfection of the self and the perfection of critical dialogue within the context of a movement that bridged Christianity and secular humanism. The success of this progressivism relied on people's confidence that public discussion was conducted with sincerity.

The Problem of Sincerity in Public Debate

While orthodox minister Horace Chapin, like Morse and Beecher, understood the pulpit as a locus of moral judgment where doctrine represents the only authentic discourse of authority, Channing and the Unitarians repositioned it as a nexus where a variety of discourses of authority intersect. To orthodox eyes, this epistemological pluralism meant that the Unitarians presented everything in "general terms" because "complex words are not reduced to simple definitions." This effort to conceptualize ideas rather than to articulate norms means that difference of "moral character is not stamped according to its value and name."[47] In their response to Unitarian practice, ministers such as Chapin objected to the Unitarians' effort to synthesize and mediate rather than to judge competing discourses of authority. Chapin feared Unitarian epistemology for two reasons. First, he objected to the democratization of epistemological hierarchy that liberal theology created by blurring the distinction between the voice of God and the discourses of science, philosophy, and other humanist intellectual disciplines. Second, he feared that Unitarian theology would divert attention away from the cosmic struggle between Christ and Satan. As he expressed it, "In a word, it appears to be the object of such a [liberal] preacher . . . to keep his people still, be prudent, and take no part in the controversy between heaven and earth."[48] By focusing on this world, the Unitarians ignored the imagery of divine magnificence and human puniness that the orthodox Congregationalists needed to sustain the immanence of the supernatural struggle.

The inversion of authority that the Congregationalists feared in Unitarianism can be seen in Moses Stuart's reply to William Ellery Channing's "Unitarian Christianity." When interpreting the Bible, Stuart argues:

> My simple inquiry must be, what sentiment does the language of this or that passage convey[?] . . . When this question is settled . . . then I either believe what is taught, or else reject the claim of divine authority. What can my own theories and reasonings about the absurdity or reasonableness of any particular doctrine, avail in determining whether a writer of the New Testament has taught this doctrine or not? . . . I must choose the course I will take; I must either believe his assertion, or reject his authority.[49]

Since orthodox legitimation hinged on the claim that scripture is the word of God and bears a level of authority that no human discourse can hope to achieve, the stark distinction that Stuart draws between human "reasonings" and the "divine authority" of biblical texts goes to the core of the difference between the orthodox and the liberal world-views. Yet Stuart's exasperated tone also reveals the difficulty that the orthodox Congregationalists faced when they engaged in debate with the liberals who were advocating a pluralist epistemology. In spite of the fifty pages of careful analysis through which Stuart tracks the history of the doctrine of the Trinity, in the end, one either believes in the uniform inspiration of the Bible, or one is an infidel. This is the simple "fact" that people must accept for orthodoxy to retain its authority. By restricting himself to this approach, Stuart modeled the imaginative challenge that proved to be both the greatest strength and the greatest weakness of the orthodox faction. At its root, the vitality of orthodox faith hinged on people's willingness to participate in the metaphysics of submission that their faith required. This in turn required them to live in the increasingly discontinuous contexts of their church and the secular society of which it was a part.

But the Unitarians' adaptation to the assumptions of the liberal public realm also created fundamental theological problems. As the Unitarians' incorporation

of critical dialogue into the center of spiritual life implies, antebellum Unitarianism was fundamentally a procedural religion. It emphasized the ongoing quest
for truth over revelation itself. As a religion that had faith in discursive democracy at its core, Unitarian spirituality encouraged the faithful to incorporate a
wide range of discourses into their faith. However, this emphasis on process
undermined the Unitarians' ability to arrive at stable doctrinal positions. Like
contemporary theorists of discursive democracy, Unitarian ministers measured
the virtue of their theology by the integrity of the dialogue it produced rather
than by the "truths" it revealed. Whereas irrational acceptance of the revealed
truths of the Gospels represents a method of attaining certainty of salvation,
the process of reasoning through defective human faculties implies an endless
process of exploration and critical revision. Since its epistemology emphasized
a progressive dialogic process over the revival-relapse pattern of orthodox spirituality, Unitarianism became less an identifiable creed and more a quest for an
ever-elusive likeness to God.

The unstable theological positions that resulted from the Unitarians' rejection
of orthodox doctrine became an object of satire for conservative polemicists.
The same Samuel Miller who had supported Codman in 1808 wrote in 1823: "It is
evident that Unitarianism, according to the statement of one of its most zealous
friends in the United States, consists rather in NOT BELIEVING."[50] Lyman Beecher
developed the same line of thought by arguing that the practice of abandoning
doctrines on the ground that they are irrational represents a descent into chaos:

> Unitarians, who have been educated in orthodoxy, abandon what they call one
> error, and adopt what afterwards they call another, and abandon this and adopt
> a third error, and abandon this and adopt a fourth, and are ever learning their
> past errors, and are confident of nothing but that in all their opinions, except
> the last, they have been wrong; while even these, as it is meet they should after
> such reiterated admonition of their frailty, they hold with such magnanimous
> uncertainty as renders confidence arrogant. (*WLB* 2:368)

Here, Beecher underscored the instability of Unitarian doctrine by characterizing
liberal ministers as prodigal sons who had left the high peaks of orthodoxy and
begun to slip from one error to another on the downward slope to infidelity
and atheism. He assumed the characteristic orthodox tone of high authority.
Beecher's slippery-slope argument ends by wending its way back to a subtle
reaffirmation of his own position of assurance. The "magnanimous uncertainty"

of the Unitarians created an ironic context for his own "confidence," which, of course, Beecher did not consider arrogant.

Unitarian rational theology thus forced the minister to think of himself not as the "herald of salvation" but as a diplomat who mediates sincere dialogues about faith. Perhaps the most important way in which New England Unitarianism anticipated Emersonian transcendentalism is in the way it shifted faith toward an effort at sincere or faithful self-expression. Since he could not unequivocally assert doctrinal truths, the minister could only seek to inspire his congregants to think and speak as people who can be like God. In effect, the logic of Unitarian faith limits the authority that a minister can legitimately project to that which derives from a heartfelt confession of faith. As Channing noted: "A minister must communicate religion, not only as a result of reasoning, but as a matter of experience, with that inexpressible character of reality, that life and power, which accompanies truth drawn from a man's own soul." Even in his sermon on "The Great Purpose of Christianity," Channing prefaced his remarks by saying: "I beg you to remember, that in this discourse I speak in my own name, and in no other" (*WEC* 3:207). Belief derives not from a dramatization of divine magnificence and human puniness, but from a religious sentiment that combines faith with rational analysis to provoke a sincere and multivocal but indeterminate quest for truth.

The secularization of worship into a critical conversation infused with faith that is at the center of Unitarian spirituality is expressed in the literary styles that Channing advocated for Unitarian ministers. Channing made an implicit contrast between the orthodox and liberal methods of meeting intellectual challenges in his 1824 sermon on "The Demands of the Age on the Ministry": "The most effectual method of expelling error, is, not to meet it sword in hand, but gradually to instill great truths, with which it cannot easily coexist, and by which the mind outgrows it" (*WEC* 3:152–53). Channing proposed that the Unitarian minister bring erroneous doctrines into public dialogue with more robust discourses of truth. There, in the realm of public debate, Channing trusted that truth would supplant error. In a world that is, as Channing put it, "tracing connexions between all objects of thought and branches of knowledge, and which cannot but distrust an alleged revelation, in as far as it is seen to want harmonies and affinities with other parts of God's system," the minister must work to harmonize disparate "branches of knowledge." He must "regard the signs, the distinctive marks and character of the age to which he belongs, and must accommodate his ministry to its wants and demands" (*WEC* 3:144, 147).

Intellect and affection, revelation and nature, past and present, the possible and the ideal, Channing argued, must all be brought into dialogue and reconciled from the pulpit. To cite just one example, in order to resolve tension between revealed and natural religion, the minister must be able to "discern and unfold the consistency of revealed religion with the new lights that are breaking in from nature; and . . . be able to draw, from all men's discoveries in the outward world and in their own souls, illustrations, analogies, and arguments for Christianity." To achieve this reconciliation, Channing contended that two tools are necessary. First, the minister should be broadly educated in the most important discourses of knowledge: "The state of the world . . . may be called enlightened, and requires an enlightened ministry. It hardly seems necessary to prove, that religion should be dispensed by men who at least keep pace with the intellect of the age in which they live." (*WEC* 3:145) To deny the explanatory force of science and of the reason through which it was progressing would be willfully to limit the quest for truth and submit to a regime of myth rather than of knowledge. Hence, the first demand of the age was that religion should support advances in "intellect" or reason rather than maintain an unchanging faith in the face of a rapidly changing world.

Second, the minister must develop a rhetorical style that facilitates morally progressive dialogue and impels it toward divinely sanctioned ends. In contrast to the jeremiads and revivals of the evangelicals, Channing offered fiction and poetry as rhetorical models. "Fiction," Channing suggested:

> is no longer a mere amusement; but transcendent genius, accommodating itself to the character of the age, . . . fiction [has been turned] from a toy into a mighty engine, and, under the light tale, is breathing through the community either its reverence for the old or its thirst for the new, [it] communicates the spirit and lessons of history, unfolds the operations of religious and civil institutions, and defends or assails new theories of education or morals by exhibiting them in life and action. (*WEC* 3:145)

To exemplify this change, Channing compared neoclassical and romantic poetry. The contrast that he drew brings into sharp focus his confidence in the harmonizing force of pluralist conversation as a principle of faith. Rather than the "regular, elaborate, harmonious strains, which delighted a former generation," Channing contended that "men want . . . a poetry which pierces beneath the exterior of life to the depths of the soul, and which lays open its mysterious workings, borrowing from the whole outward creation fresh images and correspondences" (*WEC* 3:145–46).

By presenting moral teaching as a process that borrows from "the whole outward creation," Channing characterized the Unitarian minister as a kind of Bakhtinian novelist, a figure who orchestrates and harmonizes a host of voices rather than articulating a single authoritative world-view. In Channing's model, the dialogic style raises liberal epistemology from theological infidelity to religious "self-culture" because it not only draws conflicting voices into harmony but also foregrounds the individual's ability to transform a secular quest for truth into an act of faith. Whereas for the orthodox evangelical, imaginative experience is often a form of temptation that draws one away from a godly path, for the Unitarian, attentiveness to the manifold nature of experience is itself a part of the dialogue of faith. Though "the first and most solemn duty of . . . ministers is to res[c]ue [Christianity] from . . . doctrines for which it is in no respect responsible; and to vindicate its character as eminently a rational religion," the minister has an equally sacred task to perform. He must use his imagination to expand religion so that it infuses motivation and transforms experience into an ecumenical religious pilgrimage.

The "vague but ardent core of poetic feeling" that Lawrence Buell identifies as the "basis for belief" for most Unitarians reflects faith in the power of artfully constructed pluralist dialogue to transform a combination of reason and spirituality into a faith that "bears on and touches everything human, as a universal spirit, which aught to breath through and modify all our desires and pursuits."[51] Channing reiterated this central connection between secular reason and Christian spirituality again and again. Religion, he wrote, "must be seen not only to correspond and to be adapted to the intellect, but to furnish nutriments and appeals to the highest and profoundest sentiments of our nature." Further, "the historical and miraculous proofs of Christianity are indeed essential and impregnable; but, without superseding these, the inward proofs of which I speak, are becoming more and more necessary . . . in proportion as the moral discernment and sensibilities of men are strengthened" (*WEC* 3:150, 153).

Thus, the challenge presented by the liberal public realm for orthodox ministers revolved around sustaining the vividness of God's exclusive authority against increasingly robust secular discourses of knowledge. They responded by developing instruments of publicity to call people back to the faith. But these instruments themselves extended the importance of critical dialogue as a legitimizing procedure for authoritative voices. As the work of Catharine Beecher and William Lloyd Garrison will make clear, the emergence of the evangelical press and the religious revival became central instruments of critical publicity as evangelical reform expanded into the women's rights and antislavery movements. The liberal ministers who would form the Unitarian Church responded to the orthodox assault on liberal theology as an attack on thought itself. In important respects, the Unitarian defense of liberalism was a defense of human rights as much as it was an effort to harmonize Enlightenment rationalism and Christian faith. In its willingness to respect secular discourses as legitimate sources of truth, even to use the products of what Mary Cayton calls "scientific protocols" to revise orthodox interpretations of the Bible, the Unitarians modeled the procedures of critical discourse.[52] In effect, the effort to connect scientific truth to a perfectly sincere moral dialogue that seeks to emulate perfect goodness defined the ideal of Unitarian spirituality. The Unitarian reformation was a paradoxical effort simultaneously to return the faith to its first-century predoctrinal origins and, in a very modern fashion, to incorporate into Christianity the epistemological procedures that undermined the hegemony of theology.

With dialogue at its very core, Unitarianism emerged as a reflection of the critical public sphere. But it was not a successful platform for the most influential reform movements of the antebellum period. Nonetheless, in its respect for the voice of the individual, its emphasis on sincerity in public dialogue, and its faith in moral perfectability for both the individual and society, the Unitarian movement was the vital bridge connecting the principles of liberal consensus with the religious context from which the culture of reform emerged.

The Unitarian Controversy and Antebellum Reform

Both the orthodox and the liberal factions in the Unitarian controversy represent social reform movements in their own right. In the broadest perspective, the dispute between them marks efforts to adapt the practice of Christianity to a changing epistemological and cultural environment. Yet the division between orthodox and liberal ministers also reflects foundational differences in the type of reform that the times required. As the debate over the "moral tendency" of liberal or orthodox practice indicates, both factions held that they were working not just in the interest of Protestant Christianity but in the broadest interest of the society as a whole. The Unitarian controversy is important to the emergence of reform movements because even as the disputants modeled the elements of critical publicity and developed instruments of mass media, in practice neither faction was able to extend its vision of reform to incorporate the ideal of universal access to public discourse as a central element of equality. Within both factions, there was a patronizing assumption of moral leadership, an implicit desire to reempower the minister. Hence, the Unitarian controversy brought instruments of reform into general use and legitimized the principles of critical dialogue, but it did not transform American society. It revealed a changing context more than it served as an engine of change in its own right.

An insightful reviewer of the state of the Unitarian controversy in 1826—just after the Unitarians officially separated from the Congregationalists—summarized the debate between the orthodox faction and the liberals in a way that illustrates how the theological debate became a debate about social morality in general. This anonymous reviewer broke the conflict into three phases: a "biblical" phase in which the Unitarians rejected a host of orthodox doctrines; a "philosophical" phase in which hermeneutical and epistemological issues dominated the debate; and a phase that emphasizes the moral influence of the two movements. This final phase of the conflict brought the opposing creeds "to another test, that of tendency." The main question was "which of the two systems, the Unitarian or the Orthodox [was] of superior tendency to form an elevated, religious character."[53] While the first two phases of the conflict were textual and theological, the third was social. The debate over moral tendency dealt with the ways that each creed conditioned the behavior of individuals and exemplified moral leadership for the community.

As a reform movement, the Unitarian Church increasingly sought to focus spirituality on processes of social integration rather than on the connection between obedience to doctrine and morally upright behavior. It is on this level that the Unitarians were able to establish their movement most successfully because "tendency," as this reviewer used the word, is measured in part by the success with which a creed enables an individual to establish continuity between his or her secular and spiritual lives. Even though orthodox churchgoers were to view reality through the fixed and single lens of an unchangeable doctrine, orthodox spirituality facilitated a pattern of lapse and revival as individuals proved more or less able to live by the code of laws defined by doctrine. The less doctrine-based faith of the Unitarians enabled them to see reform in terms of incremental moral growth rather than in terms of transformative born-again experiences that saved lapsed souls. The effect that this characteristic of Unitarianism had on its public character is apparent in the Unitarians' different levels of participation in the Sunday school and abolition movements. Since Unitarian spirituality makes free enquiry a fundamental principle of faith, the Unitarians could easily reconcile their institutional goals with the goals of ecumenical educational reform movements. By midcentury, Unitarian churches were sponsoring a quarter of Boston's eighty Sabbath schools. Jane and William Pease conclude that these schools were not run primarily to gain converts—one school even employed an Irish Catholic teacher.[54] In general, the Sabbath schools promoted two goals. First, Unitarian-sponsored schools tried to develop the moral character of students in a way that related more to responsible citizenship than to loyalty to any specific religious creed. The constitution of the Howard Sunday School, for example, defined the school's mission in terms of inculcating "principles of order, truth, sobriety, and goodness."[55]

Second, the schools worked to develop students' ability to reason independently and to participate in the dialogic process that is at the center of Unitarian religious practice. The Peases cite the remarks of a teacher at the Boston West school: "It should be less [the teacher's] aim to fill the minds of his pupils with his own treasures, than to excite them to think and feel for themselves. Their tho'ts should be a reply, not an echo to his own."[56] Unitarian participation in the Sunday school movement harmonized well with the principles that define the Unitarian world-view and reflect its pluralistic approach to faith. But participation in this movement was also a philanthropic activity similar to the benevolent reform movements of the early nineteenth century. As such, it was relatively uncontroversial. David Robinson and Douglas C. Stange reach similar conclusions, arguing that the relative weakness of Unitarian doctrine led church members to support philanthropic endeavors that neither forced ministers to take controversial political stands nor threatened the economic interests of Unitarian congregations.[57]

In contrast to their strong commitment to education, Unitarians were much less willing to support antislavery. Though some prominent Unitarians such as Samuel May, Thomas W. Higginson, the Weston Chapmans, Lydia Maria Child, her brother Convers Francis, and Theodore Parker were active participants in the movement, most Unitarian ministers had ethical reservations about antislavery and especially about Garrisonian immediatism.[58] Strange concludes that the power congregations held over ministers also influenced the Unitarians' position.[59] Channing's denunciation of slavery in 1835 would typify the Unitarian response well into the 1850s. Even though Channing denounced slavery as a violation of the "essential equality of men," he hewed to the strictest position that only an awakening of the conscience of the slaveholder would bring about abolition (*WEC* 2:17). Stange especially emphasizes Channing's ambivalence toward the antislavery movement, noting that "Channing coupled every statement he made in favor of the abolitionists, with one against them."[60]

The immediatist abolitionism of the Garrisonians struck Channing in a way similar to his feelings about evangelism and the debate over Abner Kneeland. Garrisonian rhetoric was, in his view, a distortion of critical public discourse. He even characterized the radical abolitionists as the victims of a fever that had infected the body politic. Channing lamented the ubiquitous presence of radical movements: "In the present age it will not do to deal harshly with the characters of fanatics. They form the mass of the people. Religion and Politics, Philanthropy and Temperance, Nullification and Antimasonry, the leveling spirit of the working man, and the spirit of speculation in the man of business, all run into fanaticism. This is the type of all our epidemics. A sober man who can find? The abolitionists have but caught the fever of the day" (*WEC* 2:125). Making a connection that would typify Unitarians as well as transcendentalists, Channing saw Garrisonian moral suasion as a mode of single-minded zealotry antithetical to the broad worldliness that they associated with fully developed consciousness. In his criticism of the abolitionists, Channing even ignored the slave's right to freedom by arguing for an antislavery that focused on the moral salvation of racists and slaveholders.

Garrison's Anti-Slavery Society, in Channing's view, also defeated the true purpose of reform because it subordinated self-culture to the objectives of the association. In an interesting parallel, Channing was suspicious of the Garrisonians for the same reason that many Unitarian ministers opposed revivals, indeed, for the same reason that Lyman Beecher was suspicious of George Finney: "The forced, artificially excited enthusiasm of a multitude, kept together by an organization, which makes them the instruments of a few leading minds, works superficially and often injuriously to the mass of people in the movement" (*WEC* 2:131). As people ethically committed to the pluralist paradigm in its own right, Unitarian ministers distinguished between intellectual opposition, which they could promote as one voice in a dialogue, and Garrisonian polemics, which they saw as an attempt to stifle dialogue by shouting down one's opponents. Elizur Wright, a Garrisonian and secretary of the Massachusetts Anti-Slavery Society, condescendingly replied to Channing's 1835 essay by highlighting the distinction between talk and action. Though Unitarians "adopted into their creed the fundamental principles of human rights, and theoretically recogniz[ed] their bearing upon the evil in question . . . when they came to the practical application [Unitarian ministers] fall into violent fits of 'worldly wisdom.'"[61]

Despite an epistemology that fostered pluralistic dialogue and rational inquiry in a host of emerging disciplines, the Unitarian church stagnated as its moral force was appropriated by secular reform and its religious identity was hemmed in by its own elitism and by the antiliberal propaganda of orthodox evangelicals. Even though they embraced key elements of critical conversation as central tenets of faith, they proved ineffective in creating a general model for social integration. Where the orthodox evangelicals responded to the fragmenting of the social by calling people back to a world of revealed authority, the Unitarians sought to fashion themselves as a critical public sphere grounded in the Protestant tradition. But Unitarianism proved to be a cipher of the critical public realm. It adopted and spiritualized the ideals of critical publicity, but it was unable to provide a dialogic forum broad enough to contain the restive forces that became the culture of reform.

Though Unitarians and orthodox Congregationalists both participated in reform movements, for my argument their primary importance is in the way they reveal the changing architecture of public discourse. As profoundly religious as Angelina Grimké was, for example, she found her voice in the Garrisonian fold, working outside the religious institutions of both the Protestantism of her youth and the Quakerism she adopted later. Equally, even though William Lloyd Garrison learned much from Lyman Beecher, the lessons he learned were tactical rather than philosophical. Throughout his career, Garrison treated churches as loci of strategic discourse and thus as the objects of some of his sharpest criticism. In his newspaper and the many reform organizations that he founded, Garrison positioned reform culture in a unique institutional middle ground between churches and political institutions. As Garrison understood it, the Massachusetts Anti-Slavery Society represented a site of sincere moral speech that not only existed outside the corrupt discourses of church and state but was made necessary by the failure of these institutions to model an authentic realm of critical publicity.

Andrew Delbanco, in his biography of William Ellery Channing, characterizes the paradox of the Unitarian imagination in relation to the antislavery movement. Delbanco treats the last years of Channing's life as an "interval of trial" in which he came to terms with his lifelong "evasion" of the philosophical implications of slavery.[62] For most of his career, Channing was able to imagine Christianity in dialogic terms and thus to integrate humankind's moral "likeness to God" into a polyvocal process in which the faithful move toward truth through critical conversation. But the dehumanizing evil embodied in the slave master represented a set of motivations that was antithetical to the moral progressivism of Unitarian spirituality. In psychological terms, the slave master embodied the trace of innate depravity within the ideals of perfectability that were at the center of Unitarian faith. Like innate depravity rerearing its face, the evil fact of the slave master required Channing to recognize a form of egotism that knew no bounds. This egotism, of course, was coupled with an equally profound philosophical cynicism that constructed a discourse of justification for slavery as a moral good. The motivations that enabled one person to claim another as a slave are the antithesis of the utopian quest that defines man and woman's likeness to God. Equally, the frame of mind that enabled one to step into the public sphere and call slaveholding a positive good is the rhetorical antithesis of the sincere dialogue that is the core of Unitarian faith and of discursive democracy.

Delbanco reformulates Channing's mature spirituality to deemphasize his poetic confidence in moral progress and focus on the struggle between the Unitarians' optimism and Channing's private recognition that the most profoundly evil motivations coexist with divinity inside the self. Delbanco concludes that "if Channing's earlier thought had construed the religious impulse as an urge toward elevation, he comes in his later years to feel it much more as a combat. The central importance of the slavery issue is that it identifies two enemies: the defenders of slavery, and the self."[63] In effect, Delbanco argues that in the last years of his life, Channing returned to an almost Puritan spirituality, but one in which the struggle between Christ and Satan was internalized and redefined as a struggle between the self's likeness to God and the reality of its satanic opposite, the slave master. This change in Channing's point of view is important to Unitarianism as a template of discursive democracy because it shows Channing internalizing the dialectical tension between critical and strategic public discourse. It also brings Channing closer to the orthodox position by recognizing the constant presence of a force that distorts discourse, spirituality, and the self.

In its fracturing of authority, both among a broadening plurality of denominations and away from ministers and toward congregations, the Unitarian controversy modeled an identification of self with voluntary associations rather than with the early republican ideal of the civic virtue of the independent citizen. In its broadly public debates among different religious communicants, it also modeled critical public discourse in a context where the stakes were very high. Even if the participants did not embrace the principle of universality, the struggle between orthodox and liberal Congregationalists reveals the diffusion of authority away from institutional settings and toward sites of public discourse. The disruption of church structures was also fully public, not just in regard to disestablishment but even in the need for towns to restructure taxation and shuffle church memberships. Ironically, though, the Unitarians fared worse than the orthodox evangelicals. The liberals' commitment to tolerance left them in a weak rhetorical position vis-à-vis the sense of crisis generated by the spectacles of evangelical revivalism. Equally ironically, the orthodox faction mastered the subtle dynamics of the critical public realm much more successfully than the Unitarians. But in some ways the orthodox strategy was also self-defeating because the fundamental assumptions of liberal epistemology and public reason were antithetical to their Bible-based faith. In a very real sense, the fact that Lyman Beecher had to establish an evangelical mission in the city of Boston, Massachusetts, demonstrates the challenge that the orthodox evangelicals faced.

The Unitarian controversy thus laid the foundation for secular reform culture in several ways. Above all, this episode describes the adaptation of an elite class to changing institutional and philosophical circumstances. While the Unitarians embraced the principles of pluralist dialogue, toleration of dissent, freedom of thought, and the value of historical, scientific, and philosophical discourse within their faith, they ultimately defined a spiritual form of civic humanism that counterbalanced the tendency to equate pluralism with chaos rather than with progressive dialogue. Orthodox adaptation to liberalization in Jeffersonian and Jacksonian culture is characterized most emphatically by intense publicity campaigns and aggressive efforts to swell their own ranks and thereby reverse the tide of events. In their crusade, the orthodox evangelicals embraced their new role as the militant guardians of Christianity, but they also hearkened back to a predisestablishment alliance of church and state and to the deferential society that went with it. In Lyman Beecher's suppression of debate at Lane Seminary in 1834 and in Moses Stuart's defense of Daniel Webster and the Fugitive Slave Law in 1850, the desire to embrace their place as missionaries to their own homeland always competed with the desire to reclaim a church-state alliance as a means of keeping demons in a bottle.

Despite their efforts to reinvent themselves, neither the orthodox nor the liberal faction was able to define a clear position on antislavery or to take leadership of the antislavery movement. The lukewarm efforts of churches to oppose the most egregious moral crime of their society created the occasion for the emergence of secular reform culture. It would be tautological to argue that the nation collapsed into Civil War because people failed to find a satisfactory discourse with which to bring slavery to an end. But crafting a discourse in which people could conduct an honest and direct discussion of slavery was an important goal for early reformers. The women's rights movement, in important respects, emerged out of just such a critical conversation about the conditions under which women could facilitate a discussion of slavery. In this dialogue, the divisiveness of religious and reform rhetoric is explicitly thematized to redefine the basic issues under discussion. Rather than explicitly engaging epistemological and spiritual questions such as the legitimate foundations of knowledge and faith, the conversation in the early woman's rights movement focused on relationships between femininity, sincerity, and publicity. Though religion was still important to this dialogue, the first major debate over women's access to the critical public realm was rooted in the problem of public sincerity.

CHAPTER TWO

Sincerity and Publicity in the Grimké-Beecher Debate

As the legitimization of the minister's authority diffused into the realm of critical public discourse, the types of authority Americans saw in womanhood were also beginning to find purchase in the public sphere. Even as Jacksonian Americans were assembling the scaffolding of antebellum domesticity, American women were defining two important pathways into critical discourse. Working as writers and social reformers, women were in the vanguard of cultural dialogues about the implications of industrialization, urbanization, and the doctrine of universal human rights. Women's participation in benevolent reform movements offered them a site where connections between femininity and privacy intersected with those between femininity, sincerity, and moral virtue. As much as the "feminization" of the clergy describes a process of privatization that reflected fundamental change in the structure of American civil society, the debate over women's participation in critical public discourse reflects both the role of the public sphere in defining equality and the extraordinary disruptions attendant on the transition to a pluralistic public sphere.

Lydia Maria Child, writing in the wake of the dispute over women's participation in the American Anti-Slavery Society, describes women's presence in reform as a transformation both of womanhood and of the society as a whole. A wizard's apprentice, Child writes, witnesses his master "cause a broom to become a man" for the purpose of housework. One day, the apprentice awakens the broom and asks it to do some of his chores. But he unleashes a force beyond his control: "With supernatural activity, the bewitched household utensil brought water, water, water, till tubs were filled, the floor overflowed, the furniture was deluged." The apprentice desperately tries to return the broom to its inert state, but "he forgot the backward spell. Thus it is," Child concludes, "with those who urged women to become missionaries, and form tract societies. They have changed the household utensil into a living, energetic being; and they have no spell to turn it into a broom again" (*Lib.* July 23, 1841). Despite the poetic justice Child conveys with this story, even to those inside the movement, women's participation in reform had the aura of a mystical event fraught with all the tensions that attend the unleashing of a new force.

Well before suffrage moved to center stage at the Seneca Falls Convention in 1848, American women reformers recognized a deep strategic divide in their ranks. Liberal reformers such as Frances Wright, Sarah and Angelina Grimké, and Margaret Fuller had begun to argue that the moral equality of women required fundamental changes in American institutions. In their view, restrictions on women's right to public speech violated philosophical principles of equality and autonomy underpinning Americans' most cherished tenets of selfhood. The liberal reformers who advanced this position assumed that the nation's values are most importantly shaped in a discursive public realm and that restricting access to public debate denies the moral equality of those who are barred from participation.

During the first half of the nineteenth century, liberal reformers contended against conservative reformers such as Catharine Beecher and Sarah Josepha Hale, who argued that women's authority must remain consistent with a social and religious tradition that treated gender spheres as a divinely ordained division that must be preserved in any legitimate structure of civil authority. Advocates of gender-sphere ideology articulated an ideal of women's authority in which political disenfranchisement legitimized women's stewardship of the moral virtue of the nation by creating a discrete discursive environment characterized by femininity, privacy, and sincerity. In the process through which Ann Douglas sees clergy and "literary women" undergoing parallel forms of disestablishment, conservative reformers such as Catharine Beecher saw something more like a paradigm shift that offered women the opportunity to claim political authority for the domestic sphere and to eclipse a factionalized clergy as the representatives of consensus.[1]

Recent histories of women's involvement in social reform have stressed points of transition at which relationships between femininity and publicity shifted to redefine the legitimizing principles of women's participation in public life. As Lori Ginzberg and others explain, at the end of the eighteenth century, benevolent organizations such as the Boston Female Asylum and the Society for the Relief of Poor Widows with Small Children emerged to relieve suffering among the "deserving poor," people such as virtuous widows and their fatherless children. Then, with the rapid social transformations that occurred in the early antebellum period, women's reform activism expanded to include work with prostitutes and prison inmates. Hence, innovations in reform movements during the 1830s increasingly brought middle-class white women into contact with "fallen" women and criminals.[2]

This expansion of women's involvement in social reform had important but unrecognized implications for both the liberal and the conservative faction of the early women's rights movement. Most importantly, it marked a telling change in women's participation in critical discourse because it introduced tension between social conventions that functioned to protect women's "virtue" by insulating them from corrupt influences and contrasting conventions of selfless benevolence that supported women's effort to reform the weakest and most vicious members of society. Although benevolence had brought women into social reform beginning in the 1790s, this form of activism in itself did not seriously violate the fictions of moral innocence that many considered indispensable to feminine virtue. However, the exposure to vice that went along with reform activism among the sinful and criminal asserted women's claim to the critical subjectivity that enabled them to work among corrupt members of the society without being morally compromised themselves. Instead of being protected in a realm of perpetual innocence, women in benevolent associations began to undertake the work of rescuers and redeemers. This demonstration of the internal resources that comprise moral autonomy gave momentum to efforts to legitimize women's access to critical public discourse, which had its own complex combination of sincerity and duplicity.

Lori Ginzberg sums up connections made by Mary P. Ryan, Nancy Cott, and others: "The very assertion of an identity based on female morality carried within it both the conservative imperative to conform and a more radical call to define and act upon women's needs."[3] Each faction, the conservatives who argued for the authority implicit in domesticity as well as the liberals who argued for the authority to be gained through women's participation in antislavery and other reform movements, was working to redefine femininity in relation to the changing norms of the public sphere.

In this respect the women's rights movement responded to the same pressures that shaped the Unitarian controversy. In his 1851 *Memoirs of Margaret Fuller*,

Emerson tries to describe the invisible topography that women faced as they stepped into intellectual and reform culture: "A woman in our society finds her safety and happiness in exclusions and privacies. She congratulates herself when she is not called to the market, to the courts, to the polls, to the stage, or to the orchestra. . . . Prescriptions almost invincible the female lecturer or professor of any science must encounter; and, except on points where the charities which are left to women as their legitimate province interpose against the ferocity of the laws, with us a female politician is unknown" (1:321–22). Women's "safety and happiness," Emerson assumes, lie in "exclusions." But he also marks out public realms in which women had achieved recognition. While some women worked in charities that the culture recognized as women's "legitimate province," Margaret Fuller faced "almost invincible" obstacles in her desire to live as a public intellectual. Most important for my purpose, Emerson notes a border where a struggle for legitimacy was taking place as women sought recognition as participants in reform politics. The "female politician," in Emerson's eyes, was an "unknown" figure to Americans. Though Emerson probably meant this comment to denote the extreme rarity of female politicians in America, it also describes a changing condition. During the course of Emerson's lifetime, the female politician emerged as a presence on the public stage and became something of a "known" figure in society.

The debate between Angelina Grimké and Catharine Beecher that occurred from 1836 to 1838 represents the first major episode in the struggle over the nature of women's participation in politics and its implications for American society. As such, it is a critical conversation about the "female politician" that defined central issues in the organized women's rights movement. In their boldest moments, Grimké and Beecher each imagined femininity as a revolutionary force, a force that could redefine institutions, transform values, and serve as the moral bedrock of a consensus society. Grimké grounded a claim to full and equal access to public dialogue in the principle that women's moral equality requires unfettered access to civil society. She argued that a feminine discourse of sincerity and sympathy can transform the norms of public debate to create an improved critical public realm. To achieve this end, as Frederick Douglass would strive to do in other ways, Grimké would have to subvert the abstract masculine homogeneity of eighteenth-century citizenship and literally embody feminine citizenship. Catharine Beecher, instead of seeking to legitimize women's participation in a pluralistic public sphere where men and women speak as equals, worked to capture critical dialogue for the domestic realm, where it would be mediated by women. Though these conflicting models of women's authority mark a public/private distinction central to women's emergence as political agents in antebellum America, they are equally important as competing expressions of women's self-understanding as members of society. Ironically, as divisive as the debate between domesticity and civil equality proved to be, both Beecher and Grimké entered the lists of reform out of a desire to heal a corrupted public discourse and to promote consensus in a society that they feared might collapse under the centripetal pressures already pulling churches into the same realm of discursive democracy as other voluntary associations.

Psychologies of Feminine Disfranchisement and Privilege

In 1836 Angelina Grimké, a member of a wealthy slaveholding family in South Carolina, published an antislavery essay titled *Appeal to the Christian Women of the South*, exhorting southern women to organize in opposition to slavery. Though much of Grimké's pamphlet is a conventional rebuttal of proslavery religious dogma, her argument that women should join antislavery societies provoked a stormy debate that reached a climax when Pennsylvania Hall in Philadelphia was burnt to the ground after she delivered an antislavery speech there.[4] Angelina and her older sister Sarah extended the argument of the *Appeal* into practice in a yearlong antislavery lecture tour in 1837 and 1838. Though Grimké's pamphlet provoked a wide variety of responses, the most substantial response came from Lyman Beecher's daughter Catharine. In a book titled *An Essay on Slavery and Abolitionism, with Reference to the Duty of American Females*, Beecher defended domesticity as a locus of civic power and argued that equality in the public sphere would diminish rather than enhance women's authority in American society.

Despite the antagonistic positions they took in this debate, Catharine Beecher and Angelina Grimké had much in common. Most importantly, Beecher and Grimké had backgrounds that gave each a sense of cultural enfranchisement. Beyond their regional differences, these similarities were strong enough briefly to bring them together in a mentor-pupil relationship. When Beecher's Hartford Female Academy was at its height in 1831, the twenty-six-year-old Grimké visited for a week. Before Grimké returned to Philadelphia, she even took Beecher's entrance examination and considered enrolling as a student. As the circumstances of this meeting indicate, when they debated the merits of Grimké's *Appeal* five years later, the two women were at different places in their lives and careers.

Gerda Lerner remarks, "At the time of their meeting Catharine Beecher must have appeared an awe-inspiring figure of female accomplishment to Grimké."[5] When Grimké visited in 1831, Beecher was already an important advocate of women's education and the professionalization of domestic labor. By contrast, Grimké was still groping for a self-image that would fulfill her own conflicting impulses and aspirations.[6]

The path that brought them into debate reveals much about the conflicted psychologies of privilege and powerlessness that characterized the margin of the critical public sphere. In Emerson's metaphor, a "female politician" was a woman whose legitimate charitable activities "interpose[d] against the ferocity of the laws." That site where benevolence meets the ferocity of law and tradition is the site where the Grimké-Beecher debate took place.

Catharine Beecher's career as a writer and educational reformer developed in an incremental process through which she mediated between deeply felt religious anxieties, intense public aspirations, and cultural expectations defined by class and gender. Though to her father's disappointment, Catharine never experienced saving grace and even questioned its necessity for salvation, she first engaged a public issue through an epistolary defense of Calvinism against Catharine Sedgwick's satirical representation of it in *A New England Tale*. This incident dramatizes an important nuance in Beecher's psychological relationship to paternal and religious authority. Although not a full member of a congregation, she was nonetheless deeply committed to the tradition of leadership that Congregationalism embodied. She was quick to defend orthodoxy both as a source of cultural authority and as a locus of metaphysical truth. As letters to her younger brother Edward reveal, she always felt herself to be a lieutenant in her family's ongoing fight against the Unitarians.[7]

Though Beecher psychologically entered the public sphere in the context of religious sectarianism, her emergence as an educator was motivated more by a quest for self-definition than by her father's role in the Unitarian controversy. Following the sudden death of her fiancé, Alexander Fisher, Beecher felt herself at a crossroads. As Kathryn Sklar explains, Beecher's romance with Fisher transformed her sense of self by introducing her to self-reflexive images of maturity and adulthood.[8] Rather than compelling her to accept a position of wifely submission, her relationship with Fisher rewarded Beecher by convincing her that making high-stakes decisions about her own life was accompanied by seriousness of identity and purpose. In the period following Fisher's death, Beecher revaluated the pre-Fisher period of her life and concluded that it represented a kind of frivolous self-indulgence that paled in value before the seriousness that she felt during her courtship and engagement. Having lost the context of this enriched identity through a tragic accident, Beecher found herself struggling to retain the seriousness of self that she had gained.

Despite some harsh self-reflection on her dilettantish life, Beecher decided, as she haltingly remarked in a letter to her father: "There is reason to believe that in more solid pursuits there is no deficiency" (*ALB* 1:318). After a period of spiritual introspection and private academic study, Beecher decided that the best way to satisfy her conflicting desires was to establish a woman's academy. In the same letter to her father, she described the problem that she was trying to negotiate. Though she aspired to live a life of "solid pursuits," she was acutely aware of the threats to conventional models of femininity that her aspirations created. She articulated this opposition through the metaphors of space that defined women's relationship to publicity: "Generally speaking there seems to be no extensive sphere of usefulness for a single woman but that which can be found in the limits of a school-room. . . . [However,] there have been instances in which women of superior mind and acquirements have risen to a more enlarged and comprehensive boundary of exertion . . . and by their talents and influence have accomplished what, in a more circumscribed sphere of action, would have been impossible (*ALB* 1:378). Beecher presented the schoolroom as a middle ground between realms characterized by narrow "limits" and the "enlarged" realms that have "comprehensive" boundaries. Shortly thereafter, she opened the Hartford Female Academy. By the time Angelina Grimké joined the antislavery movement, Beecher had founded two female seminaries, published articles on educational reform, written school textbooks, and published a book-length treatise on "Mental and Moral Philosophy" based on the capstone course she taught her students in Cincinnati.[9] When Grimké published her *Appeal to the Christian Women of the South* in 1836, Catharine Beecher was one of the most famous and accomplished women in the United States.

While Beecher's emergence as a public figure was motivated by tension between a sense of self that defined seriousness in terms of public influence and deep loyalty to traditions of faith and norms of gender, Angelina Grimké's entry into the public sphere was driven by a quest for spiritual fulfillment that ultimately intersected with reform politics. Throughout her early adult years, Grimké sought a religious denomination in which she could fully express her faith. This quest caused her repeatedly to change religious affiliations. As she converted from Episcopalianism to Presbyterianism to Quakerism, she repeated a pattern of intense spiritual commitment succeeded by disillusionment as each church failed to offer her sufficient outlets for civic spirituality.[10] While visiting her sister Sarah in Philadelphia in 1828, Grimké found herself in a community in which spiritual discourse was inseparable from political commitment. During this visit, Angelina not only embraced antislavery; she also sought to gain some expressive outlet for her emerging commitment to social reform. Soon, though, Angelina discovered that the Quakers who had worked so hard to convert her to antislavery not only were passive in their efforts to bring about abolition but also were actively hostile to women's participation in the antislavery movement. In embracing antislavery, she had gained a sense of moral commitment that had a public and political face, but she almost immediately found the desire to express her conviction repressed. Grimké's inability to find a church that satisfied her desire to combine faith with public service dramatizes the failure of existing public institutions to effectively integrate moral and political discourse. In her quest for a church, she found the antislavery society.

In the summer of 1835, an article in William Lloyd Garrison's *Liberator* impelled Grimké to write him a letter that asserted her sympathy with the abolitionists.[11] The anguish that she recorded after sending this letter indicates her awareness that by writing it she was on the verge of raising her involvement in antislavery to a new level. In September 1835, Grimké wrote in her diary:

> It is now more than 4 weeks since I tho't I felt it right to write WLG[arrison] a letter of sympathy & encouragement in regards to the efforts of the Abolitionists & the violent opposition made to them. As far as I can possibly judge, I believe that letter, penned under right feeling, in the spirit of prayer. I felt that it might involve me in some difficulty, & therefore it was written in fear. And after it was written, I hardly knew whether to send it or not, & therefore again implored divine direction. At last I sent it to the office & felt a degree of peace in doing so. (*PY* 29–30)

Although the letter was personal and not part of the public discussion of slavery, it was an unsolicited letter to a stranger, and it asserted her sympathy for a radical propagandist. Thus, without explicitly moving into public dialogue, Grimké took a half step toward the public realm by writing to the editor of the nation's most controversial newspaper.

If Grimké moved tentatively toward public discourse by writing the letter,

Garrison had few qualms about nudging her across the threshold into reform activism. Without first gaining Grimké's permission, Garrison published her letter in the September 19, 1835, issue of the *Liberator* and attached her name to it. This event was met with as much elation among the abolitionists as it was by distress among the Quakers. In its wake, a Quaker elder visited Grimké and encouraged her to publish a retraction. At the same time, abolitionists were imagining ways to draw her more fully into the antislavery movement.[12] In the same diary entry in which she recorded her anguish over writing the letter, Grimké described her feelings about the attention that its appearance in the *Liberator* provoked: "O! the extreme strain of extravagant praise," Grimké protested, "to be held up as a saint in a newspaper before thousands of people, when I felt I was the chief of sinners. Blushing & confusion of face were mine, & I tho't the walls of a prison would have been preferable to such an exposure" (*PY* 31). Like Beecher, Grimké revealed her acute sense of the threshold between private and public action by contrasting the radical isolation of a prison with the withering exposure of being "held up . . . before thousands of people." As Grimké retreated to struggle with these sentiments, the organized movement was working to enlist her as a marquee figure in its public work. In July 1836, while staying with a friend at the seashore town of Shrewsbury, New Jersey, Angelina wrote to her sister that she was composing an essay on antislavery. She also reacted to a request from Elizur Wright, secretary of the American Anti-Slavery Society, proposing that she lead a series of discussions among women "in parlor meetings." Though Grimké deferred a decision on the speaking tour until after she finished her *Appeal*, she remarked regarding her sister's interest in the proposition: [It] "increases the fear I feel that probably I may have to do it" (*PY* 34). After competing work on the *Appeal* that same summer, Grimké agreed to promote antislavery by speaking to private gatherings of women.

At the beginning of her lecture tour, Grimké spoke exclusively to women's groups. But by March 1837, she was speaking to audiences that included men as well as women. Referring to a lecture in Poughkeepsie, New York, Grimké recorded that for the first time in her life she "spoke to a promiscuous assembly . . . and found the men were no more to [her] than the women."[13] During the year they were on the road, Angelina and Sarah Grimké spearheaded a cultural debate that integrated antislavery with women's rights. As part of this debate, Angelina replied to Catharine Beecher's *Essay* in a series of letters. Her older sister Sarah also published two important texts between 1836 and 1838: *An Epistle to the*

Clergy of the Southern States in 1836 and *Letters on the Equality of the Sexes and the Condition of Women* in 1838. In this two-year period, the Grimkés developed the rights-based argument against slavery in a way that also asserted women's unfettered access to critical discourse as an indispensable element of the belief in universal moral equality. In their writing, they defined full public equality for women and blacks as an inextricable component of the moral equality of all people.

In contrast to Beecher, who emerged from the identity crisis that followed her fiancé's death by defining a vocation that institutionalized tension between publicity and privacy in her professional life, Grimké emerged from her identity crisis by embracing the public role that she had half-intentionally sought. In the debate she initiated with her friend Catharine Beecher, Grimké articulated a relationship between women and public discourse that both argued for a fundamental reconstruction of the idea of equality and, perhaps ironically, deployed an essentialist construction of gender to assert the advantages of a pluralistic public sphere.

Publicity and Equality in Grimké's Appeal

Like other American women in the antislavery movement, Angelina and Sarah Grimké understood their activism in relation to the tradition of dissent that improves the society and anticipates an eventual consensus. At the height of the controversy over Grimké's *Appeal*, for example, Maria Weston Chapman circulated a letter that compared the Grimkés to the original separatist Pilgrims. She exhorted her friends in "Female Anti-Slavery Societies throughout New England" to help the Grimkés "exalt the national character of [American] women—so inferior to that of the Maternal Ancestry who in 1620 'fled from their spheres in England and journeyed here with their little ones,' sheltered in the wintry air, that they might pursue their Christian course unimpeded by sneers of ridicule, ecclesiastical mandates or public outrage" (*WGL* 1:396). Angelina's presence on the public stage, in Weston's view, represented a return to a mythic image of maternity.

Rather than acting as rebels, the Grimkés believed they were rearticulating a tradition of heroic dissent in which women bravely left their "spheres" to advocate a better Christianity and a better society. In reply to an article in the New Haven *Religious Intelligencer* that asked the Grimkés to offer "definite practicable means" through which the North could undermine slavery in the

South, the sisters contextualized the boycott of slave produce by comparing it to the Stamp Act boycott that preceded the American Revolution: "We know full well that this [boycott] will involve much self-denial, but we presume not any more than our revolutionary fathers voluntarily imposed on themselves. . . . Our fathers and mothers knew that there was a very important *principle* involved in the right claimed by England to lay a tax upon articles exported to the colonies, and they therefore refused to pay that tax" (*WGL* 1:371). Most famously, the Declaration of Sentiments that was published following the 1848 women's rights convention at Seneca Falls used the Declaration of Independence as both an ideological and a rhetorical model.

In her *Appeal to the Christian Women of the South*, Grimké assumes that antislavery discourse functions as one voice in a broad public debate, and she explicitly calls on women to participate in it as a means of influencing public opinion.[14] As she understands it, the strategy of the antislavery movement is to argue for a set of principles that might mobilize the popular will by transforming public opinion from tacit support or apathy into active support for abolition. She works toward this end by trying to motivate southern women to embrace abolition as a moral imperative and then to speak against slavery in social discourse as well as in more public and explicitly political media. The assertion of a new, feminine form of public sincerity is at the center of Grimké's *Appeal*. In addition to bringing a new cadre of activists into the movement, Grimké aims to feminize critical public discourse and tip the rhetorical balance away from strategic discourse and toward sincere communication.

Stephen Browne emphasizes the role of the *Appeal* in reconstructing a model of feminine community that Grimké had actually disrupted by writing her letter to William Lloyd Garrison. The *Appeal*, in this sense, "is about the very possibility of community, about its formation, deformation, and reformation in a world as uncertain about the future as it was damaged by the past."[15] While the subtext of disrupted norms reflects Grimké's desire to appropriate feminine sincerity as a counterdiscourse to conventional political rhetoric, she adapts the tones of intimate, private dialogue to the purposes of public, political debate. Toward this combination of feminine sincerity and publicity, Grimké also underscores the relationship between risk-taking and sincerity. In an observation that begins to describe the assumptions Grimké makes about women's potential role in critical discourse, Gerda Lerner marks the stylistic originality of the *Appeal*, emphasizing its "simple and direct tone" and the "absence of fashionable rhetoric" that characterized many antislavery polemics.[16]

Grimké prefaces her *Appeal* with an epigram from the Old Testament that functions as a complicated metaphor of self-justification. In the story of Esther, King Ahasuerus marries Esther, not knowing that she is a Jew. When one of his ministers begins a campaign against the Jews, Esther's adoptive father, Mordecai, implores Esther to petition the king to stop the pogrom. Esther reminds Mordecai that "if any man or woman goes to the king inside the inner court without being called, there is but one law; all alike are to be put to death, except the one to whom the king holds out the golden scepter" (Esther 4:11 RSV). Despite the risk, Mordecai repeats his request and adds the following warning that Grimké excerpts for her epigram:

> Think not within thyself that thou shalt escape in the king's house more than all the Jews. For if thou altogether holdest thy peace at this time, then shall their enlargement and deliverance arise to the Jews from another place: but thou and thy father's house shall be destroyed: and who knoweth whether thou art come to the kingdom for such a time as this. And Esther bade them return Mordecai this answer:—and so will I go unto the king, which is not according to law, and *if I perish, I perish*. (Esther IV, 13–16)

This epigram can be explained on two levels. On one level, Grimké is asking southern women to emulate Esther by accepting the risk of representing slaves in political dialogue. She uses Esther to create a metaphor in which Mordecai, standing in for the slave, has no access to a discourse of power except through Esther. Esther is physically within the structure of power and even though it implies great risk, can speak for the condemned from a privileged position. Yet despite her access to the site of critical discourse, Esther is alienated from it by a taboo that underscores the danger women face by projecting their voices into the critical public realm.

On another level, Grimké is speaking as a type of Esther herself, risking punishment by making herself visible in a forum from which social convention bars her. As Catherine Henry explains, Grimké turns her transgression of the prohibition against women's political speech into a device that demonstrates her sincerity. Henry makes the point that the "rhetoric of exposure" through which Grimké calls attention to her own public presence functions as an authenticating vehicle that simultaneously underscores her sincerity and enables her to subvert taboos by appropriating their transgression as legitimating devices.[17] Working self-consciously within a national tradition of dissent and explicitly speaking in utopian terms, Grimké's *Appeal* works very much as a Bercovitchian rite of assent. Through the epigram, Grimké presents herself as an Esther who is taking a great risk in the hope of calling a whole class of Esthers into being.

Yet despite the conventionality of its place within a historical tradition, the very first sentence of the *Appeal* reveals the acute sense of vulnerability that Grimké felt as a political writer. She combines the assertion of authenticity and vulnerability as she first addresses her audience: "It is because I feel a deep and tender interest in your present and eternal welfare that I am willing thus publicly to address you" (*PY* 36). Connecting her own violation of norms with the sincerity of her voice and the moral urgency of her cause, Grimké notes that a sincere effort to communicate requires simultaneous acts of self-expression and self-denial. As she transgresses a set of gender-specific norms that require public invisibility, Grimké strives to assert a new set of norms that have a form of self-revealing sincerity at their center. She begins by speaking to close friends: "Some of you have loved me as a relative, and some have felt bound to me in Christian sympathy." She then turns to those who witnessed her religious turmoil of the 1820s, remarking: "You were generous enough to give me credit for sincerity as a Christian, though you believed I had been most strangely deceived." Finally, she reaches out to address strangers: "But there are other Christian women scattered over the Southern states, a very large number of whom have never seen me, and never heard my name" (*PY* 36–37). By addressing her audience in this ranked order of intimacy, Grimké blurs the boundary between public and private dialogue. Those with whom she is less intimate, in effect, are invited to enter her circle of friends.

Creating a rhetoric that integrates the intimate discourse of friendship with the publicity of political discourse is more than a stylistic issue for Grimké. It goes to the core of her understanding of critical conversation. Rather than writing from "the heat of passion or prejudice," her text is communicated in a desire to speak "truths in love." Indeed, her sincerity is prayerful: "It is then, because I *do feel* and *do pray* for you, that I thus address you upon a subject about which of all others, perhaps you would rather not hear anything." In this context of sympathy, she entreats her readers "to read the following pages in the spirit of calm investigation and fervent prayer" because she does "not believe that the time has yet come when *Christian women* 'will not endure sound doctrine,' even on the subject of slavery, if it is spoken to them in tenderness and love" (*PY* 37). Grimké seeks to combine conventions of private dialogue with the publicity of political discourse to create a community of women activists. This reconstructed community will contribute a new voice to critical public discourse. "It will be a great thing," Grimké exhorts in the middle of the *Appeal*, "if the subject [of abolition] can be introduced into your legislatures in any way, even by *women*, and *they* will be the most likely to introduce it there in the best possible manner, as a matter of *morals* and *religion*, not expediency or politics" (*PY* 66). Rather than writing to repatriate herself into an apolitical pre-letter-to-Garrison private realm, Grimké extends the voice that originated with that letter by describing the conventions and detailing the implications of a feminine political discourse.[18] With this suggestion, Grimké images a plural public in which a distinctly feminine voice calls the official public sphere into sincere dialogue.

The core of Grimké's antislavery argument is the assertion of America's unique commitment to the ideal of universal human equality. In her political imagination, equality is contingent on the individual's right of public self-representation. Though Grimké makes her case by connecting the human rights doctrine of the Declaration of Independence with biblical descriptions of legitimate civil authority, she always measures justice in relation to people's rights as members of civil society. In Grimké's logic, as in that of John Rawls and Jürgen Habermas, an unequal right to self-representation in the public sphere amounts to moral inequality as a human being.[19] Working from this construction of human rights, Grimké's activism is motivated by the assumption that moral equality requires the right to participate in the critical debates of the public sphere. Ultimately, in what will become the focal point of Catharine Beecher's opposition, Grimké argues for the necessity of organizing women committed to antislavery into political associations that can participate in critical conversation and thereby influence public opinion. Grimké thus proposes a radical reconstruction of the critical public. As part of her critique of Habermas, Nancy Fraser situates the type of challenge that Grimké poses into a structural context. "Dominant groups," Fraser writes, "articulate need interpretations intended to exclude, defuse, and/or co-opt counterinterpretations. Subordinate or oppositional groups, on the other hand, articulate need interpretations intended to challenge, displace, and/or modify dominant ones."[20] What is important here is not just that Grimké's challenge is structural but also that she aims to reform one of the fundamental principles regulating access to the critical public sphere. Whereas Frederick Douglass would make a case built around the problem of recognition, Grimké makes one grounded in contemporary theories of women's subjectivity. On this foundation, rather than arguing for sameness, Grimké argues for a pluralist revision of the structure of public discourse.

While Grimké's program represents a vindication of women's political equality in relation to nongovernmental political debate, it also strikingly disregards the separate-spheres dogma that was central to antebellum Americans' identities as men and women. Beginning by drawing a link between Esther's dissent in Babylon and the founders' dissent sixty years before she was writing, Grimké develops a line of argument that asserts women's authority not just to speak in public but even to serve in political office. In a letter she wrote to her sister as she was working on the manuscript, Angelina outlined the argument of the *Appeal*: "The plan I am pursuing is first to frame slavery to the contrary of our declaration, and to answer the objections that our forefathers were mistaken for the Bible sanctions slavery by showing it to be contrary to the great charter of human rights granted to Adam."[21] She follows this outline by connecting the principles that the founders articulated in the declaration with the principles that God defined for Adam: "We must come back," she begins, "to the good old doctrine of our forefathers who declared to the world, this self evident truth that '*all* men are created equal, and that they have certain *inalienable* rights among which are life, *liberty*, and the pursuit of happiness.'" After situating the declaration as the centerpiece of American moral philosophy, Grimké modulates her tone and notes: "But after all, it may be said, our fathers were certainly mistaken, for the Bible sanctions slavery, and that is the highest authority. Now the Bible is my ultimate appeal in all matters of faith and practice, and it is *to this test* I am anxious to bring the subject at issue between us" (*PY* 38). She conducts this test by comparing southern slavery to biblical representations of servitude and bondage.

In testing American slavery against the Old Testament, Grimké finds ancient civil protections that enable her to argue that Old Testament bondage protected human rights in ways that American slavery did not. Citing passages in Leviticus, Exodus, and Kings, Grimké identifies laws that limit the power of slave owners. She emphasizes norms that limit a master's power by defining his right to punish servants, the penalties that masters faced for murdering and mutilating slaves, and even legal limitations on masters' sexual power over female slaves. Grimké concludes that in the Mosaic Law, servitude is an economic state in which the individual retains the same fundamental rights as other members of civil society. This body of law, she argues, recognizes the moral equality of masters and slaves and incorporates principles of human rights to protect that equality.

As Grimké summarizes the argument of the antislavery section of the *Appeal*, she underscores the importance of the declaration as a defining text for human equality and goes so far as to deny the existence of dehumanizing chattel slavery in the world of the Bible. She summarizes:

> I have thus, I think, clearly proved to you seven propositions, viz.: First, that slavery is contrary to the declaration of our independence. Second, that it is contrary to the first charter of human rights given to Adam, and renewed to Noah. Third, that the fact of slavery having been the subject of prophesy, furnishes *no* excuse whatever to slave dealers. Fourth, that no such system existed under the patriarchal dispensation. Fifth, that *slavery never* existed under the Jewish dispensation; but so far otherwise, that every servant was placed under the *protection of law*, and care taken not only to prevent all *involuntary* servitude, but all *voluntary perpetual* bondage. Sixth, that slavery in America reduces a man to a thing, a "chattel personal," robs *him* of *all* his rights as a *human being*, fetters both his mind and body, and protects the *master* in the most unnatural and unreasonable power, whilst it *throws him out* of the protection of law. Seventh, that slavery is contrary to the example and precepts of our holy and merciful Redeemer, and of his apostles. (*PY* 54)

Despite the tautological aspect of Grimké's argument, the specifics of the case she makes against slavery reveal the importance of universal human rights to her spirituality. She implicitly, perhaps even subconsciously, sees the founders acting in a prophetic tradition. In the human rights doctrine represented by the declaration, the founders reassert a principle that has stood since God first peopled Eden. Far from articulating the results of secular philosophy, the humanism of the Declaration of Independence simply renewed a biblical doctrine in the rhetoric of an enlightened age.

While Grimké's argument for the continuity of biblical and national doctrines of human rights is scholarly and theoretical, her argument for southern women's power to end slavery has a more practical orientation. In this section of the *Appeal*, Grimké describes a process of consciousness formation that radically opposes conventional assumptions about women's intellectual lives.[22] It represents the construction of feminine selfhood in direct relation to processes of critical discourse in the public sphere. To begin, Grimké addresses women's political disenfranchisement and sketches a program through which her readers can claim authority in the antislavery movement. "But perhaps you will be ready to query," she writes:

> Why appeal to *women* on this subject? *We* do not make the laws which perpetuate slavery. *No* legislative power is vested in *us*; *we* can do nothing to overthrow the system, even if we wished to do so. To this I reply, I know you do not make the laws, but I also know that *you are the wives, and mothers, the sisters and daughters of those that do*; and if you really suppose *you* can do nothing to overthrow slavery, you are greatly mistaken. You can do much in every way: four things I will name. 1st. You can read on this subject. 2nd. You can pray over this subject. 3rd. You can speak on this subject. 4th. You can *act* on this subject. (*PY* 55)

Although Grimké acknowledges women's disenfranchisement and includes a conventional assertion of the influence women hold over those who "make the laws which perpetuate slavery," she explains this influence in very unconventional terms. Rather than emphasizing modes of moral influence that women can exert over men in the domestic realm, Grimké stresses women's self-education and the collective forms of public action that can grow out of it. She treats public activism as the culminating act of a process of self-transformation.

By Grimké's logic, the risks that antislavery women accepted were consequences of a moral commitment that compelled public action. As such, while her antislavery and her feminism were both rooted in the principle of universal equality, her feminist thought focused more narrowly on the problem of publicity. In a letter titled "Human Rights Not Founded on Sex," which she wrote in reply to Catharine Beecher's *Essay on Slavery and Abolitionism*, for example, Grimké shifts the foundation of rights discourse from gender to humanity and argues for the identical moral nature of men and women.[23] She writes that "human beings have *rights*, because they are *moral* beings: the rights of *all* men grow out of their moral nature; and as all men have the same moral nature, they have essentially the same rights" (*LCB* 114). The idea of a universal moral identity negates gender-based restrictions on women's access to critical publicity: "When human beings are regarded as *moral* beings, *sex*, instead of being enthroned upon the summit, administering upon rights and responsibilities, sinks into insignificance and nothingness. My doctrine then is, that whatever it is morally right for man to do, it is morally right for woman to do" (*LCB* 115). Eliminating the private/woman, public/man distinction by asserting a shared moral nature, Grimké holds to men's and women's equal obligation to denounce evil publicly.

In the *Appeal* she cites several biblical examples of women acting in public—Miriam, Deborah, Huldah, Anna—to underscore her argument for the legitimacy of women participating in political dialogue. Grimké even gives particular attention to biblical examples of women acting as preachers. For example, she cites Peter's assertion that in the last days women will preach equally with men:

> What did Peter mean by telling them, "this is *that* which was spoken by the prophet Joel: And it shall come to pass in the last days, said *God*, I will pour out my spirit upon *all* flesh: and your sons and your *daughters shall prophesy*. . . . And on my servants and on my *handmaidens*, I will pour out in those days of my spirit; and *they shall prophesy*." This is the plain matter of fact, as Clark and Scott, Stratton and Locke, all allow. Mine is no "private interpretation," no mere sectarian view. (*LCB* 106)

She also cites an inconsistency in biblical translation that transformed a woman into a servant and a man into a preacher.[24] Grimké explains: "[I]t appears that the very same word, *Diakonos*, which when applied to Phoebe, Romans xvi. 1, is translated *servant*, when applied to Tychicus, Ephesians vi. 21, is rendered *minister*." In a letter to Theodore Weld, Angelina anticipated that in the future "posterity will read withal *women* were *not* permitted to preach the gospel with as much amazement and indignation as we do that no *colored* man in No[rth] Ca[rolina] is allowed this *holy right*" (*WGL* 1:418). In regard to Margaret Fuller, Jeffery Steele has recently argued that women's authority to preach was a central topic of debate between Fuller and Ralph Waldo Emerson.[25] These examples do more than reconstruct a tradition of women in evangelical reform; they link moral equality to publicity by presenting women acting prophetically in public contexts. In them, women stand as moral equals of men not just in their natures but also in their roles as public speakers-of-truth. A key image of progress for Grimké is the liberalization of public sites of authoritative discourse to recognize the equality of white women and African Americans.

Grimké asserts her confidence in the moral legitimacy of full public equality most unequivocally when she rebuts Catharine Beecher's argument for the value of women's deference to masculine political authority:

Now, I believe it is woman's right to have a voice in all the laws and regulations
by which she is to be *governed*, whether in Church or State; and that the present
arrangements of society, on these points, are *a violation of human rights, a rank usurpation
of power*, a violent seizure and confiscation of what is sacredly and inalienably hers—
thus inflicting upon woman outrageous wrongs, working mischief incalculable in
the social circle, and in its influence on the world producing only evil, and that
continually. *If* Ecclesiastical and Civil governments are ordained of God, *then* I
contend that woman has just as much right to sit in solemn counsel in Conventions,
Conferences, Associations and General Assemblies, as man—just as much right to
sit upon the throne of England, or in the Presidential chair of the United States.
(*LCB* 119)

Encompassing power in both church and state, Grimké's vision for justice in
American civil society required a profound revision of American constructions
of equality and citizenship.

These changes begin with a four-stage program for the transformation of
women's sense of self and for her incorporation into critical public discourse.
The program that Grimké proposes begins with reading and culminates in
political activism. The act of reading, always coded with subversive implications
for women in antebellum America, was especially subversive in the slaveholding
states, which typically censored threatening literature.[26] Grimké recognizes that
"Committees of Vigilance," whose task it was to suppress subversive thought
and action, worked to keep antislavery propaganda out of reach. Hence, she
encourages her readers to "search the Scriptures daily" to discover the validity of
the claims she makes in the *Appeal* and when possible, to read "other books and
papers [that] might be a great help in this investigation" (*PY* 55). By making these
suggestions, Grimké asks women consciously to challenge standard justifications
of slavery rather than accepting the conventional practices of a society dependent
on slave labor. In Grimké's view, for women to read the antislavery press implies
more than just an act of dissent; it is the first stage in a process of moral self-
education.

Grimké supplements the type of autonomy that reading fosters by coupling
it with prayer. She connects the two by explaining: "I have not placed reading
before prayer because I regard it more important, but because, in order to pray
aright, we must understand what we are praying for; it is only then that we can
'pray with the understanding and the spirit also'" (*PY* 55). While reading will

enable women intellectually to recognize the moral crime of American slavery, prayer will enable them to embrace antislavery with full spiritual sincerity.

During the emergent activist's period of reading and prayer, Grimké encourages her to develop a type of moral consciousness that is intellectually autonomous and that recognizes its complicity in contemporary social conditions. The first phase through which Grimké imagines women developing a commitment to reform involves a private dialogue with scripture that can lead them to a subversive interpretation of their obligations as citizens. In the identity that Grimké maps, this process of reading and prayer lays the foundation for subsequent acts of speaking and writing because it defines the self-construction of an autonomous moral subject, a democratic personality, who has voluntarily internalized a set of values and can speak from a position of moral self-reliance. In important respects, it parallels the evolution in women's benevolent reform from work with the deserving poor to work with the sinful and criminal. By linking reading and prayer with the fact of chattel slavery in their civil society, the first phase of Grimké's plan asks southern women to develop a complex ethical consciousness that will enable responsible political citizenship.

The second phase of Grimké's plan deals with forms of social activism. After women have developed the psychology of liberal autonomy through reading and prayer, Grimké then asks them *not* to repress this new sense of self in their daily lives. She encourages women to find ways to vocalize their antislavery views. As a bridge between self-transformation and the conversion of others, Grimké introduces "speaking" through the same nuanced reference to less and less intimate communities that she deployed in introducing herself at the beginning of the *Appeal*: "It is through the tongue, the pen, and the press, that truth is principally propagated. Speak then to your relatives, your friends, your acquaintances on the subject of slavery; be not afraid if you are conscientiously convinced it is *sinful*, to say so openly, but calmly, and let your sentiments be known" (*PY* 56). When she discusses "speaking" in the *Appeal*, Grimké is not referring to the kind of public speaking that she had been invited to do as a lecturer for the American Anti-Slavery Society. She presents this form of activism as a self-reflexive, semiprivate action that sustains a speaker's desire to maintain a newly created antislavery consciousness as much as it serves the evangelical function of changing the minds of others. Conscientious private speech serves as an alternative to a hypocritical silence for women whose private self-education has led them to embrace antislavery.

In the context of private conversation as a form of political activism, Grimké takes pains to preserve sincerity as a legitimizing element of women's political speech. She underscores her conviction that women should only oppose slavery if they are "conscientiously convinced" that slavery is sinful. She even defines the tone of voice she imagines for antislavery women. If they are opposed to slavery, they should "say so openly, but calmly," rather than adopting the inflammatory rhetoric of the radical abolitionists. She concludes her discussion of "speaking" by quoting lines of verse that combine the themes of moral community, feminine sincerity, and the obligation to speak against oppression. She queries:

> Will *you* behold unheeding,
>   Life's holiest feelings crushed,
> Where *woman's* heart is bleeding
>   Shall *woman's* heart be hushed? (*PY* 57)

In these four lines, Grimké casts women's antislavery activism as a moral imperative and defines feminine speech as a model of authenticity. Witnessing the degradation that she describes in the first two lines of the quotation leads to a sympathetic reaction in the third line and a call to respond in the fourth. By the logic of Grimké's equal-rights feminism, for "*woman's* heart" to remain silent in the face of "life's holiest feelings crushed" undermines femininity far more than participation in the antislavery movement.

Despite the emphasis that Grimké places on transforming the self to lay the foundation for sincere speech, she also sees "action," in the form of organized speaking and publishing in the antislavery press, as a necessary element of women's moral obligation. Her argument for women's participation in antislavery is her most radical departure from the careful balances between traditional femininity and reform activism that sustained women's benevolent movements. Most important as a challenge to the discursive structure of the public realm, Grimké does not justify women's entrance into political organizing as a logical extension of domestic moral authority. Instead, she presents the right to public activism as a fundamental element of women's moral equality with men and as the moral obligation of all civic-minded citizens.

Women's public speaking and propagandizing is central to Grimké's program because she assumes that although human rights are a spiritual imperative, the practical means to end slavery lies in mobilizing public opinion through reform movements. Nancy Isenberg, in her analysis of the relationship between femininity and citizenship, describes the religious discourse that Grimké appropriates as an important authorizing discourse for women activists. Isenberg explains that "religion had a distinctive influence on the women's rights movement . . . as a crucial medium for debating such pivotal concerns as public opinion, the ethical foundation of rights, and the need for heresy and dissent when challenging the irrefutable authority of 'common sense' and majority rule."[27] In this respect, Grimké's advocacy of the right to participate in political speech extends an important tradition of women's reform rhetoric. As Stephen Browne notes, Grimké and Lydia Maria Child shared a confidence that the combination of free and open public discourse with the human rights doctrine that underpins the liberal public sphere would eventually create an antislavery consensus and peacefully bring about abolition. As Lydia Maria Child expressed the relationship between morality and critical conversation: "In a community so enlightened as our own, [prejudices] must gradually melt away under the influence of public discussion."[28] Browne aptly describes the millennial ideal that Grimké and Child shared. He notes that both saw "in the republican inheritance a structure of commitments and a cultural logic that could effect God's will on earth."[29] This confidence also reflects the views of the Unitarian ministry, which fundamentally saw the evangelical movement as an atavistic rejection of a divinely guided progressive dialogue.

Southern women speaking against slavery *in the South* represents Grimké's ideal of moral authenticity in the public sphere because it includes all the elements that demonstrate feminine moral commitment: personal risk, public expression of belief, and participation in a committed public dialogue. In *The Lecturess*, a cautionary novel that was inspired by Grimké's lecturing, Sarah Josepha Hale displaces the burning of Pennsylvania Hall from Philadelphia to Charleston, South Carolina. This revision in the history of Grimké's career insightfully describes the connection between danger and sincerity that was central both to Grimké's legitimation and to the context she was working to transform. In the *Appeal*, Grimké underscores the importance of transforming women's sense of self in her ideal for a revised critical public by asking: "Have I been seeking to magnify the suffering and exalt the character of woman, that she 'might have praise of men'? No! no! my object has been to arouse *you*, as the wives and mothers, the daughters and sisters of the South, to a sense of your duty as *women*, and as Christian women." She even subtly contrasts women's influence against male violence by arguing: "There are only two ways in which [abolition] can be effected, by moral power or physical force, and it is for you to choose which of these you prefer" (*PY* 64).

Stephen Browne is correct in concluding that Grimké's text "is as much about the conditions of reform as it is about specific proposals."[30] The *Appeal* marks the emergence of a voice that both insists on an expanded critical public and articulates the virtues of a public sphere that treats access to publicity as a universal human right. The foundation of the public femininity that Grimké constructs lies in a synthesis of liberal human rights doctrine and essentialist gender assumption that she integrates by encouraging women to make autonomous moral judgments and to think of their moral identities in relation to equally compelling civic obligations. The principle of universal equality that renders slavery immoral and degrades black slaves out of civil society reflects the moral death that results from barring their access to critical debate. While the universal human rights that Grimké finds in the Bible require the liberation of black slaves, the liberal tradition of thought within which she operates makes the right to participate in critical public discourse equally fundamental to moral equality. At its root, the central idea of Grimké's feminist thought is the inextricability of moral equality and access to the critical public sphere. While the moral equality of the slave was denied in every way, the moral equality of woman was denied by conventions that banned her from making political utterances. In challenging these conventions, Grimké was acting on the assumption that achieving the goal of moral equality for all people required not just freedom for African Americans but also a consensual recognition that equality in a liberal democratic society demands that all people freely participate in the discourses that define the norms of their society.

Redefining the Critical Public

In a letter to Theodore Weld on August 12, 1837, Angelina Grimké began to reckon the implications of, as she phrased it, "stepping so far out of the bounds of female propriety as to lecture to promiscuous assemblies." Self-conscious but unapologetic that women's rights had eclipsed antislavery as the issue of her public reputation, she described some of the implications of women's presence in public discourse: "The fact is it involves the interests of every minister in our land and therefore they will stand almost in a solid phalanx against women's rights. . . . It will also touch every man's interests at home, in the tenderest relation of life; it will go down into the very depths of his soul and cause great searchings of the heart" (*WGL* 1:415).

In addition to threatening the authority of ministers as the nation's dominant public voice of morality, women's public activism also implied profound changes in the meaning of domesticity and masculinity. Redefining the critical public sphere to recognize women's right to equal access would compel the redefinition of a wide variety of relationships. It would necessarily go beyond a simple adjustment in domestic relationships because it would demand that men as well as women search their souls and reconstruct the meaning of manhood and womanhood. Gently, tentatively put in this letter, Grimké argued that recognizing the public equality of women changes everything.

In the context of the opposing trajectories of antebellum domesticity and women's movement toward the political realm through benevolent reform activism, Grimké's assertion that women should join political organizations provoked a heated debate over the criteria for membership in the critical public sphere. The driving question of this debate was the compatibility of conventional models of femininity with women's political speech.

Even as they were fighting to contain the spread of liberal theology and religious pluralism, the orthodox clergy fought aggressively against women's participation in critical discourse. In response to Grimké's emergence as a type of Emerson's "female politician," orthodox ministers in New England endorsed a letter written by Nehemiah Adams, pastor of the Union Congregational Church in Boston. Adams's rhetorical strategy was to define women's authority outside rhetorical power by placing it in opposition to rhetoric as a source of moral influence. According to Adams, "The power of woman is in her dependence, flowing from the consciousness of that weakness which God had given her for her protection, and which keeps her in those departments of life that form the character of individuals and of the nation." Adams transformed what he called the "mild, dependent, softening influence of women" into a "source of mighty power" by arguing that a constant awareness of weakness and vulnerability created the sympathy that enabled women to inculcate values and promote norms that respect the rights of the weak and vulnerable. In Adams's view, this sympathetic persona could emerge only from a position of literal weakness, and this literal weakness was embodied by woman's voluntary submission to masculine discourses of authority.[31] Although he recognized the "social influences" of women's benevolent reform organizations, he defined the legitimate boundaries of women's influence in terms of "unostentatious prayers" that guide sinners to ministers who can redeem them from sin. Adams's position, in effect, was that women's benevolent reform should avoid political advocacy and that it should enhance rather than compete with the minister's moral authority.

Adams also argued that the form of influence that is consistent with feminine identity stops abruptly at the margin of the critical public. He distinguished between masculine and feminine realms of discourse by defending femininity against "the dangers which at [the time] seem[ed] to threaten the female character with a widespread and permanent injury."[32] When women participated in "associated efforts" such as benevolent societies that reflect "the modesty of her sex," Adams heartily approved. But when women entered critical discourse in their own right, their subject position underwent a transformation. Sharpening the distinction that he made between legitimate and illegitimate women's reform activism, Adams warned: "When she assumes the place and tone of man as a public reformer, our care and protection of her seem unnecessary; we put ourselves in self-protection against her; she yields the power which God has given her for protection and her character becomes unnatural." Grimké, by linking moral equality with the right of equal participation in public debate, violated what Adams saw as a metaphysical law. He interpreted the *Appeal* in a fashion characteristic of the orthodox Protestant imagination by reading Grimké's transgressions in relation to a God-given order that women violate when they adopt masculine places in the structure of public discourse. As Sarah Grimké would point out, Adams's equating this violation of a normative structure with "unnatural" character rearticulates the argument that Cotton Mather made at the witch trials in 1692.[33]

For Adams, though, the Grimkés' 1837 speaking tour represented a kind of pandemonium. To visualize the public position that Grimké appropriated was more than Adams could bear. Unable to "countenance" women who "forget themselves" and assume "the character of public lecturers and teachers," Adams adopted a posture of self-defense, trying to protect not only himself but also a moral order that he asserted was "Scriptural" and would be "permanent." The fear that Grimké elicited resulted from her literal embodiment of a pluralistic public realm. Following Robyn Wiegman's analysis of the rhetorical patterns that caused the phrase "women and blacks" to emerge as a trope for pluralist destabilization of the eighteenth-century public, Grimké faced the problem of presenting a taboo body in public that Frederick Douglass would also face. For

Grimké to achieve recognition as a legitimate participant in the critical public sphere, she could not simply appropriate the abstract persona of the enfranchised citizen. On the contrary, in order to bring woman and citizen together, Grimké had to present herself as self-consciously female in the site of critical discourse, where it could itself become the object of legitimization. In doing so, Grimké asserted the necessity of a pluralistic public sphere by claiming public recognition of her legitimacy as a critical actor.[34]

In his response to this structural challenge to a homogenous public, Adams also inadvertently articulated several implications for the critical public of the fact that the Grimkés were ignoring the norms of women's public discourse. By claiming the right to participate in critical discourse on the same terms as men, the Grimkés "yielded" the power which conventions of public deference had granted to women benevolent reformers. In the redefined critical sphere that polemics such as Grimké's *Appeal* created, masculine "care and protection" became "unnecessary" because critical debate assumes the equality of each participant in relation to rational argument. Adams's response indicates the domino effect of Grimké's call for pluralization. The question of access affected not only the boundaries of the critical public sphere; it also raised questions about the functions of ministers and churches, the relationship of manhood and womanhood, and the nature of publicity and privacy.

As disorienting and threatening as Grimké's presence was to Adams's understanding of legitimate critical dialogue, he was equally appalled by the implications of women's political speech for the boundaries of the private and public realms. In reference to women's discussion of the sexual exploitation of female slaves, he offered a rebuke: "We especially deplore the intimate acquaintance and promiscuous conversation of females with regard to things 'which aught not to be named'; by which that modesty and delicacy which is the charm of domestic life, and which constitutes the true influence of women in society is consumed."

Sexuality, in Adams's eyes, represented a private realm within the private realm. While Grimké's insistence on women's equality required a radical refiguring of membership in the critical public sphere, asserting sexual exploitation as a legitimate topic of public discussion demanded a refiguring of the norms and boundaries of privacy. In Adams's view, the public discussion of sexual violence and exploitation threatened to negate the idea of privacy altogether and "consume" woman's place by creating an all-encompassing public discourse. For women to discuss sexuality in public portended a complete collapse of the norms that defined femininity and privacy. It also implied a radical refiguring of the topical boundaries of public speech and the criteria for political agency.

The refiguring of critical discourse that Grimké provoked is also related to the expansion of religious pluralism in the early antebellum period. The sense of siege that Adams expressed reflects the clergy's fear that a class of morally motivated, publicly vocal women had begun to poach on the moral influence of the church. Indeed, by justifying women's right to public speech at the intersection of human rights ideology, benevolent reform, and religiously motivated civil dissent, Grimké appropriated a form of authority that was especially threatening to ministers. By the time William Lloyd Garrison found his voice in 1831, the authority to define and inculcate moral values had already diffused from the pulpit to an amorphous realm of personal responsibility that was spreading far from the pews of churches. In the "Divinity School Address," for example, Emerson turned his back on a minister's sermon to find moral education in a snowstorm. In *Uncle Tom's Cabin,* moral conversions take place in parlors and kitchens under the guidance of characters such as Mrs. Byrd and Rachel Halliday rather than in churches under the guidance of ministers. In fact, at the same time that they were trying to suppress Grimké, the clergy was also denouncing the Garrisonian radicals in tones that resembled Adams's. The immediatists, a group of "clerical abolitionists" wrote, "are not *properly abolitionists.*" As "radicals" rather than reformers, the ministers expelled them just as Adams barred women activists from womanhood: "Let them go out from amongst us, for they are not of us. They are the prolific fountain of all the evils which retard and injure the cause of abolition" (*Lib.* Sept. 8, 1837).

Grimké's emergence as a reformer and the hostility it elicited thus represent the complementary processes through which the ministry was feminized and women began to advocate a redefined public sphere and a transformed critical discourse. The terms of Mary P. Ryan's characterization of the role of public space for feminist analysis of the nineteenth century also apply to the relation of publicity to equality: "The term public continues to serve at least four critical purposes in feminist theory: as a reference for cultural values, as a crudely serviceable classification of social behavior, as a space denoting especially blatant gender asymmetry and inequality, and as a center of concentrated power."[35] Grimké's challenge marks both a moment of opposition to the disestablishment of literary women and a counterdiscourse of overt political dissent to the novelistic voices of sentimental dissent that critics such as Nina Baym, Jane Tompkins, and

Gillian Brown have described.[36] Grimké's argument, regardless of its emphasis on feminine sincerity, was premised on the idea that moral equality demands that critical public discourse be open to all members of the society. Far from arguing that feminized domesticity offered a counterdiscourse to Jacksonian materialism, as Tompkins holds in her chapter on Harriet Beecher Stowe, Grimké claimed that moral principle and the American liberal tradition required an egalitarian and open public sphere. For Grimké, the moral foundation of the nation lay in the realm of public discourse, especially in the liberality with which it recognized equality in civil society. Censuring women's voices undermined the legitimacy of critical public discourse not just because it violated the principle of publicity but also because it segregated a vital source of sincerity and thus promoted strategic rather than authentic critical conversation.

The diffusion of authoritative discourse into an expanded and increasingly pluralistic public sphere reflects the changing structure of critical debate in antebellum America. Whereas figures such as Nehemiah Adams and Catharine Beecher worked to claim authority for specific institutions—the church and the home—in a public sphere that they saw as hierarchical, Grimké argued for a public sphere that was pure at least in terms of access. In the version that she advocated, black and white people, as well as men and women, would participate as equals. From a historical point of view, it makes sense that the clergy would object most strenuously to Grimké's argument for equality and women's rights. When Grimké emerged on the stage in the mid-1830s, the Congregational and Presbyterian churches were weakened by several struggles. They were recovering from the Unitarian controversy, adjusting to the growth of evangelical sects, and working to reclaim their place as the preeminent spokesmen of moral authority in the society as a whole. As Nehemiah Adams's letter indicates, Grimké's assertion of equality in public discourse destabilized a host of institutions and asked Americans to redefine basic elements of their collective experience.

While the orthodox clergy defended conventional relationships between the church, women, and publicity, feminist reformers beginning with Angelina Grimké exploited principles embedded deep in the soil of liberal thought to disrupt hierarchies of authority and the homogeneity of the public realm. Grimké faded from the public scene well before the model of equality that she first articulated was adopted by the women who met at Seneca Falls in 1848, but she introduced what Nancy Ruttenburg describes as a type of "popular voice" essential to discursive democracy. Grimké's brief public career worked throughout antebellum reform as "a spectral presence now embodied, now disembodied; now univocal, now grotesquely polyphonic; but unfailingly, powerfully, audible."[37] Ultimately, the argument that Grimké introduced provoked a dialogue among women over the definition of femininity and its relationship to civil society. This is why the four-step program that Grimké defined in her *Appeal* is so important to the origins of the culture of reform. On the most basic level, she provoked a critical conversation about the relationship of femininity to publicity. But on a more subtle level, she articulated a model of feminine selfhood grounded, first, in essentialist ideals of identity and, second, in a model of equality inextricably connected to the right of access to critical public discourse.

Grimké described a model of women's subjectivity that begins with independent will-formation and culminates with political activism in institutions that shape public opinion. In the evolution of consciousness that Grimké defined, she connected the independent spirituality of Protestantism with the political conventions of Jacksonian democracy to draw an image in which both authentic selfhood and equality are defined by access to critical discourse. It is this destabilization of privacy and femininity rather than the issue of slavery that motivated Catharine Beecher to enter the debate over Grimké's *Appeal*. On its surface Beecher's response is a defense of tradition, but in truth, Beecher saw the diffusion of clerical authority into sectarian struggles as an opportunity to claim moral authority for women and the private realm. Her debate with Grimké was less about antislavery and more about the possible implications of redefining gender spheres. Though Beecher's vision for American womanhood has been overshadowed by historical reconstruction of the equal rights tradition that has come to characterize the women's rights movement, her model of feminine power dominated debates about womanhood and publicity until the early twentieth century. Even though Grimké's argument has long had the upper hand in both theoretical and political discourse, Beecher's position was much more in harmony with the philosophical and political assumptions of antebellum Americans.

Catharine Beecher and the Critical Private Sphere

In the opinion of Catharine Beecher, the path on which William Lloyd Garrison set the antislavery movement when he founded the *Liberator* in 1831 and which Angelina Grimké encouraged women to follow five years later repudiated vitally important feminine modes for shaping the values of the nation. While Garrison's brand of persuasion was public, inflammatory, polemical, and sensational, Beecher's ideal of women's power was private, nurturing, sympathetic, and pacific. Yet despite the conservatism of this model of woman's authority, Beecher's response to Grimké's *Appeal* was not an effort to deny women's legitimacy as political actors or as influential players in public affairs. Rather, Beecher articulated a grand strategic vision of how prevailing conventions of femininity could be developed to provide a model of communication that would end slavery and create a consensus society grounded in the moral authority of women.

Beecher's model of women's social power envisions a world in which the home eclipses the church and women eclipse ministers as the arbiters of moral values for the nation. While Grimké's vision of reform is primarily a project of expanding the critical public realm to recognize the implications of liberal human rights philosophy, Beecher's is one of defining domesticity as a discourse of authority that makes women the central mediators and arbiters of the values of the people. Grimké sought justice by equalizing access to the public; Beecher strove to preserve authenticity by containing political discourse in a realm of sincere communication.

Though Beecher's vision of domesticity reflects patterns of industrial specialization that were emerging in the Jacksonian period, her vision of womanhood grew out of an orthodox Protestant metaphysics that carefully distinguished between discourses of authority and the social realms that they governed. Following the hierarchical divisions that defined orthodox theology and separated divine from earthly realms, clerical from secular authority, and masculine from feminine spheres of action, Beecher understood her world in structuralist terms. In her imagination, spheres of authority carried specific attributes that fulfill specific functions within a comprehensive, divinely sanctioned structure.[38] For Beecher, the American utopia lay in the project of constructing a comprehensive set of authoritative discourses, defining the function that each would perform in the well-regulated society, and gaining consensual recognition of the boundaries that separated domestic, economic, religious, and other realms of authority. By advocating what Kathryn Sklar at one point calls "a female caste identity," Beecher worked against the cultural momentum that was making access to public discourse an indispensable element of Americans' understanding of equality. But Beecher's vision for American society is important because it adapted emerging ideals of femininity and some of the ideological implications of industrialization into a model of womanhood that paradoxically made political disenfranchisement an authorizing device in women's claim to moral power.

Though the *Essay on Slavery* that Beecher published in response to Grimké's *Appeal* is part of the debate over antislavery methodology, her early publications emphasize the pragmatics of woman's influence by defining gender-specific conventions of discourse. The conventions of thought, behavior, and speech that Beecher attributed to these realms of discourse reflect models of self that are far more important to her thought than geographical locations such as kitchens, pulpits, or lecture halls.

Early in her career as an educator, Beecher began to seek models through which women could redefine the moral authority of domestic femininity to function as a discourse of authority in the public realm. Underpinning this effort was Beecher's desire to emulate her father's pastoral authority within the boundaries of domesticity.[39] As she developed the connection between public authority and domestic femininity, Beecher constructed an ideal of professional domesticity in which American women not only provided the civic and moral nurturance of republican motherhood but also represented a locus of value that was central to the political stability of the nation. As critics such as Ann Douglas and Gillian Brown argue, Beecher's ideal of femininity functioned as a form of ballast for Jacksonian individualism. But it emphatically did not write domesticity out of the public realm. On the contrary, Beecher defined the home as a public institution similar to the church or the courts. The unique bridge between public and private that she imagined for women is especially apparent in her insistence on women's education and professional training. In her 1835 *Essay on the Education of Female Teachers*, she remarks that establishing endowed women's schools would "have the same effect on female education, as medical and theological schools have upon those professions" (*ES* 5). The professionalization of the home as an institution that is simultaneously public and private and that requires special schools and a professionally educated class of women to manage it defines the core idea of Beecher's vision of a reformed American society. But this reconstruction of womanhood primarily serves to support the enhanced ideological role that Beecher anticipates for women.

The model of womanhood that Beecher envisions supplements her structuralist imagination by fulfilling a social need that she associates with individualism and liberal freedom. She situates her call for women's education in the big-picture evolution of Enlightenment philosophy by arguing that even as expanding democratic freedoms liberate individuals, they also threaten the complete breakdown of social order. As she maintains in her *Essay on the Education of Female Teachers*:

> Man is bursting the chains of slavery, and the bonds of intellectual subserviency; and is learning to think, and reason, and act for himself. And the great crisis is hastening on, when it shall be decided whether disenthralled intellect and liberty shall voluntarily submit to the laws of virtue and of Heaven, or run wild to insubordination, anarchy, and crime. The great questions pending before the world are simply these: are liberty and intelligence, without the restraints of a moral and religious education, a blessing, or a curse? Without moral and religious restraints, is it best for man to receive the gift of liberty and intelligence, or to remain coerced by physical force, and the restraints of opinions and customs not his own. (*EE* 14)

These potential problems require that liberal societies work to inculcate moral and religious restraints that will promote voluntary submission to the "laws of virtue and of Heaven."[40] Importantly though, instead of asserting the authority of ministers to fulfill this task, Beecher appropriates it for women. She defines women—not ministers—as the mediators of virtue and the stewards of religious values:

> The necessity of *virtuous* intelligence in the mass of the community is peculiarly felt in a form of government like ours, where the people are not held in restraint by physical force, as in despotic governments, but where, if they do not voluntarily submit to the restraints of virtue and religion, they must inevitably run loose to wild misrule, anarchy, and crime. For a nation to be virtuous and religious, the females of that nation must be deeply imbued with these principles: for just as wives or mothers sink or rise in the scale of virtue, intelligence, and piety, the husbands, and the sons will rise or fall. (*EE* 9–10)

From early in her career, Beecher advocated reform in women's education not only to help maintain the home as a smoothly functioning cog in the larger machine of American society but also to inculcate the moral restraints that she saw as necessary to prevent freedom from degenerating into anarchy.

Kathryn Sklar develops this idea as the dominant theme that Beecher elaborated in a variety of ways over the course of her career. Especially, Beecher's school in Cincinnati and her visions of the West offered a kind of blank slate onto which a new role could be written. Beecher, Sklar writes, "asserted that a woman could be chiefly responsible for setting the moral tone of the community. A community could coalesce around women rather than the church." In Beecher's later work, Sklar notes that "the evangelical emphasis fell away from Catharine's work" so that she could focus on imagining and advocating the invention of a class of women who would fill the vacuum of moral authority that sectarianism created.[41] I would argue that it was not just sectarianism but the broader diffusion of moral authority that Beecher was working to counteract.

Beecher literally argued that in a democracy women should be authorized and trained to represent, even embody, the foundational principles of civil society. While Grimké focused on the implications of universal equality for the composition of the democratic public sphere, Beecher concentrated on the psychological dynamics of liberal selfhood, especially as it represented a threat to civil order. The role of moral educator that Beecher defines for women in her *Essay on the Education of Female Teachers* extends to the inculcation of "American" values to foreign immigrants and the urban poor. In her words, "The education of the lower classes is deteriorating, as it respects moral and religious restraints . . . and at the same time thousands and thousands of degraded foreigners and their ignorant families are pouring into this nation at every avenue." In Beecher's view, creating a vanguard of women teachers to serve as a bulwark against forces of social disintegration would serve several purposes. It would protect American democracy, sustain women's role as moral educators, and provide women a professional status consistent with domesticity.[42]

In time this vanguard of women teachers would expand into a quasi-mandatory form of public service. Through it, "the interest of the whole nation [could] be aroused, and every benevolent and every pious female in the nation . . . [could] be enlisted to consecrate at least a certain number of years to this object" (*EE* 19). At the end of the essay, Beecher frames her vision of women's identity in the rhetoric of benevolent reform: "Few know or realize the amount of Christian benevolence which is slumbering in female bosoms, which could be most delightfully and beneficially employed to elevate and save our country" (*EE* 21). In this early essay, Beecher thus defines women's potential to provide ideological cohesion and moral authority in a nation threatened with chaos not only by its liberal philosophical foundations but also by the pressures of religious sectarianism, divisive politics, radical reform movements, and immigration. Rather than emphasizing technical education for women as housekeepers or for immigrants as mechanics in the new economy, Beecher describes women's service in explicitly ideological terms as the definitive inculcators of the internal restraints that allow democratic autonomy to coexist with civil order.

However, despite the professional and political role she foresaw for women teachers, Beecher also strongly opposed women's involvement in radical reform and was a lifelong opponent of woman's suffrage. In the debates over political equality that followed the Civil War, Beecher continued to argue that the insulating value of political disenfranchisement, coupled with professional status as moral and religious educators, offered women a position of cultural authority more powerful than that offered by civil equality.[43] The aggressive case that Grimké made for women's participation in the organized antislavery movement compelled Beecher to defend her own model of women's authority against the argument that women's interests would best be served by gaining equal access to the critical public sphere. Though they were motivated by different senses of urgency, Beecher's response to Grimké mirrors that of Nehemiah Adams. She felt that Grimké's formulation of equality threatened to destabilize an emerging discourse of feminine cultural authority, a form of feminine enfranchisement, in the same way that Adams believed Grimké threatened further to erode a long-embattled discourse of clerical authority.

Gender and Strategic Discourse

In the *Essay on Slavery*, Beecher adapts her ideal of women's authority to the tactics and rhetoric of the antislavery movement. In this essay, femininity continues to represent the forces that stand against chaos, but Beecher offers intimate dialogue in the domestic sphere as a form of critical discourse better suited to propagating antislavery than the evangelical tactics of the radical abolitionists. As Beecher imagines a way to adapt her theory of women's authority to a specific case, she describes women less as the inculcators of virtue and more as the mediators of a political dialogue that both occurs in domestic space and follows a feminized set of conventions.

Beecher's prefatory remarks to the *Essay on Slavery* underscore her deep sensitivity to distinctions between masculine-public and feminine-private modes of discourse. The *Essay*, Beecher explains, emerged as two forms of private dialogue intersected. First, "a gentleman and a friend, requested the writer to assign reasons why he should not join the Abolition Society." As she was responding to this request, Beecher's old acquaintance Angelina Grimké published an *Appeal* intended to use "her influence among northern ladies to induce them to unite with Abolition Societies." Grimké's plan was a direct challenge to the conventions that Beecher believed to be indispensable to woman's authority and to a well-ordered society. To respond, Beecher felt compelled not only to argue against her male friend's impulse to become a partisan but also against a public call for large-scale organizing by women. She "began a private letter to Miss Grimké as a personal friend" but was convinced to combine the two projects into an essay written for publication "by the wishes and advice of others" (*ES* 3). The *Essay on Slavery* was drawn out of the realm of private dialogue by Beecher's need to rebut publicly the attractions of radical abolitionism, an attraction that was drawing both men and women into the widening sphere of the culture of reform. Beecher's desire to counteract this attraction hinged on her belief that intimate discourse was more likely to result in an authentic critical dialogue than either masculine public speech or the organization of women's associations that mimicked the rhetorical conventions of political parties.

To prepare the foundation of her argument that a critical private discourse could redeem the nation, Beecher first offers her understanding of American political debate. Reiterating the principle that she finds both fundamental to the modern age and threatening to civil order, Beecher argues that "the prominent principle, now in development, as indicating the spirit of the age, is the perfect right of all men to entire freedom of opinion" (*ES* 109). Second, describing the spirit of masculine political dialogue, Beecher argues that "at the same time another right is claimed, which is of necessity involved in the preceding,—the right to oppose, by all lawful means, the opinions and the practices of others" (*ES* 110). "These fundamental principles of liberty," Beecher contends, reasserting another position she had taken in the *Essay on the Education of Female Teachers*, "have in all past ages been restrained by coercive influences, either of civil or of ecclesiastical power. . . . But the form of our government is such, that every measure that bears upon the public or private interest of every citizen, is decided by *public sentiment*. All laws and regulations in civil or religious, or social concerns, are decided by the *majority of votes*" (*ES* 110–11). In addition to symbolizing a slackening of external controls and the consequent liberation of the individual, this realm of majoritarian public debate threatened to colonize all other realms of knowledge and truth, making them conform to the assumptions of a liberal public sphere in which rightness was defined by the will of the majority. By accepting these two basic assumptions, Beecher concludes that the rhetoric of politics and social reform represent an inherently masculine realm of struggle. In the *Essay on Slavery*, Beecher even defines masculine norms of public dialogue in terms that integrate rhetorical manipulation and physical violence. She describes legitimate norms of masculine debate by explaining that "a man may act on society by the collision of intellect, in public debate; he may urge his measures by a sense of shame, by fear and by personal interest; he may coerce by the combination of public sentiment; he may drive by physical force, and he does not outstep the boundaries of his sphere" (*ES* 99–100).

Given the oppositional nature of this model of dialogue, Beecher fears that the Garrisonian immediatists—with their denunciation of gradual emancipation and their encouragement of women's political activism—signaled the ascendancy of a mode of discourse that risked the complete disintegration of civil society. She intimates the threat that radical abolitionism posed to dialogue between gradualists and slaveholders when she asks: "Who can estimate the mischiefs that we must encounter while this dismemberment, this tearing asunder of the joints and members of the body politic, is going on? What will be the commotion and dismay, when all our sources of wealth, prosperity, and comfort, are turned to occasions for angry and selfish strife?" (*ES* 141). The rhetoric of the Anti-Slavery Society functioned to "generate party spirit, denunciation, recrimination, and angry passions" and as such, epitomized a coercive form of discourse that threatened the political stability of the nation. "In this country," Beecher summarizes, "it is party-spirit that rules with an iron rod, and shakes its scorpion whip over every interest and every employment of man. From this mighty source spring constant detraction, gossiping, tale-bearing, falsehood, anger, pride, malice, revenge, and every evil word and work" (*ES* 124). This strategic discourse, Beecher expands, is not confined to antislavery but pervades the public realm. She echoes William Ellery Channing as she describes a kind of nightmare in which processes of partisan combat undermine the foundations of public sincerity: "The present is a time when every doctrine, every principle and every practice which influences the happiness of man, either in this, or in a future life, is under discussion. The whole nation is thrown into parties about every possible question" (*ES* 111). The changing norms of reform have allowed "party spirit to take the place of Christian principle" (*ES* 15) and created a psychology of partisan opposition rather than a desire to mediate differences and work toward mutual understanding.

Beecher perceives the destabilization of traditional sources of authority that

Habermas also sees in the construction of liberal public spheres. But Beecher does not see the public sphere as a potential locus of authentic critical dialogue. On the contrary, Beecher views it as an inherently strategic site of struggle for domination rather than as one of rational dialogue oriented toward mutual understanding. This realm strikes her not as the "chastened" realm—purified and made modest by the temporariness of dominance—that George Kateb envisions, but as a place where the struggle to dominate knows no restraints. The growth of political partisanship and religious sectarianism posed such an immanent threat to Beecher's ideal of a well-ordered society that she even reiterates Jedediah Morse's fears by envisioning the United States collapsing into a kind of Babylonian chaos. In her *Essay on the Education of Female Teachers*, she had warned that without a vehicle of national moral education the nation would be "dashed in pieces, amid all the terrors of the wild fanaticism, infidel recklessness, and political strife, of an ungoverned, ignorant, and unprincipled population" (*EE* 18). In the *Essay on Slavery*, she refines this warning to highlight the potential threats to civil order posed by masculine norms of public discourse. She asks: "Must we be distracted and tortured by the baleful passions and wicked works that unrestrained party-spirit and ungoverned factions will bring upon us under such government as ours? Must we rush on to disunion, and civil wars, and servile wars, till all their train of horrors pass over us like devouring fire?" (*ES* 126).

To counteract "the storms of democratic liberty" in the public sphere, Beecher argues that women should construct a voice that functions according to different norms. In effect, she contends that women should facilitate political dialogue by modeling an ideal speech situation within the context of the domestic sphere. Jeanne Boydston, Mary Kelley, and Anne Margolis sum up Beecher's assumptions regarding the relation of domesticity and virtue: "Beecher argued that a reliable model of virtue existed only in the privacy and self-sacrifice of the family, and there, only in the role of mother."[44] In the context of an inherently strategic public, women could mediate disputes that threatened to destroy the nation by feminizing critical discourse and capturing it for the domestic sphere. For example, Beecher interprets the activists' emphasis on "immediate" abolition and their description of slaveholders as "stealers" of men as examples of a strategic discourse that inflames opposition and obstructs sincere communication. Instead of recognizing the Garrisonians' effort to recast phrases such as "immediate emancipation" and "man-stealer" as devices that move the debate away from property rights by forcing a discussion of the human rights of slaves, Beecher interprets the immediatists' discourse in relation to what she calls the "principle of expediency" in advancing the diplomatic process of mediating difference between advocates and opponents of slavery.

Far from serving as a site of ethical debate in its own right, language, Beecher argues, should function as a purely neutral substance. She concedes that "words have no inherent meaning," but she also maintains that "the question never should be asked, what *ought* a word to mean?" Rather, words should be accepted to "signify that which they are commonly *understood* to mean" by referring to "vocabularies and standard writers." By Beecher's logic, following this standard would permit the transparency that represents discursive fair play. She concludes that "if men take words and give them a new and peculiar use, and are consequently misunderstood, they are guilty of a species of deception, and are accountable for all the evils that may ensue as a consequence" (*ES* 40). For Beecher, contesting the terms of debate as the Garrisonians did represented a tactical choice that obstructed transparent dialogue and put the immediatists outside the boundaries of rational discourse. The immediatists' ethical purpose in recoding words to emphasize principles of human rights simply baffled Beecher and led her to interpret the Garrisonians' principled choice as a kind of mischievous deception. By her reasoning, disrupting conventions of shared understanding at the level of the word threatened to tear the nation apart. By succumbing to the pressure exerted by these tactics, women risked losing the claim to sincerity that both she and Grimké found integral to womanhood.

Beecher correctly understood this threat to be structural, aimed at one of the pillars of the social order, and hence she saw the expansion of discursive democracy and of the critical public sphere as a threat to the moral integrity of her society. Most disturbing, the incorporation of women's voices into a corrupt realm of public discourse threatened to make them complicit in the same process through which liberal Christianity was undermining orthodox Protestantism. It is important to note though, that in her defense of domestic discourse as a rhetoric to promote antislavery, Beecher did not attack liberal philosophy as such (though she did in some religious tracts). Rather, her criticism focused on publicity, the conventions of public and reform discourse, and their implications for women's authority.

While Unitarianism had not succeeded in displacing orthodoxy in New England, it had profoundly changed the nature of clerical authority and redefined the boundaries within which ministers could command obedience from their

flocks. Equally, integrating women's reform organizations into a culture of critical conversation structured by conventions of partisan debate threatened to
undermine cultural assumptions that connected femininity with authenticity,
sincerity, and moral integrity. Just as the liberal Christians' response to scientific
and philosophical challenges to orthodox dogma promoted a dialogic spirituality
that diffused religious authority, the erosion of woman's sphere as a distinct locus
of authority threatened to make feminine discourse just one of several voices in
a pluralistic public dialogue that continued to function according to norms that
Beecher associated with strategic discourse.

Beecher's Theory of Domestic Citizenship

As an alternative to a pluralistic critical public sphere, Beecher developed a theory
of critical discourse in which Christianity, femininity, and privacy combine to create a context for sincere dialogue. She describes the conventions she proposes as
"a system of *persuasion*, tending, by kind and gentle influences, to make men *willing*
to leave off their sins" (*ES* 46). Although Beecher calls this method of persuasion
"Christianity," its attributes are identical to those of woman's influence, and it
serves an explicitly political function. Citing the English abolitionists Thomas
Clarkson and William Wilberforce as exemplars of "Christian principles" in
a political context, Beecher endorses an antislavery rhetoric that emphasizes
"benignity, gentleness, and kind-heartedness." Clarkson and Wilberforce are
praiseworthy because they speak a "charitable language" and grant those "who
differ in opinions or measures . . . full credit for purity and sincerity of motive"
(*ES* 23). The characteristics that Beecher attributes to Clarkson especially exemplify her feminization of Christian persuasion. Clarkson succeeded, Beecher
argues, because he "avoided prejudices, strove to conciliate opposers, shunned
everything that would give needless offense and exasperation, began slowly and
cautiously" (*ES* 20).

The set of rhetorical norms that Beecher advocates shifts the locus of the
antislavery debate away from a partisan public sphere that she considers irrational
and focuses it in a feminized realm that she associates with rational dialogue.
Having defined Garrisonian antislavery rhetoric as "a system of *coercion* by public
opinion," Beecher offers "persuasion" as a form of dialogue that embodies the
norms of intimate discourse in the private realm. Yet, despite her emphasis on
the power of feminine sympathy, Beecher treats intimate political discourse as a

rational rather than a sentimental form of conversation. She identifies prejudice as the vital obstacle that Americans need to overcome before slavery can be abolished. As she phrases it, "a prejudice is an *unreasonable* and *groundless* dislike of persons or things. Of course, as it is unreasonable, it is the most difficult of all things to conquer" (*ES* 26). According to Beecher's model of critical conversation, prejudice can be overcome not by denouncing it in self-righteous diatribes but by rationalizing it in settings of intimate trust. In one of the most revealing phrases of her *Essay on Slavery*, Beecher asserts the advantages of taking the antislavery debate out of the realm of political pamphlets and conducting it "by the fire-side of the planter." This move from a context of public polemics to a context of intimate dialogue offers a metaphor for Beecher's vision of sincere critical discourse. For her the fireside represents a place where authentic dialogue can occur not only on apolitical domestic issues but also on the ethical and moral implications of all aspects of experience. It is her counterpart to the ideal speech situation.

The specific vision that Beecher offers of antislavery by the fireside is of "some southern gentleman, such for example as Mr. Birney," who might "quietly have gone to work at the South, collecting facts, exhibiting the impolicy and the evils [of slavery], to good men of the south." This intimate discussion among influential men would follow specific conventions. Beecher describes them by explaining that "the peaceful and Christian method of meeting the difficulty [that slavery creates for the country] would have been, to collect all the evidence of this supposed hurtful tendency, and privately, and in a respectful and conciliating way, to have presented it to the attention of the wise and benevolent men, who were most interested in sustaining this institution" (*ES* 24). In addition to engaging the advocates of slavery in private, rational dialogue, Beecher argues that prejudice can be successfully fought by feminizing the black population and creating an intimate relationship between African Americans and the rest of their society. In a passage that anticipates her sister's characterization of Uncle Tom, Catharine writes:

> If a certain class of people is the subject of unreasonable prejudice, the peaceful and Christian way of removing it would be to endeavor to render the unfortunate persons who compose this class, so useful, so humble and unassuming, so kind in their feelings, and so full of love and good works, that prejudice would be supplanted by complacency in their goodness, and pity and sympathy for their

disabilities. If the friends of the blacks had quietly set themselves to work to increase their intelligence, their usefulness, their respectability, their meekness, gentleness, and benevolence, and then had appealed to the pity, generosity, and Christian feelings of their fellow citizens, a very different result would have appeared. (*ES* 27)

She applies the same standards to disputes between immediatist and gradual abolitionists. "The peaceful and Christian method of encountering such opposition" within the antislavery movement "would have been . . . to have avoided all harsh and censorious language, and to have employed facts, arguments, and persuasions, in a kind and respectful way with the hope of modifying opposing views" (*ES* 38). Since the Garrisonians were in journalistic dialogue with advocates of slavery as well as with proponents of gradual emancipation, by advocating a feminized intimate discourse as a model of critical conversation, Beecher is advocating a profound change in conventions of reform discourse.

For Beecher the sympathetic self that facilitates this process of dialogue required that women sympathize with all parties—slaves, slaveholders, and antislavery activists. In contrast to Grimké, who understood the foundations of authority in relation to gender-neutral, substantive moral values, Beecher ultimately rooted woman's authority in processes of dialogic mediation. In Beecher's view, the ability to sustain a broadly sympathetic posture was indispensable to woman's authority as the mediators of a process of social evolution. Women's mediation of moral conflict took the place of the social "restraints" that had been lost as feudal tyranny evolved into modern liberalism.

While Grimké understood her argument for civil equality to be a necessary development in the synthesis of moral and democratic principles, Beecher's imagination was more historically grounded. Beecher constructed her ideal of feminine critical discourse in conscious relation to the growth and expansion of American democracy. At a moment when the risk of chaos loomed over the nation because of the conventions that had come to define the public realm, Beecher saw a world-historical opportunity for women to assume the role of the "external controls" through which religious and monarchical tyranny had maintained social order in a past era.

The psychological posture and the rhetorical norms that Beecher advocated defined a subject position that embodied more than a set of conventions for mediating dialogue. Through them, Beecher sought to define women as the professionals of a discourse equal in social authority to legal or religious discourse.

In Beecher's vision of women's role in the evolution of American society, the construction of carefully differentiated gender spheres served to ensure rather than to contain women's authority. She makes this case most emphatically at the beginning of her *Treatise on Domestic Economy* (1841). At the beginning of this text, Beecher quotes from Alexis de Tocqueville's chapters on American family life as a means of articulating the compatibility of women's political disenfranchisement with moral equality and equivalent social power to men. She begins by approving and quoting Tocqueville's assertion that democracy represents the working out of an irresistible divine plan. Tocqueville explains that *Democracy in America* had "been written under the impression of a kind of religious dread, produced in the Author's mind, by the contemplation of so irresistible a revolution. . . . If the men of our time were led, by attentive observation, and by sincere reflection, to acknowledge that the gradual and progressive development of social equality is at once the past and future of their history, this solitary truth would confer the sacred character of a Divine decree upon the change."[45] Beecher treats this idea almost like part of a Russian *matrushka* doll, with the divine plan outermost, democracy within that, and the critical private sphere at the very center.[46]

Tocqueville's presentation of gendered forms of authority and his integration of democracy into a supernatural plan are fully in harmony with Beecher's understanding of woman's divinely ordained mission as a moral force in democratic culture. Tocqueville praises American women effusively, noting their "manly" strength of intellect and their independence, as well their stoic pragmatism in reconciling themselves to unequal gender-based divisions in social roles. He also tellingly notes that "the women of the United States [were] confined within the narrow circle of domestic life," where they [were] in a state of "extreme dependence." But he attributes "the singular prosperity and growing strength" of the United States *"to the superiority of [its] women."*[47] According to Tocqueville and Beecher, this superiority was the result of a unique balancing of equality and renunciation that both see as a reflection of the true spirit of liberal democratic selfhood. Beecher quotes Tocqueville's explanation:

> The Americans do not think that man and woman have either the duty or the right to perform the same offices, but they show an equal regard for both their respective parts; and though their lot is different, they consider both of them, as being of equal value. . . . Thus, then, while they have allowed the social inferiority of women to subsist, they have done all they could to raise her, morally and

intellectually, to the level of man; and, in this respect, they appear to me to have excellently understood the true principle of democratic improvement.[48]

To Tocqueville and Beecher this rational equality does not change inherent duties they see rooted in gender. The distinction that they emphasize, women's obligation to accept "social inferiority," relates to public liberties that define political citizenship. Tocqueville and Beecher subordinate civil equality to an ideal of authority that they perceive to be rooted in women's voluntary renunciation of political citizenship. Americans' acceptance of women's rational equality in combination with women's voluntary political disenfranchisement embodied the internalized self-control that both Beecher and Tocqueville believe democracy requires. Through their self-control, American women represented the ideal of liberal selfhood and thus acquired a powerful source of authority. In Bercovitchian terms, such renunciation reflects the motives that cause Hester Prynne to return to Puritan New England and pin the scarlet letter back onto her dress. Democracies in general, Tocqueville argues, "make incredible efforts to provide that individual freedom shall be able to control itself." Americans educated woman to "give arms to her reasoning powers."[49] Yet marriage in democracies profoundly limited women's freedom. As Tocqueville puts it, "In America, a woman loses her independence forever in the hands of matrimony." He describes the transition from maidenhood into marriage by describing a rational pragmatism that motivated American women to consent to the restrictions of marriage as a paradoxical affirmation of their commitment to democratic freedom:

> When she is born into the world the young American [girl] finds these ideas firmly established; she sees the rules that spring there from; she is soon convinced that she cannot for a moment depart from the usages accepted by her contemporaries without immediately putting in doubt her peace of mind, her reputation, and her very social existence, and she finds the strength required for such an act of submission in the firmness of her understanding and the manly habits inculcated by her education. One may say that it is the very enjoyment of freedom that has given her the courage to sacrifice it without struggle or complaint when the time has come for that.[50]

Beecher appropriates this voluntary sacrifice as a legitimizing device that authorized women to represent the foundation of democratic community. In a potent rite of passage, marriage represented a transformation in which women exchanged democratic autonomy for a form of cultural authority that is legit-imized by the sacrifice of public selfhood. Renunciation legitimized women's authority as stewards of the critical public realm. Accepting self-control in marriage as a form of citizenship mirrored the cultural work of women teachers who inculcated "internal restraints" in children, immigrants, and the urban poor. These sacrifices authorized women to appropriate critical discourse and mediate its progress in a feminized private realm where rational self-control prevailed over the chaotic and combative liberty of the public sphere.

Domesticity as Critical Silence

However, by grounding women's authority specifically in the renunciation of the right to civil advocacy, Beecher defined women's influence more as a moral context than as a voice that represents a point of view in critical discourse. As such, American women successfully represented an antithesis to the irrational liberty of partisan public discourse, but in doing so they lost the authority to advocate substantive positions. Beecher preserved authenticity, but she sacrificed reciprocity and critical recognition. In the *Essay on Slavery*, Beecher situates her ideal of self-restraint and the intimate critical dialogue that it facilitates directly in the context of the antislavery debate, but as she does so, she also blunts women's ability to assert substantive critical positions:

> Is there not a peculiar propriety in such an emergency, in looking for the especial agency and assistance of females. . . . In the present aspect of affairs among us, when everything seems to be tending to disunion and distraction, it surely has become the duty of every female instantly to relinquish the attitude of a partisan, in every matter of clashing interests, and to assume the office of a mediator, and an advocate of peace. . . . While quietly holding her own opinions, and calmly avowing them, when conscience and integrity make the duty imperative, every female can employ her influence, not for the purpose of exciting or regulating public sentiment, but rather for the purpose of promoting a spirit of candour, forbearance, charity, and peace. (*ES* 127–28)

In this passage Beecher describes women's responsibilities in terms that are simul-taneously private and deeply involved in the political life of the nation. Through a rhetoric of Christian generosity, Beecher encourages women to represent a position of authentic sympathy with those who hold opposing views.

But in advocating women's role as cultural mediator, Beecher risks women's ability to advocate substantive moral positions. Rather than representing a position in a debate, she asks each woman to turn herself into a living embodiment of virtue whose influence will silently and invisibly pervade an idealized domestic realm. In a frequently quoted passage from the *Essay on Slavery*, Beecher describes the paradoxical, even impossible, combination of mediation and advocacy that she envisions for women in intimate critical discourse. In the "domestic and social circle . . . let every woman become so cultivated and refined in intellect, that her taste and judgment will be respected; so benevolent in feeling and action; that her motives will be reverenced;—so unassuming and unambitious, that collision and competition will be banished. . . . Then, the fathers, the husbands, and the sons, will find an influence thrown around them, to which they will yield not only willingly but proudly." The woman must go about "making herself so much respected, esteemed and loved, that to yield to her opinions and to gratify her wishes will be the free-will offering of the heart" (*ES* 100). In Beecher's ideal, women would transform the world around them not through direct action, not even by participating in a norm defining private dialogue, but by so fully embodying self-control, virtue, and religion that they would become perfect models of self-controlling, civic-minded, liberal femininity. Ultimately, in Beecher's ideal, women seem to dictate moral norms more than they influence rational subjects. By constructing a self that is perfect in its humility, women paradoxically attain an irresistible control over the norms and values of society. But they would do so silently, without exacerbating the context of "clashing interests" by adding yet another partisan voice to the conversation.

Though the paradoxes and contradictions of Beecher's effort to domesticate political dialogue within a forum controlled by women have left influential traces in domestic ideology, her central contribution to reform thought in antebellum America lies in her effort to define the home as a new kind of church and woman as a new kind of minister. Women's disenfranchisement functioned for her like the ideal of celibacy for Catholic priests and the vestal virgins of ancient Rome. It legitimized authority through an act of renunciation on behalf of the common good. Although Beecher never wavered in ascribing gender-based distinctions to a divine plan, her domestic theory is most accurately understood as a project in the social construction of authority by manipulating conventional definitions of masculinity and femininity. The home, in the structure she defines in the *Essay on Slavery* and especially in the *Treatise on Domestic Economy*, is not so much a place of retreat from the public realm as it is the foundation on which all other public institutions rest.

Her grand vision was to redefine the home as a public institution that would be the vital source of moral values for the nation as a whole. This effort was enabled by the broadly shared assumption that once sectarianism and religious pluralism had come to characterize American Christianity, the home remained the only institution that could serve as a stable focal point for consensus. For Beecher the domestic realm not only represented a feminine site of moral education and personal authenticity; it also called to mind a consensually recognized site of virtue untainted by the partisan rifts that were affecting religious and political discourses. Even as religious institutions were reproducing the divisions of partisan politics and radical reformers were beginning to argue for disunion, the domestic realm still retained the aura of a prelapsarian community. It was the only institution to which Americans could turn as a model of both civic virtue and political autonomy. By constructing a model of authority that defined domesticity in terms of a professional discourse, Beecher sought to reassert a voice of consensus that could take the place once claimed by the orthodox minister. Far from understanding the private sphere in terms of civil disenfranchisement, Beecher presented the home as an institution responsible for mediating conflicts that were too threatening to trust to the public sphere. As a site that linked moral authority with ideological consensus, the home represented an extremely powerful source of authority for women's voices. In her construction of domesticity, Beecher sought to define and codify this authority, to gain professional status for the women who would wield it, and to reposition the home as an institution that bridged private and public functions.

In their debate over women's participation in antislavery, Grimké and Beecher thus offered competing models of critical conversation grounded in conflicting assumptions about femininity and human nature. In the process, they also articulated opposed assumptions about the nature of public dialogue in democratic society. At the center of their disagreement is the relationship of sincerity to publicity. Grimké's model assumes the possibility of sincere critical dialogue in the public sphere. She pitted feminine sincerity against the problems of strategic discourse in a principled assertion of the right of access to the public sphere as a necessary dimension of democratic equality. In the process, though, Grimké also argued that equality requires a pluralistic public sphere that recognizes a multiplicity of identities. Though the tradition of women's rights activism that

Grimké helped to found has been more influential in shaping the boundaries of critical publicity in the United States, the distinction Catharine Beecher emphasized between feminine/private/sincere and masculine/public/strategic also still importantly influences critical public discourse. In truth, Beecher was less an essentialist than a pragmatist, and her construction of woman's influence was an effort to provoke or catalyze a paradigmatic shift in the way Americans understood authority. In a way, Beecher seems to have felt that the changing nature of public institutions and the danger that authentic dialogue would be completely eclipsed by strategic action had left critical authority up for grabs. Hers is one of the first assertions of what has become the rhetoric of family values, insisting on the private realm as the sole locus of virtue and marking the public as a site of inauthenticity that inherently threatens the ability of the individual to remain moral. In an important respect, by moving the locus of sincerity from the church to the home, Beecher strove to collapse the public into the private and succumbed to the forces of privatization that also compelled clerical disestablishment. This effort was based on the belief that the home was the only place where people could speak sincerely and the only institution that still represented the possibility of critical conversation.

CHAPTER THREE

Garrison, Douglass, and the Problem of Politics

Frederick Douglass's fight with the slave breaker Covey was clearly an act of liberatory self-assertion. But as Frank Kirkland points out, it is also a parable of recognition, a story that demonstrates Douglass's ability to compel a white man to recognize him as an equal, at least in terms of brute force.[1] After defeating Covey, Douglass puzzled over his master's response and wondered why Covey did not have him "taken by the constable to the whipping-post and there regularly whipped" (N 79). He interpreted this failure on Covey's part by contextualizing the fight as a challenge to Covey's public standing, his "unbounded reputation for being a first-rate . . . negro-breaker" (N 79). The change this fight marked in Covey's attitude toward Douglass also reflects an important transformation in Douglass's understanding of the forces that structure social relationships. It marks a moment in which Douglass paradoxically rose out of slavery at the same time that his effort to assert autonomy drew him into animal violence.[2] The fight with Covey began a sequence of self-transformations through which Douglass linked equality to the culture of reform and its role in provoking a pluralistic public. The tensions between moral perfectionism and political antislavery that do so much to animate both Douglass's and Garrison's career dramatize the emergence of important links between the early culture of reform and efforts to imagine a pluralistic public sphere.

In the long view of the relationship between Frederick Douglass and William Lloyd Garrison, the moral perfectionism that drew Angelina Grimké to Garrison's Anti-Slavery Society serves primarily as a foil against which Douglass rethought the relationship of race to the structure of American civil society. Thinking along lines similar to Angelina Grimké, who linked equality, gender, and publicity, Douglass sought to instantiate pluralism by making his claim to public recognition inseparable from his blackness. Yet in contrast to Grimké, who underscored sincerity as a site where femininity and republican virtue in civil society could intersect, Douglass grounded his claim to equality in the very act of critical participation in debates over divisive issues. For Douglass such an appropriation of public presence, particularly in the debate over the legitimacy of the Constitution during the 1850s, created a necessary intersection of the African American struggle for liberty and the construction of citizenship in antebellum society.

Though Douglass always revered Garrison as an exemplar of courage, Douglass's effort to legitimize an African American presence in the official public sphere eventually compelled him to abandon Garrison's moral perfectionism and integrate himself as fully as he could into the political structure of the nation. In important respects, Douglass's career illustrates a movement from the private into the public realm as a means of transforming himself from a chattel into a citizen. This movement is especially striking in relation to the perfectionist dynamic of Garrisonian moral suasion. As deeply as William Lloyd Garrison was committed to equality, one thing he was never able to understand about Frederick Douglass was that for a black man and an escaped slave, the position of the perfectionist come-outer did not offer the same rhetorical authority that it offered to the white male New Englander.[3] Unlike Garrison, Douglass had no franchise to repudiate, no citizenship to come out of, and no legal standing to renounce. He was barred from service on juries. Churches, schools, and railroads were almost totally segregated against him. On the public stage, Douglass could assume no public presence or recognition in critical conversation.

A comment President Johnson made in a meeting with Douglass shortly after the end of the Civil War tellingly describes the almost total opposition white Americans understood between blackness and citizenship. In discussing the possibility of expanding the franchise to include African Americans, the president explained to Douglass that "the White man was permitted to vote before Government was derived from him. He [was] a part and parcel of the political machinery" (*FDP* 4:101). In the president's imagination, public authority was less a civil right than an inborn entitlement of white men that simply required an instrument for its realization. As much as the private realm subsumed the African American as dehumanized private property, the construction of citizenship in the public realm represented a commensurate elision of blackness. The case that Douglass made for equality was rooted in the problem of achieving recognition on the public stage. But achieving this goal required not just the redefinition of the ideas of citizenship and equality to include blackness but also the transformation of the public sphere to recognize a plurality of identities, especially African Americans and women. Moreover, this redefined public would recognize plural identities not by subsuming difference into a universal ideal of rational subjectivity but, as Grimké and Douglass insist, by recognizing the self-identified differences of a plurality of citizens.

Garrison's theory of reform does much to illustrate the position from which Douglass sought to instantiate African American equality in a revised public realm. In a poem that compares Garrison to Martin Luther and Christopher Columbus, James Russell Lowell emphasizes the long years Garrison worked in the wilderness of an unpopular cause: "In a small chamber, friendless and unseen, / Toiled over his types one poor, unlearned young man." But as Lowell goes on to explain, with the resources of a burgeoning print culture at his fingertips, Garrison's isolation and invisibility were trivial obstacles: "What need of help? He knew how types were set, / He had a dauntless spirit, and a press."[4] Lowell's offhand remark, "What need of help?" indicates the boundaries of class, race, and gender that defined access to critical public discourse in Jacksonian America. Though Garrison was "unlearned," without influential friends, and from the laboring class, his gender and race gave him an "inborn" right to claim a place in critical dialogue. He may have faced class prejudice, but his legitimacy as a voter, as a freeholder, even as a candidate for political office would have gone unquestioned. With these forms of enfranchisement built into his status as a member of the critical public, Garrison's decision to renounce political entitlements and speak from the margins of the official public sphere represents a rhetorical strategy that made authoritative institutions themselves the subjects of a critical conversation. Further, by embracing a perfectionism that compelled him to abstain from voting, denounce organized churches, and "come out" from corrupt institutions of all kinds, Garrison was not only responding to the demands of his conscience. He was also constructing an outsider position that required him to invent reform institutions that were independent of churches and the state.

As much as any other figure in American history, William Lloyd Garrison defined the terms of a major cultural debate. His combination of tireless propagandizing and pacifist nonresistance has influenced contemporary reform at least as much as Thoreau's civil disobedience. Yet Garrison's career also represents an important irony in the historical evolution of the culture of reform. Even though his commitment to moral suasion defined a basic paradigm of reform activism, it was founded on a perfectionist model of self that stood in opposition to the integrationist models of citizenship and community that emerged in his own lifetime and that continue to characterize the most influential reform movements in American society.[5] Garrison established a tight-knit alternative community and a model of association that enabled the culture of reform to emerge as a permanent feature of American civil society. But people such as Angelina Grimké and Frederick Douglass ultimately did more to articulate a public sphere in which the equality of diverse identities is defined by reciprocal recognition in a pluralistic environment. The politics of recognition that Douglass would articulate in his analysis of American publicity during the 1850s is more representative of contemporary American reform methods and goals than the explicit utopianism of Garrisonian come-outerism.

Despite this irony, Garrison's model of public selfhood defined the secularization of evangelical morality in a pure and representative form. Above all others, Garrison embodied the spirit of Stephen Mintz's "moralists and modernizers" who built the institutional structure of the culture of reform.[6] But Garrison's legacy, connected as it is to forms of public action, ultimately emerged out of the demands of the private self rather than as an intentional effort to redefine publicity. At its foundations, Garrison's construction of moral authority was grounded in a series of conscientious repudiations through which he sought to purge himself of the corrupt influence of a slaveholding society. By self-consciously positioning himself in a realm of moral purity outside church and state, Garrison constructed a Jeremiah-like stance from which to denounce a sinful society. Garrison's extremely public life was paradoxically always a quest to achieve a Platonic ideal of moral purity on a personal level. Because Garrison placed the moral authority of the private self at the root of his model of public authority, his career as an activist drew its energy from a desire to establish continuity between his private and public lives. Garrison's rhetorical persona, as unwavering and sensational as it was in its publicity, always mirrored a deeply held desire to live a pure and good life.[7]

In contrast to the evolutionary progression of Douglass's career, William Lloyd Garrison's thought exhibited remarkable consistency. Even as antislavery activists feuded over women's rights in the late 1830s and then moved toward political participation during the 1840s and 1850s, Garrison's commitment to a perfectionist ideal of nonresistance remained fundamentally unchanged. His adoption of causes such as women's rights, anti-Sabbatarianism, anticlericalism, and disunion mark stages in the unfolding of a single idea about the nature of virtue and its role in legitimizing claims to public authority. For Garrison, the rifts and schisms that divided the abolitionist community were not political or tactical challenges. On the contrary, to him they were tests of commitment, temptations in which opportunities to gain practical influence sought to lure him away from the true faith.

Garrison, Publicity, and Perfectionist Authority

Garrison's moral-suasion antislavery extended the methods of Lyman Beecher's revivalism into secular debates. As Garrison was sorting out his commitments in the 1820s, he frequently attended Beecher's church in Boston. Beecher, of course, considered his mission to Boston an effort to throttle Unitarianism by grabbing it at the throat. When Garrison founded the *Liberator* in January 1831, he was already a well-known editor who had written for both political and philanthropic journals.[8] Like most journalists in the early republic, Garrison got his start editing and writing for papers that unabashedly engaged in partisan political debate. At the very start of his career, he worked on Federalist newspapers in Massachusetts and Vermont. He also briefly worked at a newspaper that supported Lyman Beecher's temperance crusade. While working as the assistant at this newspaper, the *National Philanthropist*, Garrison met Benjamin Lundy, with whom he would enter the antislavery movement as coeditor of the *Genius of Universal Emancipation* in Baltimore. From the very beginning of his career as a political writer, Garrison earned a reputation as a sharp rhetorician who relished the slang-whanging of political journalism. In the modest Lundy's words, Garrison wrote with "nerve." During this formative phase of his career, Garrison both refined his literary style and clarified his moral commitments. He became an early advocate of immediate emancipation, and his simultaneous rejection of gradual abolition and the colonization movement represents a major turning point in his effort to live a life that integrated moral purity with combative reform activism.[9]

The first issue of the *Liberator*, published New Year's Day 1831, dramatizes Garrison's desire to construct a voice that combined institutional independence with uncompromised moral purity. As he introduces himself to the public,

Garrison refers to his recent imprisonment for libel and presents his felony conviction as a bona fides that demonstrates the contrast between his own virtues and the corrupt norms of the official public sphere. In 1830 Garrison was jailed in Baltimore for a report that he published in the *Genius of Universal Emancipation*. In this article, Garrison exposes a Massachusetts merchant as a participant in the slave trade. Garrison writes:

> I have stated that the ship Francis hails from my native place, Newburyport (Massachusetts), is commanded by a Yankee captain, and owned by a townsman named
>
> FRANCIS TODD
>
> Of Captain Nicholas Brown I should have expected better conduct. It is no worse to fit out piratical cruisers, or to engage in the foreign slave trade, than to pursue a similar trade along our coasts; and the men who have the wickedness to participate therein, for the purpose of heaping up wealth, should be ☞ SENTENCED TO SOLITARY CONFINEMENT FOR LIFE; ☜ they are the enemy of their own species—highway robbers and murderers; and their final doom will be, unless they speedily repent, to occupy the lowest depths of perdition.

After describing the cargo of slaves that Todd carried from Baltimore to New Orleans, Garrison continues: "I recollect that it was always a mystery in Newburyport how Mr. Todd contrived to make profitable voyages to New Orleans and other places, when other merchants, with as fair an opportunity to make money, and sending at the same ports at the same time, invariably made fewer successful speculations. The mystery seems to be unraveled" (*Lib.* Jan. 1, 1831).

By defining himself as a spokesman for uncompromising sincerity who has been imprisoned for "libeling" a slave trader, Garrison made a stark distinction between moral authority and the conventions of public discourse that prevailed when he began the *Liberator*. As Lundy would have preferred, he could have avoided the libel suit by moderating his denunciation of Francis Todd. But according to Garrison's logic, such moderation would have implicated him in a form of strategic discourse. His willingness to risk legal sanction by unflinchingly denouncing the slave trader/"merchant" is central to Garrison's construction of his own critical authority. He introduced the *Liberator* with the article that—literally— *was* his crime and thus demonstrated that arrest, trial, and imprisonment had not caused him to recognize the legitimacy of a corrupt public sphere. In effect, he turned the "libel" inside out and defined it as an act of virtue and sincerity that underscored the importance of creating a discourse of moral authority standing outside the conventions of the benevolent reform movements that Catharine Beecher used as models for her educational programs.

Further, in the same issue in which he republished his libelous article, Garrison also published a manifesto in which he justifies the inflammatory style that would become his trademark. As an articulation of Garrison's sense of the connection between the rhetorical tone of his public voice and his sense of moral integrity, this article is especially important. In it Garrison replies to critics by explaining: "I am aware that many object to the severity of my language; but is there not cause for severity? I will be as harsh as truth, and as uncompromising as justice. On this subject I do not wish to think, or speak, or write, with moderation. . . . I am in earnest—I will not equivocate—I will not excuse—I will not retreat a single inch—AND I WILL BE HEARD" (*Lib.* Jan. 1, 1831). In these lines, Garrison commits himself to speaking in tones that reflect his sense of the occasion. He treats his tone of voice as a moral register in which style is calibrated to the seriousness of the sin he is denouncing. In sharp contrast to the conciliatory voice that Catharine Beecher advocated or the calm sincerity that characterizes Angelina Grimké's writing, Garrison's tone is self-consciously sensationalistic. The difference between Garrison's voice and Beecher's or Grimké's is that Garrison's style is fundamentally self-referential. In a very real sense, in order to be true to the motivating spirit of his antislavery, Garrison had to reinvent established conventions of reform discourse. As much as he was working to convince his readers of the justice of his cause, he was also speaking self-reflexively, making a public revelation of his most heartfelt sentiments. As a mode of self-expression, almost as a confession of inner experience, Garrison worked more to harmonize his tone with an internal moral sense than to integrate it into a multivocal process of dialogue.

Later in the same article, Garrison underscores the source of his motivation as he compares his own inflammatory tone to rhetorical occasions in which the individual's right to adopt a "severe" mode of expression goes unquestioned. He writes: "Tell a man whose house is on fire to give a moderate alarm; tell him to moderately rescue his wife from the hands of the ravisher; tell the mother to gradually extricate her babe from the fire into which it has fallen;—but urge me not to use moderation in a cause like the present" (*Lib.* Jan. 1, 1831). In these comparisons, Garrison describes moments of immanent crisis that he sees as analogies for the moral imperative of immediate abolition. To speak with "moderation" on such a profound violation of human rights, in Garrison's view, would not only be inconsistent with the foundations of his authority; it would misrepresent the urgency of the occasion. His defense of radical speech thus reiterates the oppositional dynamic of his libel conviction. Just as he recast his conviction to assert a moral law that trumped the criminal law, the voice of the *Liberator* hearkened to a sense of crisis that trumped the social stability implicitly represented by the discourse of benevolent reform.

Garrison's motives in the libel case and his use of them to launch the *Liberator* indicate his debt to the jeremiad tradition. In adopting this voice, though, Garrison was not just harking back to a mythic Puritan era of communal spirituality and civic virtue. As Emerson remarked in 1831, the Puritans merit admiration because "they were the pious men who kept their integrity in an unholy age." Garrison was also working to keep his integrity in an unholy age, and for him this meant speaking in immoderate tones. Indeed, Emerson referred to Garrison and his followers as "the continuation of puritanism" in his own day. Sacvan Bercovitch also situates the intersection of moral integrity with social criticism as a key element of the jeremiad tradition. Like Garrison, "from the start the Puritan Jeremiahs had drawn their inspiration from insecurity; by the 1670s, crisis had become their source of strength. They fastened upon it, gloried in it, even invented it if necessary. They took courage from backsliding, converted threat into vindication, made affliction their seal of progress. Crisis became both form and substance of their appeals."[10] In William Lloyd Garrison's world, the "threat" and "crisis" that even benevolent reform created was the sublimation of antislavery within gradualist political speech and the apologetic language of colonizationist ministers such as Lyman Beecher.

In adapting the combination of spirituality and social criticism to serve secular reform culture, Garrison grounded his voice in a form of faith that sought to redefine the legitimizing principles of social institutions. As Gregg D. Crane notes, "Arguing for God-directed self-control . . . Garrison's conception of government stressed conscience and moral absolutes not consent and human experiment."[11] Lewis Perry explains Garrison's reform zeal and his anti-institutionalism by connecting his faith to the principles of Puritan antinomianism. As Perry phrases it, the Garrisonians connected the come-outer stance to the establishment of legitimate authority. They rejected most political institutions "because they detested anarchy. In their categories, human government was synonymous with anarchy and antithetical to the rule of Christ and moral principle." [12] Perhaps ironically, other reformers' criticism of Garrison's adoption of causes beyond antislavery actually reveals the depth of his commitment to nonresistance. After renouncing church and state as analogous instruments of coercion, Garrison set about creating a set of alternative institutions—the *Liberator*, the Massachusetts and American Anti-Slavery Societies, and the Massachusetts Non-Resistance Society—that could embody his broad vision of universal equality.

Leo Tolstoy, in a letter to Garrison's son, defined the idea of nonresistance and described its implications for Garrisonian human rights philosophy. The central idea of human rights, Tolstoy remarked, is the moral necessity of renouncing "the right of coercion on the part of certain people in regard to certain others." But in practice, noncoercion requires far more than opposition to slavery. Tolstoy continued: "Garrison, understanding that the slavery of Negroes was only a particular instance of universal coercion, put forward a general principle . . . that under no pretext has any man the right to dominate, i.e., to use coercion over his fellows." [13]

Tolstoy also advocated the Garrisonian model of nonresistance for the leaders of reform movements. One of the major pretexts that reformers use to ignore noncoercion in practice, Tolstoy argued, "has always been that men regarded it as possible to eradicate or diminish evil by brute force, i.e., also by evil. Having once realized this fallacy, Garrison put forward against slavery neither the suffering of slaves, nor the cruelty of slaveholders, nor the social equality of men, but the eternal Christian law of refraining from opposing evil by violence, i.e., of 'non-resistance.'" [14] In the model of nonresistance that Garrison both proselytized and sought to practice, the renunciation of the power of coercion was the defining principle of equality. Rather than grounding his ideal in political enfranchisement, economic opportunity, or other familiar modes of imagining equality, Garrison based it on the moral recognition of other people's autonomy. For Garrison the core of perfectionist faith and the path to utopia lay in a daily effort to understand and to act according to the Christlike pacifism that Tolstoy recognized and admired in Garrison's ethics.

As a man seeking moral perfection on both a personal and a social level, Garrison was as much a pilgrim working toward a Christian utopia as he was an antislavery propagandist. The spiritual adventure of his life lay in the difficulty of remaining true to a moral idea that had constantly expanding implications for his behavior the longer he lived within it. Garrison and those who remained close to him from the 1830s through the 1850s sought to live in two worlds simultaneously. The utopian world that moral perfectionism anticipates represented the imaginative and spiritual world of Garrison's highest hopes; but that world and the norms that govern it inevitably clashed against the institutions of a slaveholding nation. Rather than withdraw into an alternative community like Brook Farm or present Thoreauvian autonomy as a model of reform, Garrison sought to exploit what he understood to be a manly commitment to moral perfection as the foundation of a radical public voice. As David Leverenz and E. Anthony Rotundo have described it, Garrison deployed a model of masculinity rooted in self-control in regard to sin and vice on a personal level, civic mindedness in denouncing the crimes that undermine the integrity of the nation, and Christlike endurance in the face of social ostracism.[15]

In the July 10, 1831, *Liberator*, Garrison outlined the pragmatics of the crusade that would occupy the next thirty years of his life. The first requirement was, as Garrison describes it, a form of cleansing through "the entire abstinence from products of slavery." Second, abolitionists who were members of churches must purify themselves in a first step toward purifying their religions. As he phrases it: "Religious professors, of all denominations, must bear unqualified testimony against slavery." These individual commitments should also be coupled with two forms of collective public activism. First, Garrison argues: "The formation of an American Anti-Slavery Society is of the utmost importance"; second, by arguing for the value of an antislavery press that would publish "at least one hundred periodicals over the land, expressly devoted to the cause of emancipation," he converts the authorizing effect of nonparticipation from an act of self-purification into an act of reform. The journals of antislavery societies would "consolidate the moral power of the nation, so that Congress and the State Legislatures [might] be inundated with petitions;—to scatter tracts like raindrops, over the land, on the subject of slavery." This early editorial also articulates Garrison's commitment to critical discourse as the sole legitimate means of persuasion. Thinking along lines similar to those of Lydia Maria Child and Angelina Grimké, Garrison concludes that the "eloquent agents" who would "plead the cause" and the one hundred periodicals that could influence public opinion were necessary because, as he states, "The people, at large, are astonishingly ignorant of the horrors of slavery. Let information be circulated among them as prodigally as the light of heaven, and they cannot long act and reason as they now do" (*Lib.* July 10, 1831). With this description of the effect that antislavery propaganda would have on the thoughtless public, Garrison articulates the process of persuasion through which moral suasion becomes a masculine, Christian force to redeem the nation.

Yet the key for Garrison was the authority to be derived from moral purity. In reply to a letter in which a black reader of the *Liberator* argued for violence in the tradition of the American Revolution, Garrison remarked: "The work of reform must commence with ourselves. Until we are purified, it will be fruitless and intrusive for us to cleanse others" (*Lib.* July 10, 1831). Once purity was attained by stepping outside the slave economy, however, the reformer's voice would take on quasi-divine attributes. Abolitionist "tracts" would work like manna, redeeming the souls of the American people as they moved individuals to recognize universal equality. This process of moral education would culminate in a consensus as the nation unified behind the reformer's vision. To the extent that his efforts facilitated a consolidation of "moral power," the reformer's voice was comparable to the "light of heaven." In Garrison's model of the culture of reform, the perfectionist reformer, not the orthodox minister or the perfect wife, becomes the "herald of justice."

The commitments that Garrison articulated in 1831 form the foundation for the broader doctrines of nonresistance and universal equality that he embraced later in the 1830s and during the 1840s. Even as the antislavery movement was building momentum toward its eventual integration into the political system, Garrison was developing the doctrine of nonresistance into a comprehensive alternative to the norms of the antebellum public sphere. His movement further and further away from participation in electoral politics was marked by his principled defense of women's rights in 1840, his rejection of the U.S. Constitution, and finally his advocacy of disunion.[16] Though the motivations behind these acts are implicit in his writing from the time of his conversion to immediate abolitionism in 1829, he had not always recognized them as part of the same idea that underpinned his antislavery. Thus, Garrison's reform philosophy did not really evolve over time. More accurately, it filled out through a series of ethical realizations that he experienced over the course of fifteen years. The most recognizable turning points in his career—the shift from colonizationist to immediatist antislavery, the advocacy of women's rights, anticlericalism, anti-Sabbatarianism, and disunion—represent successive stages in Garrison's recognition of the implications of the doctrine of nonresistance. The great schisms

over women's rights and political action in the late 1830s do not mark transitions
in his philosophy; they represent tests of Garrison's integrity, challenging his
ability to remain uncompromisingly true to his original motives.

The Peace Convention that Garrison helped to organize in 1838 reveals the
vital principles of his mature thought.[17] He wrote two documents for this convention, a Declaration of Sentiments and a constitution for the newly formed
Massachusetts Non-Resistance Society. These texts are revealing because the
pride he took in them reflects a personal sense that he had successfully joined
internal conviction with public expression. Following the example he set in 1832
when he founded the New England Anti-Slavery Society to provide an immediatist alternative to the American Colonization Society, the Peace Convention that
Garrison, Samuel J. May, and Henry C. Wright organized during the summer
of 1838 was motivated by their dissatisfaction with the accommodationist tone
of the American Peace Society. Garrison, May, and Wright sought to form a
society that would take pacifism to its logical conclusion by speaking out against
capital punishment, arguing for conscientious objection to military service, and
denouncing nationalism.

The proceedings of the convention reflect the organizers' desire to found
a pacifist institution in which commitment to principle was more important
than practical viability as a reform organization. In a portent of more serious
divisions to come, the minutes record a split between pro– and anti–women's
rights reformers. Soon after Samuel J. May called the convention to order on the
morning of September 18, 1838, several men "withdrew from the Convention,
on the ground of the admission of women to take part in its proceedings" (*Lib.*
Sept. 28, 1838). Garrison later told the story to his mother-in-law, remarking
that "there were more than 150 persons, who enrolled their names as members—
among them, quite a number of women, several of whom were immediately
put on committees. This so horrified some of the clergy, and others, that they
ordered their [own] names to be erased from the rolls." However, Garrison also
noted happily that "only about ten or twelve left the convention" (*LWLG* 2:395).
This rift set the stage for a symbolic affirmation of the right to free speech as
the marker of equality within the organization. On a motion from Henry C.
Wright, the convention passed a resolution that "any persons present be allowed
to take part in discussions of the Convention." This debate over women's access
to the alternative critical public sphere of the antislavery community directly
anticipates the divisions that occurred at the World Anti-Slavery Meeting in
London in 1840, which spurred the meeting at Seneca Falls in 1848.

The central statement of the convention was a resolution introduced by Amasa Walker: "Resolved, that human life is inviolable, and can never be taken by individuals or nations, without committing sin against God." This resolution revised an earlier one that specifies some of the practical implications of radical pacifism:

> Resolved, that it is contrary to the spirit and precepts of the gospel, repugnant to reason and to the common sympathies and principles of human nature, and destructive to the peace and good order of society for man to take the life of man, in any case, or in defense of property, liberty, life or religion;—and that, consequently, to threaten or endanger human life, or make preparations for its destruction, is a sin against God, and detrimental to the best interests of individuals and nations. (*Lib.* Sept. 28, 1838)

This draft reflects the radical pacifism that rejects the legitimacy of self-defense, military resistance of any kind, and even the maintenance of a police force. Walker's revision compressed the enumerations of the original resolution into a single sentence. After one of the remaining ministers moved to table the motion, Garrison defended it and forced it to a vote. The resolution passed and became the central ideal of the Non-Resistance Society.

The constitution that grew out of this document functioned almost as a first draft of the Declaration of Sentiments that Garrison wrote the next day to sum up the conclusions that the conferees had reached. In describing these texts to his wife, Garrison explained: "I first wrote the Constitution, radical in all things, and presented it without delay. It created much discussion, which lasted during the evening, but was adopted by a decisive majority." Then, as he put it, "I absented myself to write the Declaration. In the afternoon, it was reported to the Convention, and never was a more 'fanatical' or 'disorganizing' instrument penned by man. It swept the whole surface of society, and upturned almost every existing institution on earth" (*LWLG* 2:391). To his mother-in-law, he abbreviated the story: "A committee of nine was appointed to draft a Declaration of Sentiments. I drew it up, and put into it all the fanaticism of my heart and head" (*LWLG* 2:395).

Whereas many of Garrison's peers in the reform community, not to mention subsequent historians, have treated this Declaration of Sentiments as the example par excellence of Garrison's susceptibility to fads and quixotic causes, the declaration usefully defines the intersection of his various reform impulses. Most importantly, it explains the connection between radical pacifism and confrontational public debate. The text has a two-part structure. In the first section, Garrison describes the "principles and purposes" of the new organization. In typically Garrisonian fashion, it revolves around a series of renunciations through which the nonresistant might purify the self and claim the moral sincerity that authorizes him to make demands on others. The central issue is the withdrawal from state-controlled instruments of coercion. Garrison mixes concrete reform principles with an allegorical sketch of the nonresistant's utopia:

> We cannot acknowledge allegiance to any human government; neither can we oppose any such government by a resort to physical force. We recognize but one KING and LAWGIVER, one JUDGE and RULER of mankind. We are bound by the laws of a kingdom which is not of this world; the subjects of which are forbidden to fight; in which MERCY and TRUTH are met together, and RIGHTEOUSNESS and PEACE have kissed each other; which has no state lines, no national partitions, no geographical boundaries; in which there is no distinction of rank or division of caste, or inequality of sex; the officers of which are PEACE, its exactors RIGHTEOUSNESS, its walls SALVATION, and its gates PRAISE; and which is destined to break in pieces and consume all other kingdoms. (*Lib.* Sept. 28, 1838)

Rather than repudiating civil society altogether, Garrison renounces loyalty to national identities and to the political institutions that sustain them. As a cadre of civil antinomians, the nonresistants viewed nation-states as invidious associations that usurp God's direct authority over the individual.

But alongside the broad renunciation of nationalism and the violence it breeds, Garrison includes a metaphoric description of the authority that the nonresistants recognized as legitimate. Garrison seeks to mark a direct, virtually unmediated path from the Godhead to the Peace Convention and from there to a perfectionist public sphere. Loyalty to the ecumenically Christian "JUDGE and RULER" requires him to strip away all intermediary institutions. Nationality, ethnicity, race, and gender, all become irrelevant in an imagined heaven-on-earth of universal equality. In place of the restraints and controls that Garrison attributes to "human government," he anticipates a world in which the principles of Christian pacifism are internalized and form the core motives of public behavior. Where Catharine Beecher imagined a society in which women blunt a looming anarchy by privately inculcating the internal restraints of republican virtue, Garrison imagined a nation that was being consumed by anarchic violence but that could be reformed by Christian noncoercion. The critical discourse that he built around this principle stands both as a practical alternative to the realm of party politics and as a utopian critique of the official public sphere.

Moral authority, in Garrison's logic, is grounded in the self, and the individual can either emphasize discontinuity between a divine realm where "righteousness and Peace have kissed" and a public sphere where the discussion of the slave trade is libelous, or he can compromise his moral authority by accepting the discursive conventions of a slaveholding nation. As Garrison phrases the internal origins of reformers' moral authority: "We conceive, that if a nation has no right to defend itself against foreign enemies, or to punish its invaders, no individual possesses that right in his own case. . . . If one man may take life, to obtain or defend his rights, the same license must necessarily be granted to communities, states, and nations." The state, in Garrison's view, is simply an externalization of the values of the self. The moral relation between self and society that Garrison articulates is similar to that which Thoreau offers in his essay "Resistance to Civil Government." "If *one* man," Thoreau explains, "in this State of Massachusetts, *ceasing to hold Slaves*, were actually to withdraw from this copartner ship, and be locked up in the county jail therefor, it would be the abolition of slavery in America."[18] Thoreau here asserts an ideal of moral suasion, the power of the virtuous individual who has repudiated the relations that make slavery possible and thereby made himself representative of a better world. For both Garrison and Thoreau, the state is simply a projection of the virtue of the citizen. At the 1838 Peace Convention, Garrison sought to describe the citizen who authorizes himself or herself to participate in critical dialogue through withdrawal from the national "copartnership" similar to that which Thoreau describes—and that in different ways both Thoreau and Garrison tried to enact. The key difference, of course, is the uniquely divisive voice that Garrison defined through the *Liberator*.

While Garrison understood come-outer perfectionism to be a necessary act in the legitimatization of the reformer's authority, he also directed the moral authority of perfectionism toward public debate. As he makes the transition from principles to tactics in the Non-Resistants' Declaration of Sentiments, he writes:

> But, while we shall adhere to the doctrine of non-resistance and passive submission to enemies, we purpose, in a moral and spiritual sense, to speak and act boldly in the cause of God; to assail iniquity, in high places and in low places; to apply our principle to all existing civil, political, legal, and ecclesiastical institutions; and to

hasten the time, when kingdoms of this world will have become the kingdoms of
our LORD and his CHRIST, and he shall reign forever.

Far from avoiding controversial political dialogue as a form of strategic discourse
that compromised their integrity, as Emerson would do well into the 1840s, the
nonresistants understood reform propaganda as a form of preaching. Garrison
continues: "We expect to prevail, through THE FOOLISHNESS OF PREACHING. . . .
From the press, we shall promulgate our sentiments as widely as practicable. . . .
The triumphant progress of the cause of TEMPERANCE and of ABOLITION in
our land, through the instrumentality of benevolent and voluntary associations,
encourages us to . . . employ lecturers, circulate tracts and publications, form
societies, and petition our state and national governments, in relation to the
subject of UNIVERSAL PEACE" (*Lib.* Sept. 28, 1838). The Declaration of Sentiments of the 1838 Peace Convention is Garrison's densest articulation not just of
the central assumptions of his reform thought but also of the principle he placed
at the center of the emerging culture of reform. Authentic reform, in Garrison's
view, must be grounded in the spiritual challenge of working toward virtue on
an individual level.

What is often missed in commentary on Garrisonian perfectionism is that
it is not primarily about social perfection. Social elevation is the effect of the
individual's effort to achieve moral perfection on a personal level. As much as
they are social manifestoes, statements like the 1838 Declaration of Sentiments are
forms of religious testimony that express the faith of individuals. This pattern
links Garrison and the moral perfectionists to nineteenth-century communitarians and to the evangelicals, all of whom sought to provoke individual moral
conversion by modeling crucible-like communal environments.

Above all, the authority of the perfectionist reformer's voice was contingent
on his moral rectitude and willingness uncompromisingly to follow the voice of
conscience wherever it led. For Garrison, this led him beyond the boundaries of
antislavery as the principle of noncoercion compelled him to embrace equality
in an ever-widening set of contexts. It also compelled him to reject political abolitionism as a form of strategic action that would undermine his claim to moral
authority. The *Liberator*, as the voice of a spiritual pilgrim, must be understood
almost as a spiritual autobiography as well as an organ of reform propaganda.
As the uncompromising and consistently radical voice of its editor, it details
Garrison's ongoing declarations of independence from corrupt institutions. In

each of his radical positions, each of his radical editorials, Garrison sought to convert himself and to instantiate his own moral authority by integrating private conviction and public utterance. In its tone, its intentional radicalism, and its range of advocacy, the *Liberator* allowed Garrison always to define himself as virtue's hero, as the voice of uncompromising dissent. This remained true even as the immediatist movement, in whose founding he had played such an important role, was moving into the political camp. As Lawrence J. Friedman and more recently Robert A. Fanuzzi emphasize, the institutions that Garrison created mark the construction of alternative publics that are highly visible within the realm of critical discourse but that measure their moral integrity partly by provoking the hostility of legislatures and other organs of the official public sphere.[19]

During the two decades that preceded the Civil War, especially after the passage of the Fugitive Slave Act in 1850, the antislavery movement became increasingly involved in political organizing and in working to influence political elections. Abolitionists defected to the political wing of the movement in increasing numbers and left the moral suasionists in much the same relation to society as that of the Congregationalist ministers after the Unitarian controversy. Like the Congregationalist minister, Garrison represented a strong model of moral authority, but he was ultimately loyal to an ideal of perfectionist consensus in a public realm that was moving toward structural pluralism as a permanent feature of discursive democracy. As the institutions he was influential in creating found means of participating in politics that did not compromise their integrity, the perfectionists' come-outer stance, based on the evangelical born-again experience of saving grace, found ways of integrating into the "chastened" reciprocities of the pluralistic public sphere.

During the 1850s, Garrison remained true to the disunionist and antiviolence principles that had always characterized his brand of moral suasion. James Russell Lowell, as early as 1848, offered a kind of premature eulogy for Garrison: "Garrison is so used to standing alone that, like Daniel Boone, he moves away as the world creeps up to him, and goes farther *into the wilderness.* . . . But with all his faults (and they are the faults of his position) he is a great and extraordinary man. His work may be over, but it has been a great work. Posterity will forget his hard words, and remember his hard work. I look upon him already as an historical personage, as one who is in his niche."[20] By 1852 Garrison was assuming the tone of a retiring veteran and lamented: "The period might have been when

I was of consequence to the anti-slavery movement, but it is not now" (*LWLG* 4:210).

As political abolitionism grew in the wake of the Fugitive Slave Act, the Anthony Burns case, and the Dred Scott Decision, Garrison and the come-outer perfectionists who had reinvented reform culture in the 1830s occasionally even presented their antinomian independence in terms of political authority. In response to the Fugitive Slave Act, Henry C. Wright reaffirmed the moral suasionist's commitment to working on public opinion from outside the official political system: "Men do not go to Congress, they are coerced there. They do not act—they are acted upon. The active vote does not belong to Congress at all" (*Lib.* Aug. 29, 1850). In 1853 Charles C. Burleigh reflected the fissures in the come-outer philosophy: "No more effective vote is ever cast, in its bearing upon the politics . . . of the nation, than that which is cast from lips denouncing the Constitution" (*Lib.* June 3, 1853). Even Garrison hemmed and hawed during the election of 1856, concluding that the Republican Party had emerged as "the legitimate product of moral agitation" and admitted: "If there were no moral barrier to our voting, and we had a million ballots to bestow, we should cast them all for the Republican candidate."[21]

Despite the failure of moral suasion to end slavery, Garrison was the single most important figure in creating the institutional structure of the culture of reform. In the connection he emphasized between the moral character of the individual and the authority to make political demands in the secular public sphere, Garrison integrated the ideal of republican virtue with self-purifying evangelical conversion into a single model of democratic citizenship. In doing so, he shifted the source of the jeremiad from the pulpit to the reform convention and redefined the reformer not just as a social visionary but also as a model of aspiring liberal selfhood. In his effort to define moral virtue in a civil context, Garrison thus shared much with Emerson and Thoreau. In some ways Garrison's ideal of selfhood is very Emersonian, at least in their shared desire to achieve continuity between the private and the public self. But unlike the two transcendentalists, Garrison had a profound impact on the institutional structure through which Americans pursue reform. It was Garrison, above all, who adapted the revival format and the propaganda instruments of the evangelicals for the purposes of secular reform. He is the key bridge between the context of the Unitarian controversy and the contemporary structure of ideologically driven voluntary associations struggling to shape public opinion.[22]

Yet it is important also to recognize that the reform persona Garrison constructed reflects a race- and gender-based position of enfranchisement in critical public discourse that was not available to his most important protégé, Frederick Douglass. As a man who was disenfranchised not just by law but by a growing body of racist philosophy and pseudoscience, Douglass's Garrison-style renunciations of political enfranchisement could have no authorizing effect in critical public discourse. On the contrary, to Douglass the come-outer position primarily defined the context from which he reconciled moral authority with public activism.

As Douglass's public career evolved from his speech in Nantucket in 1841 through the growth of political abolitionism in the 1850s, he came to believe that the path to equality was grounded in the public sphere rather than in the combination of liberal and Christian perfectionism that underpinned Garrisonian thought.[23] In the Garrisonian example, slavery, racism, and inequality would end as a result of innumerable private conversions through which individuals cast off moral corruption. Thus, in a sense, racial equality is the by-product of a fundamentally self-reflexive act of personal purification. Garrison sought to project Habermasian transparency not primarily to set a standard for civil discourse but to verify his own sincerity.[24] Shifting away from authority grounded in perfect continuity between private and public, Douglass constructed a Rawlsian model of public selfhood grounded in recognition and reciprocity. In his chapter titled "Public Reason and the Ideal of Democratic Citizenship," Rawls links equality not just with the right of rational self-expression in the public sphere but also with access to the coercive force of democratic government. The paradigm of mutual recognition that Rawls places at the heart of reasonable pluralism indicates the public sphere that Douglass would substitute for Garrison's Christian perfectionist utopia. Rawls contends that democracy involves the willingness of people to recognize in one another the legitimacy of "an equal share in the coercive political power that citizens exercise over one another by voting and in other ways. As reasonable and rational, and knowing that they affirm a diversity of reasonable religious and philosophical doctrines, they should be ready to explain the basis of their actions to one another in terms each could reasonably expect that others might endorse as consistent with their freedom and equality."[25] Despite the coercive relations of interest and identity groups, Rawls insists on a critical public mediated by reciprocity in the sense that each party can explain "actions" in terms that all other groups can reasonably "endorse as consistent with their freedom and equality." It is this universal internalization of the recognition of universal human rights in a society comprising a multiplicity of identities that Douglass aimed to promote by converting to political abolitionism. In contrast to the utopian assumptions of Garrisonian thought, Douglass's thought models a pragmatics of democratic equality in a pluralistic society.

What is important, and allows Rawls's theory to illuminate Douglass's contribution to the culture of reform, is their shared emphasis on the relationship between equality and the structure of public discourse. Despite his official disenfranchisement, Douglass could begin to claim recognition by assuming a position of structural equality in the critical public sphere. Achieving this structural equality was only possible by breaking away from the Garrisonians and establishing an autonomous position from which to speak. As a means of claiming subjectivity out of the negations of slavery and then as an intentional effort to transform the structure of the public sphere, the development of Frederick Douglass's persona occurred in dialogue with the structure of public discourse. Though his relationship with the debates of the public sphere began when he was a slave in Baltimore, two transitions that he made after escaping to the free states are especially important. First, his move away from the Garrisonians indicates the growing importance of racial identity politics to Douglass's goals. By starting his own newspaper, Douglass positioned himself as a structural equal to Garrison within the critical public sphere. By linking the *North Star* explicitly to racial advancement, Douglass began to model the pluralistic public sphere that would allow full recognition of racial equality. Second, Douglass sought to move from a position of structural equality in the critical public sphere to a position of equality in the official public arena by changing his opinion on the Constitution and endorsing political abolitionism.

Race and the Struggle for Critical Recognition

A variety of newspapers reported an outburst that occurred during a speech Frederick Douglass gave at the 1848 meeting of the American Anti-Slavery Society. As he sometimes did, Douglass mimicked a minister who defends slaveholders and advocates gradual emancipation. At one point, he got "some popular pulpit orator in his mind's eye," and ridiculed the complicity of churches in supporting slavery. The *New York Herald* reported that Douglass "indulged in a good deal of low, sarcastic representations" of ministers.[26] The substance of Douglass's speech, for example, his claim that "it [was] a notorious fact that men were sold to build churches—women were sold to pay the expenses of missionaries—and children were sold to buy Bibles," was standard fare at antislavery rallies, especially those sponsored by Garrison's American Anti-Slavery Society. But Douglass's parody of a white preacher's voice outraged many people, even those attending a convention of radical abolitionists. As the crowd began to walk out on the speech, Douglass stopped them and asked a question:

> Suppose you yourselves were black and that your sisters and brothers were in slavery . . . and that the Church sanctioned such infamy, would you not feel as I do? There is no use in being offended with me. I have a *right* to address you. There is no difference except of colour, between us. . . . I am your brother—(the crowd erupts in cheers and laughter)—yes I am, and you may pass me by as you will and cut me and despise me, I'll tell everyone I meet that I am your brother. (Cheers and laughter). (*FDP* 2:129)

This moment, especially Douglass's assertion of his "right" to speak and of his brotherhood with his white audience, dramatizes the struggle for recognition that defined his public career as an antislavery activist and an advocate of equality for African Americans.[27]

In 1840s America, parodies and criticism of the clergy were by no means uncommon. The first two-thirds of Emerson's "Divinity School Address" is a critique of ministers' failure to preach an authentic spirituality. Even Emerson paid a price for this effrontery, and there was a world of difference between the latitude his countrymen would grant the ex-minister and that which they would allow an ex-slave. For Douglass to appropriate the voice of a white minister and transform it into a kind of minstrelesque parody transgressed racial norms even more than some of the Garrisonians could bear. Just as Nehemiah Adams could not "countenance" the redefinition of publicity represented by Angelina Grimké's discussion of slave women's sexual degradation, Douglass's audience could not accept the appropriation of public authority represented by a black man satirizing one of the most revered and learned of the "white" professions.[28] In important respects, certainly in the eyes of people like Nehemiah Adams and Catharine Beecher, by mocking the voice of the minister, Douglass was mocking the very idea of public authority itself. Further, neither Adams's response to Grimké nor the response of Douglass's audience to his speech addressed the substantive issue under discussion. No one supported the sexual exploitation of slaves, and clerical apologists of slavery were widely derided as hypocrites. The problem was in the appropriation of public authority embodied by the voice that was doing the denouncing.

Douglass's speech at the Anti-Slavery Society convention brings the problem of critical recognition for the black social reformer fully into the foreground. As members of the Anti-Slavery Society turned their backs on him, Douglass's reply pushed beyond the natural rights argument that Angelina Grimké also made by asserting that he has made himself a fixture in the public sphere and will not withdraw from that equalizing arena.[29] Though he addressed the reformers with the quasi-religious appellation "brother," Douglass did not talk about equality in terms of either nature or religion. He presented himself as a brother in philosophical terms, but he also emphasized that he would stand as their equal in terms of public presence. "I have a *right* to address you" he told them and vowed: "I'll tell everyone I meet that I am your brother," so "there is no use in being offended." On the contrary, taking offense at Douglass's public presence simply represented a kind of ironic recognition. Douglass, in effect, forced his racist auditors into a corner. They could haughtily pretend they were above response to such antics from a black man. But this path would leave the forum open for Douglass to assert his brotherhood and his right to equal recognition. They could also engage Douglass in critical debate, but no matter how condescending the actual rhetoric, this path accorded Douglass exactly the type of critical recognition he sought.

The famous encounter between Douglass and Isaiah Rynders in New York on May 7, 1850, exemplifies this kind of recognition. Rynders, a Tammany operative and Five Points gang leader, forced his way onto a stage with Douglass and tried to intimidate him with racist taunts and threats of violence. Douglass replied by calling attention to his own blackness: "Look the negro in the face, examine his wooly head, his entire physical conformation; I invite you to the examination, and ask this audience to judge. . . . Am I a man?" To which Rynders retorted, "*You* are not a black man, you are only half a nigger." Douglass shot back, "He is correct; I am, indeed, only half a negro, a half-brother to Mr. Rynders" (*FDP* 2:228–29). Douglass's wit made this little sparring match legendary, but it also indicates his effort to situate himself, as Robert Fanuzzi and Robyn Wiegman emphasize, as a self-consciously black presence in the critical public sphere.[30] In Douglass's view, explicitly linking blackness with critical public discourse could instantiate an image of public equality that would serve as the foundation for a public sphere that recognized the racial pluralism of American society.

Critics have formulated this problem of racial recognition in a variety of ways, most notably in relation to cultural production and to the containment of African American subjectivity within the private realm. Henry Louis Gates Jr. and Robert Stepto argue that Americans' construction of black racial identity defined blackness in opposition to the forms of cultural, intellectual, and moral awareness that marked authority in public discourse.[31] This lack of a recognized claim to critical stature, as Kristin Hoganson and Karen Sanchez-Eppler explain, feminizes blackness, which further disconnects black men and women from recognition as participants in critical public discourse.[32] Robyn Wiegman, in her analysis of links between constructions of race and femininity, has integrated the feminization of blackness into a model of liberal democratic citizenship that emphasizes the tension between racial embodiment and the abstract construct of liberal citizenship. Taking Douglass's 1855 story "The Heroic Slave" as her case study, Wiegman notes that through the rebellious hero, Madison Washington, "Douglass fashions a version of the democratic public sphere, allowing the black body to achieve the disembodied abstraction that ascendancy to citizenship routinely confers." But as Wiegman explains and Douglass's exchange with Rynders dramatizes, Douglass faced the problem of overcoming the elision of blackness that occurs as Madison Washington achieves the very "disembodied abstraction" that is simultaneously white and invisible.[33] Indeed, in the private realm Douglass was at risk of being subsumed into property, and in the public realm, his subjectivity either was not recognized or was at risk of being deracinated into a generic rational subjectivity. In their own way, each of these critics strives to frame the problem of constructing a universal model of citizenship that takes into account the fact of racial pluralism and the specific history of race-based slavery in the United States. Douglass also addressed this configuration of race and publicity as he grounded his identity ever more fully in the public sphere.

When viewed in contrast to the cowering slave boy of the *Narrative*, a boy who was unable to prevent the sado-sexual abuse of his aunt in the private realm of the slave household, Douglass's integration of his fictional hero, Madison Washington, into a tradition of Revolutionary dissent articulates a long process through which he constructed African American masculinity in relation to presence in critical public discourse. Yet even in the *Narrative*, he traces an identity grounded in public discourse all the way to his childhood, where he discovered it emerging from the national debate about slavery. The lecture against slave literacy that Thomas Auld gave to his wife, for example, served as a "special revelation" that helped him to understand "the white man's power to enslave the black man." This revelation ushered Douglass into a pluralistic world of power and discourse that allowed him to recognize himself as a disputed figure in the public life of the nation.

Auld's lecture on slave literacy occurs in the same chapter in which Douglass notes that he had managed to ferret away a copy of the *Columbian Orator*, which included an antislavery dialogue between a master and a slave. After describing the impact of this collection of political speeches on his understanding of the world, Douglass ruminates on the role that the word "abolition" played in his adolescent imagination.[34] This meditation, worth quoting in full, describes a political awakening. "Every little while," during the period in which he was learning to read and write, Douglass explains:

> I could hear something about the abolitionists. It was some time before I found what the word meant. It was always used in such connections as to make it an interesting word to me. If a slave ran away and succeeded in getting clear, or if a slave killed his master, set fire to a barn, or did anything very wrong in the mind of a slaveholder, it was spoken of as the fruit of *abolition*. Hearing the word in this connection very often, I set about learning what it meant. The dictionary afforded me little or no help. I found it was "the act of abolishing;" but then I did not dare to ask what was to be abolished. Here I was perplexed. I did not dare to ask anyone about its meaning, for I was satisfied that it was something they wanted me to know very little about. After a patient waiting, I got one of our city papers, containing an account of the number of petitions from the north, praying for the abolition of slavery in the District of Columbia, and of the slave trade between the States. From this time I understood the words *abolition* and *abolitionist*, and always drew near when that word was spoken, expecting to hear something of importance to myself and fellow-slaves. (*N* 62)

Before this paragraph ends, Douglass has decided that he must escape from slavery. This sequence of events—Auld's lecture on literacy, finding the *Columbian Orator*, learning the meaning of abolition, and resolving to escape slavery—is important in relation to Douglass's discursive construction of equality because it shows Douglass situating himself in a dialogic community that was inherently subversive to the ideological hegemony of slave society.

In addition to revealing a world characterized by ideologically motivated violence, through these events Douglass realized that the community of abolitionists was actively engaged in a debate about justice with the community represented by Thomas Auld.[35] The sequence of specific revelations that led him to claim a right to freedom enabled Douglass to see himself in a dialogically complex world, a world where authority is not simply articulated by a homogeneous class of masters but emerges out of pluralistic debate among different world-views.[36] By laying a foundation for self-recognition as a member of the abolitionist community, this sequence of events also describes a slave developing the antinomian relationship to the official public sphere that will enable him to speak the discourse of radical abolitionism.

Douglass's orientation toward publicity is most vivid as the plot of the 1845 *Narrative* builds toward the moment when he stood up and spoke in Nantucket. With his first political speech to an interracial audience, Douglass self-consciously writes himself onto the public stage in an act that models equality in a racially plural public. In his earliest recorded addresses, as he was groping to imagine himself as a man with a voice in public affairs, Douglass began speeches with remarks like the following from the fall of 1841: "I feel greatly embarrassed when I attempt to address an audience of white people. I am not used to speak to them, and it makes me tremble when I do so, because I have always looked up to them with fear" (*FDP* 1:5); or like the slightly less abashed remark from 1843: "I have never had the advantage of a single day's schooling in all my life; and such have been the habits of life, as to instill into my heart a disposition I never can quite shake off, to cower before white men. But one thing I can do. I can represent here the slave" (*FDP* 1:21).

By the time Douglass wrote his *Narrative* in 1845, his sense of public selfhood had changed enough that he could look back on his "cowering" rhetorical self with considerable critical distance. In the famous lines with which he concludes that text, Douglass explains: "While attending an anti-slavery convention at Nantucket . . . I felt strongly moved to speak. . . . It was a severe cross, and I took it up reluctantly. The truth was, I felt myself a slave, and the idea of speaking to white people weighed me down. I spoke but a few moments, when I felt a degree of freedom, and said what I desired with considerable ease. From that time until now, I have been engaged in pleading the cause of my brethren" (*N* 104). Douglass here encapsulates a long-term adjustment to speaking out in multiracial gatherings into a single moment of hesitation and self-doubt that describes the transition from a slave-bound sense of self to a self legitimized and authenticated by its recognition within a multiracial public sphere. In contrast to Grimké, who deployed public presence as a referent to sincerity, Douglass deployed it as a founding moment for African American equality. In the *Narrative*, this moment of presence literally calls the story into being and anticipates a public sphere transformed to recognize its own racial pluralism. As Robyn Wiegman notes, the 1841 speech begins to "undo the negations attending blackness in the public sphere."[37]

However, the Garrisonians' focus on moral purity created a rhetorical position that was inherently contradictory to Douglass's effort to claim equality. The apparatus of Garrison's antislavery society helped Douglass achieve public presence and enabled him to integrate into a community of breathtakingly radical reformers. But at best the Garrisonian community could offer Douglass only a simulated equality. Garrison's most important contribution to Douglass was his embodiment of an independent model of authority grounded in conscience that offered a philosophically strong position from which to denounce slavery. Yet while the privileges of whiteness and masculinity enabled Garrison simultaneously to repudiate politics and to claim recognition in the critical public, Douglass had no civil status to repudiate, and thus he could claim the authority of the come-outer only through association with Garrison. As long as he remained within the Garrisonian fold, Douglass's claim to public authority inevitably piggy-backed on Garrison's.[38] In this sense, Douglass's decision to found the *North Star* reveals the limitations of Garrisonian legitimization as a model for establishing a critical presence that could achieve authentic recognition.

Publicity and Critical Presence

Without belaboring the story of Douglass's feud with Garrison and his subsequent conversion to political abolitionism, I want to situate that narrative as part of Douglass's evolution toward a model of equality grounded in the reciprocities of a pluralistic critical public sphere.[39] As much as it was an act of Oedipal rebellion, Douglass's decision to team up with Martin Delany and start a newspaper underscores the opportunities embedded in the changing role of public discourse in procedures of legitimization. Both the Unitarian controversy and the Grimké-Beecher debate reveal the explicit emergence of cultural authority and civil recognition out of print culture and other vehicles of publicity. Equally, the fact that the major players in each of these debates about the structure of publicity were objects of dispute themselves emphasizes the increasingly popular face that such debates were assuming. Most importantly, Grimké's and Douglass's consciousness of the public presence of their bodies as emblems of a transformed public underscores the instability that attended antebellum processes of public mediation. On the one hand, both Grimké and Douglass were trying to claim access to an exclusive locus of social authority by appropriating eighteenth-century models of citizenship that coalesced around a universal subjectivity. On the other hand, their insistence that they spoke not simply as abstract rational citizens but as woman and as African American indicates the premium they placed on compelling the pluralization of the public sphere.

As a self-conscious vehicle for instantiating a pluralist public, Douglass's *North Star* began as an exercise in identity politics through which he sought to claim critical authority in a way that could begin to integrate the ex-slave with the republican citizen. The editor of another black journal argued that Douglass's racialized presence in print culture made the public sphere more pluralistic, observing that "Frederick Douglass's ability as an editor and publisher has done more for the Freedom and elevation of his race than all his platform appearances."[40] Emphasizing the other side of this tension between pluralism and abstract homogeneity in print, Eric Sundquist situates Douglass directly in the Revolutionary tradition, noting that "not simply the voice but the pen was the key to liberty, no less for black Americans than it had been for the pamphleteers of the Revolutionary period."[41]

Even though Douglass's commitment to moral suasion did not change with his move to Rochester, New York, this move away from the center of Garrisonian abolitionism signaled a significant dissatisfaction with the position of his voice in the antislavery community and the public sphere more broadly.[42] Douglass summed up the frustration he felt as an operative of Garrison's organization by explaining: "It did not entirely satisfy me to narrate wrongs; I felt like denouncing them" (*MBMF* 220).[43] The distinction between narration and denunciation that Douglass made here marks the boundaries within which the Anti-Slavery Society recognized his ability to claim authority for his own voice. In effect, the leadership of the movement used Douglass to create a mind/body dichotomy within antislavery rallies. Douglass would take the stage and describe the material conditions of slavery, while the white speakers who followed him to the podium would interpret the meaning of his narrative. Although he had achieved public presence, it was a descriptive rather than a critical presence. Quoting the almost offhand remark of George Foster, Douglass claimed that the leaders of the

Anti-Slavery Society would try to "pin [him] down to [his] simple narrative" by saying, "Let us have the facts" as he took the podium. He quoted John Collins's advice: "Give us the facts, we will take care of the philosophy," and rankled at his own objectification by pointing out that he "was generally introduced as a *'chattel'*—a *'thing'*—a piece of southern *'property'*—the chairman assuring the audience that *it* could speak" (*MBMF* 220).[44]

With the founding of the *North Star*, however, Douglass established a critical public presence by positioning himself as Garrison's equal in the structure of public discourse. This structural change in his relationship to the public sphere is as important as the buffer the move to Rochester, New York, placed between Douglass and Garrison. It is also noteworthy that when he moved to Rochester, Douglass made no programmatic distinction between his newspaper and the *Liberator*. In some ways, a programmatic justification would have defeated Douglass's purpose. By creating himself as the editor of a rival journal to the *Liberator*, Douglass appropriated membership in the select group of editorial professionals who mediated cultural and political discussions. Indeed, where Garrison saw the *North Star* as a kind of redundant competitor, Douglass saw the duplication, the very mirroring of the *Liberator* under ex-slave control as a revolutionary fact that necessarily restructured critical public discourse by insisting on equal recognition for the black reformer.[45] As Robert Levine indicates, Douglass and Delany even reproduced the organizational structure of the Garrison-Douglass relationship at the *Liberator*, with Douglass making editorial decisions and Delany traveling as subscription agent.[46]

In his analysis of Douglass's and Martin Delany's partnership during the first years of the *North Star*, Levine argues that Delany was "at times debating with himself . . . on the 'duties' of free blacks in a slave culture."[47] When they founded the *North Star*, this concern with racial "duty" was equally central to Douglass's thought. As they strove to carve out a niche for their newspaper, Douglass was in some ways working to imagine a pluralistic public sphere that did not yet exist. Unable yet to see an ethical path into the political institutions of the nation, Douglass groped for a way to contextualize his aspirations for racial advancement in a framework other than moral suasion. As Levine argues, like Delany, Douglass began with the assumption that racial self-reliance would be the best means of countering internalized inferiority and of making practical advances.[48] In the inaugural edition of the *North Star*, Douglass printed an article titled "Our Paper and Its Prospects," in which he highlights the independence of his voice and defines the impact he hoped to have by positioning it alongside Garrison's: "We are now about to assume management of the editorial department of a newspaper, devoted to the cause of Liberty, Humanity, and Progress. The position is one which, with the purest motives, we have long desired to occupy. It has long been our anxious wish to see, in this slave-holding, slave-trading, and Negro-hating land, a printing press and paper, permanently established, under the complete control and direction of the immediate victims of slavery and oppression" (*LWFD* 2:280). Douglass introduced his newspaper as the vehicle of a self-consciously racialized voice. Yet rather than tending toward separation, from the start he tried to imagine an interracial mode of critical public discourse that recognized blackness rather than erased it within an abstract and homogeneous construction of citizenship.

The carefully, almost painfully articulated connections through which Douglass imagined collaboration between white and black abolitionists expressed his desire to imagine a discourse of pluralistic recognition. As he put it, he was motivated to claim the authority of the editor "from a sincere and settled conviction that such a journal, if conducted with only moderate skill and ability, would do a most important and indispensable work, which it would be impossible for our white friends to do for us. . . . It is evident we must be our own representatives and advocates, not exclusively, but peculiarly—not distinct from but in connection with our white friends" (*LWFD* 2:280). Douglass did not try to claim for black abolitionists the exclusive authority to advocate the abolition of slavery, but he did assert a unique authority of self-representation. Even though Douglass tried to describe the multiracial collaborations that would necessarily characterize reciprocal recognition in a pluralistic society, soon after assuming the editor's chair of the *North Star* he began to analyze intensively the structure of racial prejudice that defined American society. Between January 1848 and May 1849, he published or delivered a series of articles and lectures—"Colored Newspapers," "What Are Colored People Doing for Themselves," "An Address to the Colored People of the United States," "The Destiny of Colored Americans," and "Colorphobia"—which analyze relationships between race, publicity, and critical authority.

In the first of these articles, "Colored Newspapers," Douglass articulates the identity politics that justified founding the *North Star* as a rival to the *Liberator*. He writes: "We have, sometimes, heard, persons regret the very mention of color, . . . and to counsel its abandonment. We confess to no such feelings; we are in no wise sensitive on this point. Facts are facts, white is not black, and black is not white. There is neither good sense, nor common honesty, in trying to forget this distinction. So far from the truth is this notion that colored newspapers are serving to keep up that cruel distinction, the want of them is the main cause of its continuance." A black critical presence created not by antislavery newspapers, as Garrison would have it, but by "colored newspapers," was Douglass's ideal for beginning to break down invidious distinctions that had material consequences ranging from that between "white editor, and black street cleaner" to that between slave and free (*LWFD* 1:290–91).

In March 1848, Douglass denounced segregation in an editorial titled "The Folly of Racially Exclusive Organization." Later, in an "Address to the Colored People of the United States" that he delivered in the summer of 1848 and printed in the *North Star* on September 29, he argued for public action of all kinds and in virtually any context through which African Americans could work against racial degradation. He singled out the press as a particularly potent means of reproducing racist norms. The antiblack press had "brought to the aid of prejudice, a thousand stings. Wit, ridicule, false philosophy, and an impure theology, with a flow of low black-guardism, come through this channel into the public mind" (*LWFD* 1:236). To work against this mode of publicity, Douglass argued for black participation in public organization of any "complexion" that might propagandize against prejudice. "Although it may seem to conflict with our view of human brotherhood," Douglass argued, "we shall undoubtedly for many years be compelled to have institutions of a complexional character, in order to attain this very idea of human brotherhood." But Douglass took this position reluctantly, not because he sought racial separation but because white prejudice required it. Douglass encouraged his readers with the admonition: "Act with white Abolition societies wherever you can, and where you cannot, get up societies among yourselves, but without [racial] exclusiveness" (*LWFD* 1:233). As he groped toward an imagined society in which black and white could collaborate as public equals, Douglass tried to tread a fine line between assimilation and integration.

It would be easy to conclude that the priority Douglass gave to multiracial organizations reflects an assimilationist agenda. But this conclusion is obviated by the identity politics that motivated the *North Star* and does not do justice to the complex structural problems he sought to mediate by constructing a self-consciously black critical presence. In the context of the broader culture of reform, by claiming the editor's chair, Douglass walked a fine line between a racial representativeness that permitted him to move the critical public sphere toward racial pluralism and a colorblind articulation of republican citizenship that enabled him to deploy traditional rhetorics of political influence.[49] Assimilation, with its implications of erasing difference in favor of homogeneous similarity, fails to characterize Douglass's project. He certainly sought an integrated society, but this implies not just a one-way process of incorporation but a transformation of the underlying structure of the public sphere.

Ironically perhaps, Garrison's own obsessiveness in creating associations, participating in conventions, and even writing constitutions provided the template that shaped Douglass's desire to claim an independent stage for himself within the critical public sphere. Dissenting from his own adopted community of radicals and outsiders, Douglass performed a Bercovitchian rite of assent that allowed him to stand as a structural and institutional equal with his hero. It offered him not just independence but also a position of structural importance in the critical public sphere. From this position, Douglass began to develop the voice through which he would demand racial recognition during the political phase of the antislavery struggle. Indeed, the strictures of Garrisonian legitimization that are so central to the culture of reform would cause Douglass to remain in a no-man's-land between moral suasion and political abolitionism for several years. As he moved toward political abolitionism, the questions of sincerity that underpinned his reluctance to abandon the Garrisonian paradigm dramatize the important and subtle ways in which standards of public sincerity shaped the origins of the culture of reform. Before Douglass found a way conscientiously to ground his claims to equality in partisan politics and debates about constitutional authority, he was compelled to engage the two sides of the movement in critical conversation about the relationship between moral and political authority.

Reconstituting the Critical Public Sphere

Douglass's conversion to political abolitionism is one of the most important events in the origin of the culture of reform. By investing himself with the potential power of full citizenship, Douglass established the precedent for appropriating constitutional authority to incorporate outsider groups into an official public sphere characterized by structural pluralism. He thus is paradigmatic in defining the links between the critical public and the realm of official political recognition. At the same time, however, Douglass was utterly serious about maintaining his own integrity as a social reformer. Before he could claim the advantages of partisan politics under the Constitution, he had to achieve an authentic reconciliation between the principles of Garrisonian moral integrity and active participation in the political system.

From early in the process of rethinking the authority of the Constitution, Douglass conceded the principle that the Constitution can reasonably be read as an antislavery text. But two considerations still prevented him from joining the political abolitionists. First, he believed the antislavery reading of the Constitution was a form of sophistry because the original intent of the framers was to defend slavery. Second, he felt his own moral integrity was wrapped up in the come-outer stance, and thus he could not convert to political abolitionism until he had sincere confidence in its legitimacy. This second consideration is especially important in defining the role of the culture of reform in American society. The movement of antislavery as a whole toward political abolitionism, and Frederick Douglass's conversion especially, established a symbiotic relationship between reform organizations and political parties that continues to shape the way Americans deal with divisive issues in their society. In important respects, the political abolition movement actually saved the Constitution by arguing that it needed to be relegitimized through a renewed public debate rather than annulled and replaced to mark a national born-again experience.

Even as the political culture was polarizing into the slave and free-state blocs that would signal the Civil War, the culture of reform was defining forms of political influence that would become vital to mediating social tensions after that conflict ended. Equally, as autonomous expressions of ideological commitment, the reform organizations embodied both a type of public sincerity and a structure for ideological dialogue that was unavailable to political parties focused on assembling majorities. In important respects, then, Douglass's conversion to political abolitionism can be understood as a symbol for the emergence of a long-standing relationship through which independent reform organizations both maintain themselves on grounds of sincere commitment and form a substructure that shapes action in the official public sphere.

For Douglass the linkage between politics and equality was the almost necessary culmination of a process that began with his fight with Covey and required him to negotiate deeply imbricated relationships between race, selfhood, and the public sphere. His gravitation toward the public sphere was necessary because as an ex-slave, Douglass could never base civil equality on paternity in the same way that Garrison and other white male reformers could. Robyn Wiegman has linked the slave's exclusion from civil identity through the private realm to the "slaver's imposition of a mother-bound kinship system onto the slave." This kinship system defined public "paternal rights and privileges as definitely white racial ones."[50] Since in civil terms the slave was descended from the mother rather than the father, the slave was both denied access to publicity and tied to the household as property rather than family. Founding the *North Star* was an intermediate measure that enabled Douglass to claim rhetorical equality in the structure of the critical public sphere but also highlighted the difference between the foundations on which he and his white colleagues could claim moral and civil authority. The *North Star*, as long as it grounded its voice in Garrisonian perfectionism, not only embodied the paradox of the black come-outer but also underscored Douglass's inability to claim a patronymic right to masculine equality and citizenship. In an especially cutting blow, Garrison's rejection of the *North Star* is analogous to a denial of paternity because it contested the legitimacy of Douglass's claim to equality even in the critical public sphere.

In Douglass's process of coming to terms with the political system, the Constitution ultimately proved to be a form of public refuge through which he could move antislavery rhetoric away from himself and focus it on a collective text. Among the Garrisonians, Douglass was himself the disputed text. By shifting debate from the slave to the Constitution, however, Douglass repositioned himself as an equal participant in a critical debate about authority rather than standing as the object that was to be mediated by the dialogue itself. After two years as editor of the *North Star*, Douglass oriented himself in this direction by positioning the *North Star* as a locus for critical debate on the legitimacy of the Constitution. He proposed a debate, with the *North Star* as the forum: "If our friend Gerrit Smith desires to be heard [as an advocate of the antislavery reading of the Constitution], the columns of the *North Star* are at his service. We can assure him that he cannot have a stronger wish to turn every rightful instrumentality against slavery, than we have; and if the Constitution can be so turned, and he can satisfy us of the fact, we shall readily, gladly, and zealously turn our feeble energies in that direction" (*NS* Mar. 16, 1849). Shortly after issuing this invitation, Douglass debated the constitutionality of slavery on two occasions: first, with Samuel Ward in May 1849, then, in January 1850, with Gerrit Smith, among others, in Syracuse, New York (*FDP* 2:194–97, 217–35).[51]

By the spring of 1849, even as Douglass was developing an increasingly focused theory of racism, the legitimacy of the Constitution emerged as one of his principal preoccupations. On March 16, he published articles by Gerrit Smith and Robert Forten that describe the pro- and antislavery interpretations. He prefaced these articles with one of his own, titled "The Constitution and Slavery," in which he assumes the persona of a judge who will impartially assess the merits of the conflicting arguments. In this persona, Douglass begins to discover the language that eventually will justify his change of opinion. "Of one thing . . . we can assure our readers," Douglass explains, "and that is that we bring to the consideration of this subject, no partisan feelings, nor the slightest wish to make ourselves consistent with the creed of either Anti-Slavery party, and that our only aim is to know what is truth and what is duty in respect to the matter in dispute. . . . The only truly consistent man is he who will, for the sake of being right today, contradict what he said wrong yesterday" (*LWFD* 1:361). Douglass's movement from a Garrisonian to a neutral stance underscores his desire to claim autonomy and position himself as a rational subject in critical public debate. He presents himself here not as a disenfranchised black man seeking to assert his rights but as a responsible citizen looking to solve an intellectual problem. In doing so, he quite literally models the disembodied abstractness of the rational citizen that simultaneously empowers his voice and erases his presence as a black speaker.

However, although Douglass assumes a stance of impartiality at the beginning of the article, he also quickly abandons this new voice and retreats into the rhetoric of the jeremiad. As he brings his article to a close, he reverts to the denunciatory tones of the Garrisonians, asking whether "pandemonium [could] devise a Union more inhuman, unjust, and affronting to man and God, than this? Yet such is the Union consummated under the Constitution of the United States. It is truly a compact demanding immediate disannulment" (*LWFD* 1:366).

Two weeks later, on March 30, 1849, Douglass published an article in which he emphasizes tension between Garrisonian sincerity and the coercive power of politics. He admits that he is not opposed to political participation in principle, but only because he believes the Constitution to be morally compromised: "Could we see the Constitution as the [political abolitionists] do, we should not be slow in using the ballot box against the system of slavery, or urging others to do so. But we have learned enough of the elements of moral power, to know that a man is lame, impotent, worse than weak, when he ceases to regard the clear convictions of his understanding, to accomplish anything, no matter how desirable that thing may be" (*LWFD* 1:319). There is a certain poignancy to this admission, for here Douglass draws into sharp focus the paradox of Garrisonian orthodoxy. He admits the practical potential of political organizing and of bringing the leverage of antislavery societies to bear through party politics. But he is also restrained by the internal standards that define Garrisonian moral authority. At this point, "moral power" grounded in a perfectionist conscience stands in direct conflict with the instrumental power of the official political system. For Douglass to convert to political abolitionism at this point would be consciously to embrace strategic action.

Despite this tension, Douglass's eventual change of opinion marks a process of integration that in some ways parallels his long involvement in the mechanics of the Garrisonian movement. The radical abolitionists did not in principle oppose constitutions, and they certainly did not oppose partisanship. They felt compelled to reject the Constitution because its complicity in slavery threatened to undermine their moral authority. In theory, a new constitution, even one based on the 1787 draft, could satisfy the objections of the come-outers as long as they could understand it as a document that was consistent with their perfectionist ideals. Douglass's reconsideration of politics and the Constitution did exactly this. He contained the debate over the Constitution within the official political culture and thus, in effect, recognized a nation that was trying to live under two mutually exclusive constitutions.

As Charles W. Mills and David E. Schrader have demonstrated, Douglass was well aware of the debates that shaped the drafting of the Constitution.[52] In Douglass's debate with Samuel Ward in May 1849, both debaters assumed that the Constitutional Convention was a contentious setting in which a multiplicity of conflicting interests were represented. Ward argued: "No matter what were the intentions and sentiments of the framers of the Constitution, or what was the understanding of the slave-holding and non-slaveholding states had [*sic*] on the matter, that Constitution in no portion of it acknowledges the right of property in human beings" (*FDP* 2:195). In rebuttal, Douglass quoted the claim in the *Madison Papers* that John Rutledge of South Carolina proposed the language on taxation that counted slaves as three-fifths of a white person. Douglass then described a debate over slavery that ended when "the North bowed to the mandates of Slavery" (*FDP* 2:197). But simply by referring back to the debates that defined the Constitutional Convention, Douglass revealed the multiplicity of positions represented by the framers and highlighted their inability to achieve consensus. He recognized as much in an 1851 analysis of the internal logic of original intent. By looking for meanings in the varied interests that the framers brought to the table, Douglass concluded, "We shall find conflicting and irreconcilable intentions. One state may have adopted the Constitution, intending that it should serve one end; while another may have adopted it intending that it should serve another quite different end" (*FDP* 5:198).

In the Syracuse debate in January 1850, Douglass and Smith focused on the problem of sin that attended a Garrisonian's conversion to political abolitionism. Douglass introduced the theme: "I hold that to swear to support a Constitution which requires us to put down slave insurrections and send back fugitive slaves, is a sin. It is a sin to support that which is a sin—which can require us to sin." He also responded to the political abolitionists' distinction between the text of the Constitution and the conflicting intentions of its authors. At this point, though, Douglass saw this distinction between corrupt intent and virtuous text as a kind of hair-splitting sophistry. Gerrit Smith and the political abolitionists, Douglass held, were actually advocating disunion: "Under the sham of upholding the provisions of the Constitution," the political abolitionists were actually "waging a war against the Constitution." In contrast to their "sham," the disunionists with whom he aligned himself, stood for "downright honesty, in dealing even with slaveholders" (*FDP* 2:221).

But by May 1851, Douglass had resolved the contradictions he perceived between the political and the moral authority of the Constitution. He announced his willingness to recognize the Constitution during the 1851 convention of the American Anti-Slavery Society. Edmund Quincy, who edited Garrison's *Liberator*, submitted a resolution proposing that several newspapers, including Douglass's *North Star*, receive the official endorsement of the Anti-Slavery Society. Samuel May suggested that this list be supplemented by the *Liberty Party Paper*. Garrison, however, opposed this addition because the *Liberty Party Paper* held that the Constitution was an antislavery document. As the debate over endorsements was in progress, Douglass interrupted. Speaking in what Samuel May characterized as a "hesitating and embarrassed manner," Douglass announced that he had become convinced that the Constitution could serve the ends of the abolitionists and that recognizing it was no longer inconsistent with his own understanding of moral authority. If the society could endorse only papers that repudiated the Constitution, then they would have to strike the *North Star* from the list. At Garrison's request, the convention obliged.[53] Two weeks later, Douglass explained his reversal in a short editorial titled "Change of Opinion Announced." In it, Douglass asserts: "We have arrived at the firm conviction, that the Constitution . . . might be made consistent in its details with the noble purposes avowed in its preamble; and that hereafter we should . . . demand that it be wielded in behalf of emancipation" (*LWFD* 2:155). The subtlety of the grounds on which Douglass justifies this change of opinion is often overlooked in discussions of the drama of the reversal itself.

In contrast to Catharine Beecher, who saw the debates among religious sec-tarians and political partisans as an opportunity to assert the home as a locus of consensus and thereby define women as the stewards of the nation's unifying discourse, Douglass saw debate over the Constitution as an opportunity for African Americans to redefine the nature of American equality by claiming the rights of citizenship on the public stage. Douglass underscored the enfranchising character of the change of opinion by contrasting the advantages of combin-ing moral with political action against the disadvantages of emphasizing the intentions of the framers:

> We found, in our former position, that, when debating the question, we were compelled to go behind the letter of the Constitution, and to seek its meaning in the history and practice of the nation under it—a process always attended with disadvantages; and certainly we feel little inclination to shoulder disadvantages of any kind, in order to give slavery the slightest protection. . . . It is the first duty of every American citizen, whose conscience permits so to do, to use his *political* as well as his *moral* power for its overthrow. (*LWFD* 2:155–56)

Douglass's use of the word "duty" in this context reveals much. In 1849, when he began to investigate the nature of constitutional authority, he had set out to discover "what is truth and what is duty." In the "Change of Opinion" editorial, Douglass brings that process to closure. He concludes that what he had referred to as the "elements of moral power" were not incompatible with political action under the Constitution. By achieving this reconciliation between conscience and politics, Douglass appropriated the constitutive text of American democracy for his own purposes and established the foundation for the political career that he would pursue during and after the Civil War.

Robert Fanuzzi links Douglass's appropriation of republican citizenship to his work at the *North Star*, and that is certainly true in relation to the equality implied by critical public discourse. But after he converted to political abolitionism and claimed the authority to define the legitimacy of the Constitution, Douglass situated himself at the point of conception for citizenship. By concluding in the "Change of Opinion" editorial that it is "the first duty of every American citizen, whose conscience permits him so to do, to use his *political* as well as his *moral* power" to overthrow slavery, Douglass implicitly reset the clock back to 1787 and nullified the proslavery history of constitutional interpretation.

Situating the Constitution in a dialogic context in which it is being either annulled or reratified enabled Douglass finally to link blackness, civil equality, and moral authority in a single relationship between the self and the public sphere. He connected the moral authority of the individual and the political integrity of the nation in a single struggle in much the same way that Emerson would do in response to Daniel Webster and the fugitive slave law. Emerson would affirm Douglass's conclusion that "as a condition of its own existence, as the supreme law of the land," the Constitution required the abolition of slavery.

The ambiguity of original intent thus changed the nature of constitutional authority in Douglass's imagination. It enabled him to believe that the tradition that had grown up around the doctrine of "original intent" not only misrepresented the context of the Constitutional Convention but also marked a strategic usurpation of the founding text of the nation. Douglass's conversion to political abolitionism became possible when he was able to see the Constitution as an internally conflicted text that had been appropriated by the forces of strategic discourse. In a speech he gave in Scotland in 1860, he argued that the framers themselves explicitly rejected the doctrine of original intent: "The framers sat with closed doors, and . . . this was done purposely, that nothing but the result of the labours should be seen, and that result should be judged of by the people free from any bias shown in the debates." The framers sought to present a text that contained rather than resolved the debates that created it. This perspective on the Constitution projects it into the public sphere as an object of dialogue rather than as reified sacred writ. It is this dialogue, which Douglass could join not as Garrison's proxy but as an equal, that would constitute the nation and define the terms of citizenship. Even getting an authentic bearing on original intent is impossible. "It would be the wildest of absurdities," Douglass continued, "and lead to endless confusion and mischief, if, instead of looking to the written paper itself, for its meaning, it were attempted to make us search it out in the secret motives and dishonest intentions of some of the men who took part in writing it. . . . These debates were purposefully kept out of view, in order that the people should adopt, not the secret motives or unexpressed intentions of any body, but the simple text of the paper itself" (*LWFD* 2:469).

From this position, redeeming the Constitution from a corrupt tradition of interpretation placed Douglass at the center of the process of legitimization. As such, it enabled him to integrate the ideal of a pluralistic public sphere with the act of constituting the United States. Douglass's "What to the Slave Is the Fourth of July?" speech demonstrated the vitality his relationship to the public sphere derived from the idea of a Constitution grounded in sincere public discourse conducted from positions of mutual recognition. After asking whether his audience meant to mock him by inviting him to commemorate the Fourth of July, Douglass closed the speech with a defense of the Constitution and its framers. To accept a proslavery reading of the Constitution, Douglass concluded, is to accept that the founding fathers, "instead of being the honest men" he had "before declared them to be, . . . were the veriest imposters that ever practiced on mankind." In place of a hypocritical proslavery reading, he explicitly situated the question of constitutional interpretation in the broadest public sphere, even one that theoretically permits a proslavery reading: "I hold that every American citizen has a right to form an opinion of the constitution, and to propagate that opinion, and to use all honorable means to make his opinion the prevailing one" (*FDP* 2:385).

This conclusion to his long process of incorporation into the public realm connects Douglass's claim to equality very closely with his structural position in public discourse. In his movement away from the Garrisonians, the most important distinction between Douglass and his former mentor is that Garrison focused on the problem of sincerity while Douglass focused on the problem of equality. In some respects Douglass was never able to claim the full civil equality he sought, but by drawing structural parallels between Garrisonian moral suasion, which did so much to define the culture of reform, and the political sphere that it contrasted, Douglass's career articulated the emergence of vital relationships between the pluralistic identities that comprise American society and the role that critical public discourse has come to play in defining equality.

The expansion of the critical public sphere signaled by Douglass's presence as a newspaper editor refracts in several directions. Most importantly, it established the African American voice as an autonomous participant in critical discourse. In achieving this end though, Douglass's project demonstrates the logic of legitimization in discursive democracy. Among the Garrisonians, Douglass was certainly a presence on the public stage and gained recognition as an eloquent speaker. But his adherence to the come-outer position on the Constitution underscored his disenfranchised position without allowing him the compensating authority that it offered Garrison. Only by accepting the idea of a Constitution defined and authorized through a constant progressive dialogue among citizens could Douglass imagine himself as an equal in critical discourse. Further, by balancing his assertion of critical presence with his instantiation of black citizenship, Douglass did much to model the structure of contemporary debates about equality, citizenship, and the nature of pluralist society.

CHAPTER FOUR

Emerson's Self-Reliance as a Theory of Community

When Emerson remarks in his 1841 essay "Man the Reformer," "What is a man born for but to be a Reformer," he is only half thinking about reform associations and organized movements (*CW* 1:156). More directly he is considering the processes and forces that transform selves and communities. In this early essay on the emerging culture of reform, he speaks in self-reflexive terms and argues that at his or her best, the reformer is a model of utopian selfhood, a spokesperson for better people living in a better society. As a model of selfhood, the reformer is "a renouncer of lies; a restorer of truth and good" who improves himself or herself as well as the society. Even though the concept of reform had strong attractions for Emerson, he was deeply ambivalent about the activist movements that had become prominent in New England. The problem, in Emerson's view, was that the reformers too often used their worthy causes as surrogates for authentic moral or critical self-reflection. He admired the energy people such as William Lloyd Garrison, Angelina Grimké, and Bronson Alcott introduced into the social body, their ability to "threaten" traditional institutions by dragging them into the public square and insisting that they justify their norms and practices. A rough master, the "demon of reform" is nonetheless as natural as storms or forest fires.

Perhaps thinking of the religious sectarians, Emerson scolds conservatives: "It is when your facts and persons grow unreal and fantastic by too much falsehood, that the scholar flies for refuge to the world of ideas, and aims to recruit and replenish nature from that source" (*CW* 1:146). For brittle defenders of the status quo, he has very little sympathy. But the abolitionists and the advocates of women's equality also meet harsh criticism. Man the reformer, in Emerson's view, can hardly enhance either self or society by embracing the associations, traveling agents, rallies, and newspapers that were so much a part of William Lloyd Garrison's world. In fact, in the passage just quoted, the reformer somehow permutes into a "scholar" who seeks to correct unsound or hypocritical institutions not through activism but by drawing on the energy of nature. This elision of the reformer in favor of the scholar says much about Emerson's importance to the culture of reform taking shape in antebellum America. More than any other student of antebellum culture, Emerson presents reform as a heroic act that is the chief engine of personal growth and social progress. In Emerson's sense of the term, no one can be an individualist without being a reformer. No one can even be an individual.

One of the points I want to make in this book is that the emergence of the culture of reform is connected to changes in the structure of public discourse, and that these changes, in turn, instantiate forms of publicity implicit in liberal selfhood. Emerson saw the growth of associations of all sorts—religious, political, reform—as a serious threat to the autonomy of the individual. He saw the process of association building almost as an ideological confidence game in which the individual allows his or her moral resources to be siphoned off into a world of false benevolence. Among Emerson's deepest fears was that the expansion of public institutions of all types was evacuating the self of autonomous meaning and creating simulated people who feigned selfhood, faith, and thought. Ministers, political partisans, and reformers received some of Emerson's harshest criticism. Even after he began working closely with the radical abolitionists in the mid-1840s, he maintained deep reservations about their inner lives. Sometime in 1853 or 1854, he mused:

> Of Phillips, Garrison, and others I have always the feeling that they may wake up some morning and find that they have made a capital mistake, and are not the persons they took themselves for. Very dangerous is this thoroughly social and related life, whether antagonistic or *co*-operative. In a lonely world, or a world with a half a dozen inhabitants, these would find nothing to do. The first discovery I made of Phillips, was, that while I admitted his eloquence, I had not the faintest wish to meet the man. He had only a *platform*-existence, and no personality. Mere mouthpieces of a party, take away the party and they shrivel and vanish. (*JMN* 13:283)

These figures represent a conundrum in that they speak for moral progress but do not speak as authentic individuals and thus symbolize both the greatest hope and the greatest danger Emerson saw in his society. But rather than abandoning reform, Emerson embraced it as the essential link between liberal selfhood and authentic community. In doing so, he became the most important contemporaneous theorist and critic of the culture of reform. At the same time that Grimké and Douglass were arguing for the importance of access to the critical public, Emerson was grafting the idealistic reformer onto the skeleton of American individualism. He published *Nature* in the same year that Grimké published her *Appeal,* and his first book of essays appeared in the year that Douglass spoke at the antislavery meeting in Nantucket.

As the disenfranchised and their advocates were pushing the boundaries of the public sphere outward in order to take advantage of the recognition offered by critical public discourse, Emerson was thinking about the implications of publicity for selfhood in general. The call to seek an inner spirit that will enable self-reliance and justify participation in civil society, of course, is Emerson's great counterweight to the pressures that can make even the best men "mere mouthpieces" for parties. But where spirit serves to counteract pressure and thus ward off danger, Emerson's theory of self-reliance is a model of liberal utopia because it makes autonomous and individualistic selfhood the necessary foundation of authentic community. Self-reliance brings two aspects of liberal democratic selfhood into sharp connection. First, it requires self-respect in the sense of autonomous thought without regard to party, tradition, ideology, or public opinion. This mode of self-reflection permits a public realm comprising authentic individuals. From a political perspective, it replaces material independence with intellectual independence as the crucial litmus test for citizenship. Also, in contrast to the consensus that defines Rousseau's model of civil society, the Emersonian public is radically pluralistic and positions the individual citizen rather than the party or interest group as the foundational institution of democratic society.

Second, self-reliance is a mode of public dialogue. It cannot exist in a private, head-in-the-clouds communion with spirit. It only realizes itself in the acts of conversation, or "conversion," through which the mind is transformed. Though the dominant tradition of commentary on Emerson emphasizes his work on questions of selfhood and spirituality, these issues are inseparable from questions about the conversion of thought and prayer into public speech. Emerson's lifelong meditation about public sincerity articulates the problem of strategic discourse as one of the most important forces at work in the emergence of the culture of reform. From at least the time of the "Divinity School Address," Emerson strove to imagine a rhetoric of public sincerity and argued for the reinvigorating effect it could have on his society.

Christina Zwarg, in her chapter on Emerson's correspondence with Margaret Fuller, emphasizes the Emerson-Fuller friendship as an effort to model sincere communication through private dialogue. What is important to Zwarg is that Emerson and Fuller sought to bracket contextual considerations as a means of facilitating authentic communication.[1] Emerson, Zwarg argues, believed that if he and Fuller could find a way to communicate that transcended the forces blunting sincerity, they would have taken a step toward a more egalitarian society. Citing Emerson's assertion that he wanted to be "pommelled black & blue with sincere words" (*L* 2:240), Zwarg defines his relationship with Fuller as an experiment in which the act of sincere self-expression was as important as substantive communication.

Emerson's friendship with Fuller and their effort to model an ideal speech situation is significant to understanding critical public discourse in antebellum America because it reveals some of the intersecting assumptions that Emerson and his countrymen made about publicity, gender, and sincerity. From its beginnings in 1836, the Emerson-Fuller friendship evolved on a track parallel to Emerson's authorship of his most important essays on autonomy. His construction of liberal individualism in the years after he wrote *Nature* took place not only in the context of a personal effort to reimagine dialogue through an innovative friendship with Fuller but also in the light of a society in which the conventions of public dialogue were very much in flux. The models of publicity represented by the *Liberator*, the Grimké-Beecher debate, and even the negative example of the gag rules that began in the mid-1830s all mark efforts to influence the terms and conventions of public debate.[2]

As comments in his journals and early lectures demonstrate, the radical reformers were a significant influence in Emerson's thought from the mid-1830s onward. Zwarg even describes the utopian desires of Emerson's dialogue with Margaret Fuller as a specific reaction against conventions of thought and action that he associated with radical reform and masculine violence. Zwarg concludes that "by his own admission, [Emerson] wanted to experiment with and, if necessary, break open sacrosanct notions; but he did not like the idea that a certain amount of what he considered masculine aggression was necessary to do so. For that reason, he recoiled from the social reform of the day, especially those focusing on the role of women, because he felt that there was an abusive virility at work in that model of experimentation."[3] This reaction, of course, also describes the motives for his recoiling from the debates between liberal and orthodox ministers. Zwarg's phrase "abusive virility" describes Emerson's sense that sites of public debate were being appropriated by egotistical voices and that these voices abused the legitimate issues of religious faith and secular value by allowing personality or private interest to drive critical debate.

In a passage assessing the strengths and weaknesses of Daniel Webster, Emerson offers a model of political dialogue built around the pure rationality of the ideal speech situation. At his best, in senatorial debate Webster "saw through his matter" and "went to the principal or essential" of a topic. He analyzed issues with a critical detachment that respected the autonomy of the idea, understanding it as something separate from his own interests. Though "Webster knew very well how to present his own personal claims, yet in his argument he was intellectual, and stated his fact pure of all personality" (*AW* 76). In effect, Webster had the capacity to participate in the debates of discursive democracy with a kind of integrity that Emerson admired. Of course, Emerson's attitude changed radically after the spring of 1850, but until that point Emerson looked to Daniel Webster as a model politician. In contrast to the public and political context in which Emerson saw Webster, his friendship with Fuller underscored his implicit association of sincere discourse with private conversation. Emerson's relationship with Fuller brought him to the brink of a radical reconsideration of the norms that structured his domestic life, and it revealed to him "the liabilities of his traditional marriage where the roles of husband and wife became sacrosanct and unyielding."[4] This conventionalized restraint, Zwarg concludes, led Emerson to recognize that the only way to transcend unyielding roles is through "relations." As he put it in an early letter to Fuller, it is only when "relations shall rule" that "realities shall strike sail" so that self or spirit can become the master of commodity (*L* 3:105).

The dialogic community that Zwarg uncovers in the Emerson-Fuller conversation in some ways answers the euphoric solitude of the transparent eyeball. Like the transparent eyeball, it disrupts conventions and norms in order to liberate spirit. Yet the conversation Zwarg reconstructs embodies a dynamic of disruption not just within a social setting but also within a communicative setting. While the paradoxes of the transparent eyeball disrupt boundaries of selfhood, the taboo dimensions of the Emerson-Fuller friendship disrupt communicative norms that regulate privacy and publicity, and femininity and masculinity. This example of utopian conversation from early in Emerson's career anticipates a form of self-reliant community. Though Emerson's thought is widely appreciated for its rejection of social conformity and its effort to harmonize equality with individualism, it has rarely been understood as a theory of social identity or of communal relationships. But as deeply invested as Emerson was in autonomy, the Emersonian self is never far from conversation with his counterparts. Indeed, Emersonian self-reliance comes into being through several types of conversation. These conversations work in a dialectic with introspection to define Emerson's model of autonomy. George Kateb goes so far as to see Emersonian self-reliance as a model not of autonomy through withdrawal from community but of citizenship that can facilitate authentic political discourse. As a form of critical public discourse, self-reliance is about communally shared attempts at truthfulness as much as it is about individual transcendence.

While the Beecher-Grimké debate and Frederick Douglass's movement toward political abolitionism demonstrate the efforts of disenfranchised people to redefine publicity on the grounds that equality in a democratic system requires equal access to critical public discourse, Emerson's critique of reform culture harks back to the paradigmatic redefinition of publicity that was reflected in the structural transformation of the church during the Unitarian controversy. Emerson worked both to imagine "man thinking" as the foundational institution of civil society and as the vital force of an endlessly progressive democratic dialogue. As a direct product of Christian sectarian conflict, Emerson's spirituality carried the sectarians' struggle into the realms of political and cultural theory. By working through the question of sincere spirituality outside a commitment to doctrine, he carried the question of faith beyond the margin of Christianity. Emerson asked: How can one be faithful? How can one express his or her most deeply held sentiments? Who can understand prayers? Who can reply to my prayers in the spirit in which I speak?

In rejecting the forms and observances of Christianity without rejecting their spiritual and salvific goals, Emerson did exactly what both orthodox and liberal ministers most feared: He regrounded the questions of Christian faith outside the narratives of the Holy Bible. But this means more than simply ignoring Christ in sermons or shifting the locus of divine power from heaven to the soul; it also means integrating the goals of worship and the processes of religious community into nonreligious discursive contexts. By carrying the momentum of liberal

Christianity outside the boundaries of religion, Emerson inescapably carried it into a realm where religious, political, and cultural discourses intersected. In the prospectus to the *Dial* (1840), for example, Emerson writes: "The spirit of the time is felt by every individual with some difference— . . . to one, coming in the shape of special reforms in the state; to another, in modifications to the various callings of men, and the customs of business; to a third, opening a new scope for literature and art; to a fourth, in philosophical insight; to a fifth, in the vast solitude of prayer."[5] From the late 1830s to the late 1850s, Emerson's thought developed from a reaction against the sectarian disputes of his father's generation to a critique of the norms of American public discourse as his countrymen worked to reconcile the principles of liberal philosophy with the traditions of American culture, especially slavery. As this evolution proceeded, the focus of Emerson's advocacy of sincerity shifted from an effort to model sincere spiritual experience to an effort to imagine sincere civil dialogue. In theoretical terms, Emerson began his career by developing self-reliance as a theory of recognition that can allow an authentically liberal spirituality. Then, as he shifted his focus toward explicitly political questions, self-reliant conversation of the type he imagined with Margaret Fuller served as the standard against which he measured conventions of public discourse.

In this trajectory, "Self-Reliance" anticipates political essays such as the 1854 "Fugitive Slave Law" because the terms of dialogue he defines in the former serve as the standard against which he tests the failure of democratic dialogue in the debate over slavery during the 1850s. Within his sharp critique of public discourse, Emerson articulates a theory of critical conversation that he believed could reestablish authentic civil society and prevent the drift toward disunion and war. When viewed in relation to the goals of self-culture that he pursued in his friendship with Fuller, Emerson's call for public sincerity links his individualism to the constitutional issues that Stanley Cavell has emphasized in his reading of Emerson's essay "Fate."[6] For an individual to speak insincerely is both to articulate a falsely constituted self and to inject a false voice into the body politic. If selfhood is inauthentic, if it lacks autonomous thought and heartfelt commitment, it cannot contribute to an authentic critical dialogue in the public realm. In this respect, Emerson's theory of conversation is also a theory of the legitimation of democratic political authority. For Emerson, the representatives of parties, those who speak from material interests or in conformity to institutions other than the self, embody forms of strategic action that always threaten to corrupt critical public discourse by simulating processes of legitimization for civil authority.

Self-Reliance and Civic Spirituality

Emerson's self-reliance stands in a paradoxical relationship to critical public discourse. On the one hand, it calls for withdrawal from public life to facilitate an authentic recognition of the natural truths of what it means to be human. In this respect, self-reliant society is a method of "averting," to use Stanley Cavell's term, the self from alienating social norms. On the other hand, though, self-reliance seeks authentic or unalienated engagement in the community. The self-reliant individual must be invested in society but must not heedlessly succumb to communal norms or thoughtlessly internalize social conventions. Equally, the community has a role to play in sustaining self-reliance. In Emerson's imagination, the community must be "self-reliant" as an organic form; it must look to itself, to its "selves" rather than to tradition, doctrine, or myth in order to foster the authentic relationships that can keep it healthy.

Emerson's remark, "I like the silent church before the service begins" (*CW* 2:41), implies the religious context of self-reliance as a theory of community. For Emerson the fragmentation of New England Congregationalism represented a failure of community. Instead of articulating an aspiring spiritual community, ministers of his day resembled the "retained attorney[s]" who defended material interests. As he expresses it: "If I know your sect I anticipate your argument. I hear a preacher announce for his text and topic the expediency of one of the institutions of his church. . . . Do I not know before hand that not possibly can he say a new and spontaneous word? . . . Do I not know that he is pledged to himself not to look but at one side, the permitted side, not as a man, but as a parish minister? He is a retained attorney, and these airs of the bench are the emptiest affectation" (*CW* 2:32). In contrast to the partisan minister, the individual sitting quietly in the church represents an effort to renew spirituality either through authentic individual communication with the Divine or through communal anticipation of worship. The silence before the service begins is the moment before the congregation falls from the truthfulness of organic community into the partiality of sectarian discourse. This utopian moment in which consciousness, silence, and spirituality intersect represents a kind of aporia for

Emerson. The collective silence makes vivid the lack of sincere critical conversation. In his view, the church embodies a form of aspiration, a place where people fix their minds on perfection—individual, social, metaphysical. But the silence that precedes the formalized service, as full as it is, represents a problem. What language can bridge the gap that separates the silent worshippers? How can private communion with the Godhead become a public discourse without distorting the worshipper's intentions?

The problem of creating a site of reform discourse, in Emerson's eyes, is the problem of modeling an ideal speech situation through which individuals can honestly discuss issues of general concern. Commentary on this problem has a long history in Emerson criticism and partly accounts for the tendency to define transcendentalism as a solitary, apolitical, even antipolitical philosophy. Perry Miller contains Emerson's transcendentalism within a largely religious framework and rarely connects his early spiritualist thought with his later political thought. John Carlos Rowe, extending a line of thought first developed by Arthur Schlesinger, argues for the incompatibility of Emersonian transcendentalism with communal action. Rowe concludes that "Emerson's political writings from 1844 to 1863 remain so profoundly divided internally between Transcendentalist values and practical politics as to be practically useless, except as far as the value of their political rhetoric might be measured."[7] Critics in the tradition of Schlesinger and Rowe also see the dilemma of silence in the church, but they see Emerson responding by retreating from community into solitude because the institutions of collective life are necessarily conventional and thus antitranscendental.

Schlesinger and Rowe represent extreme examples of this line of Emerson criticism. At root their almost contemptuous dismissal of Emerson's value as a theorist of democratic community is grounded in their sense that Emerson's individualism is too easily appropriated as justification for the combination of transcendentalist creativity with bourgeois material greed. Rowe summarizes the logic: "If Emerson's radical individualism cannot be aligned with his political activism in the 1850s—that is, with the explicit instances of his work toward social reform—then the argument that Emersonianism supports, rather than refutes the values of Jacksonian America seems strongly supported."[8] Though I do not want to get sidetracked into specifically rebutting this reading of Emerson, I do want to emphasize connections between Emerson's radical individualism and his antislavery writings. These links revolve around the problems Emerson saw in sincerity as a mode of self-reliant individuality and authentic or sincere dialogue as a constitutive practice for a democracy.

Individuality and democracy are both blunted, in Emerson's view, by the forces that stand in the way of communal expressions of sincere interest or heartfelt desire. Emerson's ambivalence toward reform movements, political parties, and churches is thus connected to the problem of the congregation sitting silently in the church. In his political thought, Emerson sought to imagine the kind of sincere communication that would characterize discursive democracy. In my view, Emerson's very real impulse to turn away from the political realm embodies a knee-jerk reaction against the mockery that conventional public discourses made of sincere self-expression.[9] Rowe is certainly right that Emerson's antislavery writings are "internally divided between Transcendentalist values and practical values," but essays such as *Nature* and "Self-Reliance" are equally divided between contradictory lines of thought within transcendentalism. For example, Emerson vacillates between describing selfhood as a form of godlike creative empowerment and describing it as absolute submission to the universal laws of impersonal nature. Perhaps ironically, the passivity that Christopher Newfield finds central to Emerson's legacy and uses in a creative critique of its value for progressive, political thought echoes the Protestant minister's effort to serve as a transparent medium of the Holy Spirit.[10] While Newfield emphasizes passivity and submission, it is also important to stress that the submission to spirit that Emerson sought is a means to the end of undistorted communication, or as Lawrence Buell characterizes it, to the writing of scriptural testimony grounded in the self.[11]

This tension between listening and speaking also resonates in Emerson's modeling of self-reliant community. In a sentence in which Emerson describes self-reliance in terms of one reclining like a child in the maternal "lap of immense intelligence," he also describes self-reliant individuals in active terms: they are the "organs" of the spirit's activity. One aspect of the quest for truthfulness that is at the center of self-reliance is the effort to serve as an undistorting mediator of spirit, submissively allowing the spirit to pass through a transparent medium. As Emerson posits: "When we discern justice, when we discern truth, we do nothing of ourselves," but allow a passage to the "beams" of spirit (*CW* 2:37). Yet even this mode of submission marks a form of communicative action as the paradoxically passive speaker communicates the truth of the spirit. Even in its strictest form, self-reliance cannot accurately be understood as a solitary euphoria in which the individual communes with the Divine. Rather, self-reliance necessarily represents an ongoing and restless process of mediation, transference, and passing through.

By Emerson's logic, the "self" of self-reliance is not the property of any individual but rather is the location, or energy, or force that allows people to constitute authentic individuality. Just as the inspirational dimension of self-reliance is about seeking the self by avoiding conformist thought, its expressive dimension concerns seeking truthfulness by listening and speaking sincerely. In famous lines from the "American Scholar," Emerson focuses not just on the discovery of truth but also on its sharing through public discourse. For the poet to remember and record his "spontaneous thoughts" is only the first challenge. Emerson then casts him as an orator who seeks an authentic relationship with his auditor: "The orator distrusts at first the fitness of his frank confessions, his want of knowledge of the persons he addresses, until he finds he is the complement of his hearers." His act of self-revelation allows him ultimately to collapse the distinction between private and public selfhood. His hearers listen because "the deeper he dives into his privatest, secretest presentiment, to his wonder he finds this is the most acceptable, most public and universally true" (*CW* 1:63). In addition to being a form of dissent from conventional religious and social practices, self-reliance also asserts an ideal standard of public sincerity that Emerson sees as closing the gap between private and public modes of communication.

This construction of self-reliance revises the traditional Protestant duty for the individual to maintain a personal relationship with Jesus and re-presents it as a process of self-reflexive thought that requires the individual to seek pure insight and expression outside conventional institutional restraints. Although the echoes of Protestant spirituality are important in understanding the historical context of Emerson's revision of public sincerity, the real importance of Emersonian sincerity lies in his description of it as an identity that integrates the individual's spiritual quest for selfhood with the society's momentum toward authentic community.[12] Rather than calling people back to traditional models of faith, Emerson's theory of self-reliance as a form of community is built around the emergence of a new form of critical public discourse.

Initiating a theme in "Self Reliance" that he would develop more fully in essays such as "Man the Reformer" and "New England Reformers," Emerson criticizes the clergy and moral reform movements for their failure to create an authentic critical public sphere. In Emerson's view, the ministers of his day actually degraded authentic communication by corrupting processes that could lead to legitimate self-understanding. Warning people away from ministers who could not articulate spirituality as a contemporary discourse, Emerson writes: "If . . . a man claims to know and speak of God and carries you backward to the phraseology of some old mouldering nation in another country, in another world, believe him not" (*CW* 2:38). Later, in a parallel movement, he criticizes political parties and reform associations for subsuming individuals into the mechanics of publicity. He mimics the rallying cries of political conventions to dramatize their sublimation of individuality: "The political parties meet in numerous conventions . . . and with each new uproar of announcement, The delegation from Essex! The Democrats from New Hampshire! The Whigs of Maine! The young patriot feels himself stronger than before by a new thousand of eyes and arms. In like manner the reformers summon conventions and vote and resolve in multitude. Not so, O friends! Will the God deign to enter and inhabit you, but by a method precisely the reverse" (*CW* 2:50). These phenomena of Jacksonian America—the mass political organization and the reform convention—embody hoaxes that threaten to draw young patriots into a world where self-reliance is forfeited by a willing sublimation of self into a mass. The minister's rhetoric thus could guide individuals down a false path and lead them away from truthfulness, just as political parties and reform associations literally modeled the alienation of the self. The problem, despite the enthusiasm and progressive desire that churches, reform movements, and political parties articulated, is that while boilerplate speeches motivate resolutions that are voted up or down, the will of the individual is eclipsed by a ritual of mass assent, and the idea of individuality is structurally subordinated in the assertion of a collective voice. Political and reform conventions thus move away from rather than toward self-reliance. For "the God to deign to inhabit" them, the reformers and partisans would need to develop a "method precisely the reverse" of the procedures of mass democracy that the Jacksonians developed in politics, religion, and reform.

Self-Reliance as Critical Conversation

As a way of responding to existing platforms for public discourse, Emerson redefined the norms that govern critical dialogue. Rather than imagining a new institution, Emerson imagined a new way of talking. In "Self-Reliance," he introduces the issue of committed dialogue by describing a conversation with a friend: "I remember an answer which when quite young I was prompted to make to a valued advisor who was wont to importune me with the dear old doctrines of the church. On my saying, 'What have I to do with the sacredness of traditions, if I live wholly from within?' my friend suggested—'But these impulses may be from below, not from above.' I replied, 'they do not seem to me to be such; but if I am the Devil's child, I will live then from the Devil'" (*CW* 1:30). In this passage, Emerson shifts the foundations of duty from tradition to the self. The "valued advisor," a role in which William Ellery Channing can easily be imagined, questions his conversant's movement away from the "dear old doctrines of the church" and reminds him of tradition as a time-honored ground of legitimate authority. Emerson, equating obedience to tradition with spiritual alienation, adjusts his advisor's metaphor from one that emphasizes the potential heavenly or hellish source of "impulses" to one that emphasizes internal versus external sources of motivation. The duty to be truthful to a place "above" becomes a duty honestly to represent a place within. In switching metaphors, Emerson partially neutralizes the moral implications of "living from the Devil" because he reframes the context of duty to focus on the obligation to be sincere.

In "Self-Reliance," the conversation with the "valued advisor" is followed by a conversation with an abolitionist. In Emerson's view, rather than living a virtuous life, a life authentically motivated from within, the radical reformers had adopted reform as a kind of accounting procedure, a moral "penance" for a life that was fundamentally alienated. Hence, he scorns the abolitionist's propositions in the same way that he dismisses the lawyerly minister as a partisan. In a gesture that Emerson calls a "rude truth," he writes: "If an angry bigot assumes this bountiful cause of Abolition, and comes to me with his last news from Barbados, why should I not say to him, 'Go love thy infant: love thy wood-chopper'?; be good-natured and modest; have that grace; and never varnish your hard uncharitable ambition with this incredible tenderness for black folk a thousand miles off" (*CW* 1:30). In encouraging the abolitionist to love his woodchopper and his infant, Emerson seeks to call him back home, away from the distant Barbados, to a place of intimate relationships. In response to social reform as a system of penances that reproduce rather than disrupt alienation, Emerson offers intimate community as the necessary foundation for authentic reform. By his logic, the problem is not the philanthropy but the alienating conventions of the dialogue that the reformer perpetuates. Contempt for an invitation to enter into a dialogue he believes to be rooted in a false morality drives Emerson's disgust and underpins his sense that the abolitionist had missed the point of his own desire to do good. The abolitionist's invitation is "spite at home" because in the virtuous act of exchanging support for slave emancipation on the abolitionist's terms, Emerson and the reformer only simulate authentic dialogue. The abolitionist's "news from Barbados" mocks the idea of speaking "from within" in the same way as the sectarian minister's "airs of the bench" or the partisan patriot's cheer. In their smug affirmations of virtue, there is no recognition, no intersubjective sincerity, no giving or receiving of self, no self-reliance. To create a context for mutual recognition, Emerson invites the philanthropist to live from "within," not in the sense of solitary contemplation, but to live and speak from a locus grounded in the community with whom he can conduct intimate dialogue.

In his criticism of conventions of public dialogue in "Self-Reliance," Emerson is arguing less for a withdrawal from civic commitment than for an improved form of civic self-representation. Indeed, self-reliance is a necessarily social idea, in that a constant form of "aversive" engagement or "creative antagonism" is central to it. Participation in, or even just aspiration to, genuine critical dialogue allows the self to affirm all participants in conversation. This dialogic context of sincerity and authentic self-representation obviates categories of public and private and of masculine and feminine. In a passage that echoes the sublimity of the transparent eyeball, Emerson describes the "highest truth" in terms that combine the nirvana-like rapture of self-reliance as solitude with the radical motion and transformation of self-reliance as a form of community:

> And now at last the highest truth on this subject remains unsaid: probably cannot be said; for all that we say is the far-off remembering of the intuition. . . . The soul raised over passion beholds identity and eternal causation, perceives the self-existence of Truth and Right, and calms itself with knowing that all things go well. . . .
>
> Life only avails, not the having lived. Power ceases in the instant of repose; it resides in the moment of transition from a past to a new state, in the shooting of the gulf, in the darting to an aim. (*CW* 2:39–40)

The loss Emerson associates with repose underscores the restlessness he sees as a necessary element of self-reliance. Richard Poirier interprets this act as

Emerson's most basic form of self-defense. It allows Emerson to overcome the permanent insufficiency of speech or writing as acts of self-representation. Though Poirier treats the necessity of action as a response to problems in signification, his emphasis on the provisionality of identity expresses the dimension of Emerson's thought that is foundational to the emergence of reform culture. Authentic selfhood constantly needs to be in a state of transformation because, as Poirier contends, "When you put yourself into words on any given occasion you are in fact not expressing yourself. In choosing to be understood, you are to some extent speaking in conformity to usages and in harmony with assumptions shared by your auditors. At best, then, you are expressing only some part of yourself. And since speaking or writing are by nature forms of emphasis, even that part or fragment of self so revealed probably misrepresents the full measure of your feeling." [13] Jonathan Levin takes this line of thought one step farther by adjusting Poirier's emphasis on authentic self-expression to stress the "shooting of the gulf" as Emerson's response to the problem of moral progress. In regard to the problem Emerson tries to solve with the "shooting of the gulf," Levin concludes that "this is the fundamental paradox at the heart of Emerson's writing: we only ever recognize the good as it is embodied in some particular circumstance, but any particular embodiment is a limitation of the good and so a hindrance to its further development." [14] This restless activity that always seeks to subsume existing conventions is also the dynamic force that drives Cavell's and Kateb's readings of Emerson's thought. Though Cavell does not situate self-reliance as a necessarily intersubjective process, he describes it in inherently dialogic terms. [15] Conversion requires an oppositional dialogue in which the self-reliant individual is in critical conversation with his or her society. It represents the dialogue that links the individualism of moral perfectionism to the broader social dialogue explicit in the constitutional quest for a "more perfect union." The self-reliance that Kateb and Cavell contain within the psychological realm of the individual, even if it develops as an unspoken dialogue between the individual and the society, is similar to the dialectic of expansion and containment that characterizes "Circles":

> The life of a man is a self-evolving circle, which, from a ring imperceptibly small, rushes on all sides outwards to new and larger circles, and that without end. The extent to which this generation of circles, wheel without wheel, will go, depends on the force or truth of the individual soul. For it is the inert effort of each thought,

having formed itself into a circular wave of circumstance—as for instance an empire, rules of an art, a local usage, a religious rite—to heap itself on that ridge and to solidify him in the life. But if the soul is quick and strong it bursts over that boundary on all sides and expands another orbit on the great deep, which also runs up into a high wave, which attempt again to stop and to bind. (*CW* 2:180–81)

What is valuable in this passage for understanding Emerson's thought as a theory of community is not just the dialectic of willful self-expansion and institutional containment but also the specific forces that Emerson defines as the instruments of containment. The original "ring" of the self-reliant individual's thought represents a vital image of liberation. But this generative force then instantly boomerangs as the thought loops back to form a new set of social institutions. These institutions represent repose and function to lure the individual away from the "shooting of the gulf" quest of self-reliance. The ring of "circumstance" describes the pressures that ask people to live uncritically, without the aversive thought that mental self-reliance requires.

In both its creative and aversive dimensions, self-reliance is inextricable from its social context. As a creative force, the motion of original thought shatters existing norms. But "in the instant of repose," the solidifying wave becomes the forces of convention that characterize the sectarian, the partisan, and the abolitionist. In the one truly Derridean moment of his thought, Emerson characterizes power and authentic self-reliance as a form of shooting the gulf. In doing so, he identifies the same problem of signification that Derrida does in his classic essay "Structure, Sign, and Play in the Discourse of the Human Sciences." The gap itself represents the "absent center" or lack of transcendental signification in communicative action.[16] This lack is satisfied, however, by the act of "shooting" the gulf and the constant motion along the chain of the signifier that it implies. In this definition, as in the passage from "Circles," Emerson recognizes that all words and institutions are provisional and temporary, that pretending they have stability represents a fall from the highest level of sincerity. Though this process of "endless mutation," as Emerson describes it in the penultimate sentence of "Self-Reliance," can occur through a Kantian internal dialogue about the condition of the self, it is also necessarily a critical public dialogue involving social institutions and the people that inhabit them. In this respect, self-reliance is both a reaction against an insincere public realm and a model of critical conversation that seeks to make an authentic public dialogue possible by provoking individuals to speak and listen with sincerity.

This ideal of perfectionist truthfulness defines Emerson's relationship to the reform culture of the 1830s and 1840s. It also positions Emerson unambiguously against the pressure of strategic discourse. In theoretical terms, the priority Emerson placed on truthfulness anticipates an essential criterion of public reason that Rawls and others have incorporated into models of discursive democracy. In fact, the problem of strategic discourse became the central issue in Emerson's relationship to the antislavery activists. As the antislavery movement began to take a prominent place in his thought in the early 1840s, and the implications of slavery took hold in his intellectual life from the mid-1840s onward, the problem of achieving authentic dialogue in the democratic public sphere acquired a new urgency. In "Politics," an essay that began as a lecture in 1837 and finally made it into print in *Essays, Second Series* in 1844, Emerson compares and contrasts his ideal of legitimate civil society with his countrymen's actual practice of democracy.[17] Echoing the Rousseauvian ideal of consensus under the oak tree, Emerson argues for the organic and consensual origin of government: "Governments have their origin in the moral identity of men. Reason for one is seen to be reason for another, and for every other. . . . Every man finds a sanction for his simplest claims and deeds, in decisions of his own mind, which he calls Truth & Holiness. In these decisions all the citizens find a perfect agreement" (*CW* 3:124). Yet as he searches for a model of legitimate consensual government, Emerson reverses Rousseau's terms. He posits that "all public ends look vague and quixotic besides private ones" (*CW* 3:125). But by "private" Emerson means ideals or "laws" that reflect the critical commitment of living "from within." Private signifies a locus of authentication or verification of truthfulness more than a contrast to community.

Public and private in this specific instance typify the difference between the dear old doctrines of tradition and the authenticity of motivations that originate "within." While for Rousseau "private considerations" mark the eclipse of the general will by individual interest, for Emerson they mark the necessary starting point for intersubjective recognition. As he notes in "Politics:" "If I put myself in the place of my child, and we stand in one thought and see that things are thus or thus, that perception is law for him and for me." This putting "myself in the place of" as an act of critical conversation is crucial to Emerson's understanding of the legitimation of democratic authority. He continues this line of explanation by contrasting the recognition required in the act of putting a sincere self in the place of another against its strategic opposite, the construction of a false or simulated sympathy: "But if, without carrying him into the thought, I look over into his plot, and, guessing how it is with him, ordain this or that, he will never obey me" (*CW* 3:127). This false claim to community signifies the difference between private and public recognition and represents the conditions Emerson saw emerging in antebellum civil discourse.

By analogy, Emerson's preference for literary over political life is motivated partly by the higher standard of sincere self-expression it requires: "Senators and presidents have climbed so high . . . as an apology for real worth. . . . Like one class of forest animals, they have nothing but a prehensile tail, climb they must, or crawl" (*CW* 3:127). This image of a simulated civic virtue Emerson contrasts with the wise man who can afford to be sincere: "If a man found himself so rich-natured that he could enter into strict relations with the best persons and make life serene around him by the dignity and sweetness of his behavior, could he afford to circumspect the favor of the caucus and the press, and covet relations so hollow and pompous as those of a politician? Surely nobody would be a charlatan who could afford to be sincere" (*CW* 3:127).

As in "Self-Reliance," where metaphors of passivity stand in tension with metaphors of dynamism, in "Politics" metaphors of radical individual autonomy stand in tension with metaphors of shared civic obligation. In one important sentence, these contrasting images merge into a single metaphor through which Emerson integrates self and nation: "The tendencies of the times favor the idea of self-government, and leave the individual, for all code to the rewards and penalties of his own constitution; which work with more energy than we believe whilst we depend on artificial restraints" (*CW* 3:127–28). By bringing the idea of "self-government" and "constitution" together as terms that signify on both the individual and the national level, Emerson underscores the dialectical energy of a politics that harmonizes private and public by imagining government flowing from a paradoxically private and consensual source within the self. In "Politics," as in "Self-Reliance," Emerson specifically identifies sincere dialogue as the means of reinventing or legitimizing relations on the social or national level. The ideal of intimate relationships and the discourse through which they can be conducted frames the essay. Emerson introduces "Politics" with a poem that ends with the lines:

> When the Church is social worth,
> When the state-house is the hearth,
> Then the perfect State is come,
> The republican at home. (*CW* 3:129)

He closes the essay with the lines: "I have just been conversing with one man, to whom no weight of adverse experience will make it for a moment appear impossible that thousands of human beings might exercise towards each other the grandest and simplest sentiments, as well as a knot of friends, or a pair of lovers" (*CW* 3:129). These bookends to an essay that Emerson revised for seven years are packed with images of intimate dialogue that anticipate a democratic utopia in which institutional discourses of authority are synthesized into critical conversation. The church is transformed from a debating society into an instrument of authentic social reform, the legislative arena is domesticated so that the statehouse is merged with the center of familial intimacy, and political identity is indistinguishable from domestic selfhood. Emerson's metaphors are strikingly like Catharine Beecher's even to the use of the hearth as the site where the strategic norms of politics can be eclipsed by the sincerity of conversation among intimates. This set of images is reiterated in prose at the end of the essay, where Emerson offers the possibility of intimate conversation among multitudinous crowds as the ideal alternative to the conventions of churches, reform societies, and political parties.

Critical Conversation and the Rhetoric of Consensus

In relation to democratic dialogue, Emersonian intimate conversation resembles deliberative democracy as John Rawls, Jürgen Habermas, and Richard Rorty formulate it. Emerson's formulation is especially close to Habermas's in that both imagine consensus grounded in a Platonic ideal of transparent utterance. In contrast to the assumptions that underpin dialogue itself, though, the context of Emerson's model of critical conversation more closely resembles the paradigm that John Rawls constructs. The structure of overlapping consensus on basic assumptions about democratic culture coexisting with irreducibly contrasting value systems arrayed around the institution of slavery closely resembles the fragmented social world that Emerson felt himself to be in. In the Rawlsian paradigm, a civil society can continue to avoid crisis despite such an irreducible pluralism of value systems as long as there is consensual agreement that voices representing all value systems are engaged in a sincere and fair dialogue about the legitimacy of norms. When the population ceases to trust the sincerity of the dialogue, the legitimacy of representative authority and the stability of civil society are both at risk. In Emerson's view, a breakdown in sincerity among people with conflicting values characterized the debate over slavery. Emerson felt that American politicians were cynically redefining terms that grounded democratic consensus as a means of masking irreducible conflicts of values. Rather than engaging in a critical conversation, Emerson saw his countrymen conducting strategic dialogues in which the foundational principles of democratic society were distorted to throttle sincere discussion of slavery.

Sacvan Bercovitch's analysis of Emersonian dissent clarifies Emerson's association of public sincerity with the legitimation of democratic civil authority. In his analysis of Emerson's thought about socialism, Bercovitch argues that Emerson's disgust with the hypocrisy of American materialism pushed him to the "edge of class analysis" as a means of challenging the domination of a greed that was masking itself inside a strategic discourse of liberal autonomy and equality. Bercovitch cites Emerson's journals of 1836: "When I spoke or speak of the democratic element I do not mean that ill thing vain & loud which writes lying newspapers, spouts at caucuses, & sells its lies for gold. . . . There is nothing of the true democratic element in what is called Democracy, it must fall being wholly commercial." But as disgusted as Emerson was, Bercovitch also finds him quickly retreating from the critique of capitalism. "By 1839," Bercovitch writes, "he had recoiled not only from the exaggerations of actual individualism but from the system itself, as from a vast commercial lie."[18] This recoiling drove Emerson back to his roots in spirituality rather than toward radical materialist experiments such as Fourierism and the communities.

Citing the "playfulness" of Emerson's discussion of the Fourierists and other communitarians, Bercovitch positions the radicals as antagonistic figures for Emerson's political imagination. In opposition to their efforts to harmonize the individual and the society, "Emersonian dissent reminds us that ideology in America works not by repressing radical energies but by redirecting them into a constant conflict between self and society."[19] Bercovitch's construction of Emersonian dissent as a form of romantic tension between a sincere self and a corrupting society echoes the emphasis Kateb and Cavell place on ideological or philosophical conflict against the homogenizing effect of mass culture as a means for the individual to practice aversive thought. Bercovitch's construction is especially similar to Cavell's in that both define Emersonian dissent in explicitly utopian terms.[20]

But whereas Cavell emphasizes the linked political and personal meanings of the word "constitution," Bercovitch homes in on paradoxes in the word "union" as it was used in the antebellum period. Quoting Emerson's remark in a journal entry of late 1842 that "the Union is only perfect when all the Uniters are absolutely isolated," Bercovitch draws the paradoxical nature of Emersonian self-reliant community into the foreground. Authentic democratic community can only occur, by Emerson's logic, when citizens act from a position of self-reliance. This position alone can validate a consensus. By analogy, authentic democratic dialogue can only occur when it overcomes the alienation not only of the "great commercial lie" but also of the false communicative relations promoted by reform societies and other institutions. As Bercovitch notes, Emerson condenses the problem into a paradox: "Union ideal,—in actual individualism, actual union."

By Emerson's logic, the problem with democracy is the same as the problem with the utopian communities: both seem to require the subordination of the self to the institutional structures in which the citizen lives. The solution, Emerson held, is in individualism understood as a form of self-reliant community. When Bercovitch and, more directly, Robert Milder seek to define an Emersonian radicalism in economic terms, they ignore Emerson's construction of a utopian democratic theory rooted in an anarchistic individualism combined with sincere dialogue. Indeed, any commentary on Emerson that seeks to find him advocating redistribution of wealth as the path to justice will always find Emerson wanting. Though he vacillated and at times seems attracted to the clear justice of equal material relations, he never abandoned the belief that spiritual forces dominate material power. Where the materialist critic hopes to discover an epiphany in Emerson's recognition of the violent foundations of capitalist property and labor relationships, he or she will inevitably find Emerson sublimating materialist critique into an advocacy of reformed communicative or spiritual relationships. Thus, the democracy of the antebellum United States would fail not so much because it was rooted in the dehumanizing greed that made slavery possible but because cynical commercial voices were appropriating the terms of civic idealism and dressing up radical domination in the rhetoric of democratic consensus. Rhetoric such as Daniel Webster's, which defined "union" as a civil good that trumped the crimes of slavery, became Emerson's prime example of the transformation of critical conversation into strategic action.

The scorn Bercovitch finds in Emerson's criticism of the late 1830s, a scorn Emerson directed at the tendency of churches to mimic the hypocrisies of business, anticipates the scorn that he leveled at the rhetoric of the slavery debate between the U.S. annexation of Texas and the beginning of the Civil War. As Emerson's critique of culture moved into the political realm, his focus on authentic and sincere conversation did not change. In Emerson's ideal world, churches are far more important than legislatures, and the integrity of both is defined by the ideals that motivate utterance and conversation within them. Just as sectarianism had degraded the church, the hypocrisies that enabled Americans to reconcile liberalism and slavery were degrading the idea of a national union founded on authentic consent. The come-outer positions he adopted in the 1850s replay his resignation from the ministry two decades earlier. Emerson's antislavery writings draw into stark relief the danger that he felt from hypocritical conventions of public discourse. In his writings of the 1850s, Emerson speaks not just in defense of the slave but also in defense of sincere public dialogue. The defense of slavery in the United States represents a perfect corruption of the ideals of intersubjective recognition that are necessary for critical conversation. By Emerson's logic, this failure of recognition makes it impossible for any individual to be fully human, let alone free. The importance Emerson placed on sincere dialogue in the construction of the self and in the foundation of legitimate democratic authority becomes clear in his thought about the culture and practice of the radical reformers.

Sincerity and the Radical Reformers

As his use of metaphors of domesticity in "Politics" indicates, Emerson's construction of critical public discourse shares some basic similarities with Catharine Beecher's ideal of domestic citizenship. But Beecher's formulation was contained within a feminized domestic space, whereas Emerson deployed the rhetoric of domesticity to convey the importance of sincerity to his ideal of political dialogue. Also, like virtually all his contemporaries who wrote about cultural values, Emerson was responding to the Garrisonian perfectionists. While Catharine Beecher could see Garrison and his clique as the model of partisan divisiveness and thus the perfect foil for her effort to relocate critical discourse to the home, Emerson developed a subtle and ambivalent relationship with the radicals.[21]

Most simply put, Emerson recognized Garrison as a sincere speaker but also felt that Garrison was incapable of the type of intimate conversation that he associated with authentic selfhood and legitimate community. Lawrence Buell is correct in recognizing an important similarity in Emerson's and Garrison's ideal of "universal reform." Garrison's willingness to stand against the drift toward political abolitionism by continuing to advocate "a multilateral, absolutist, no-government approach to reform" throughout the 1850s drew Emerson toward his wing of the antislavery community.[22] But Emerson always saw the associations, conventions, and publications of the antislavery movement as a form of masquerade that stood in the place of genuine conversation. The pattern of Emerson's antislavery, his willingness to speak at events but reluctance to join antislavery societies, reflects his simultaneous appreciation of Garrison's sincerity and his disappointment with the methods that characterized the antislavery movement.

The critique of strategic action through which Emerson denounced antebellum political discourse emerges as a refinement of his ambivalence toward radical abolitionism. In "New England Reformers," Emerson addresses the methodological differences that distinguish the transcendentalist from the radical reformer. As he criticizes the reformers for their partisanship and sublimation of self into association, Emerson strikes chords that he had been hitting since the 1830s. In this essay, however, he also explicitly introduces intimate conversation as an alternative to the polemics of the antislavery societies. On one level, in "New England Reformers" Emerson sees conversation in terms of communication that reinforces individuality in a way that he believes to be unattainable within the conventions of antebellum public discourse. On this level, intimate conversation means sincere self-expression that minimizes the "charlatan" quality of personae such as the sectarian minister or the partisan politician. On another level, though, Emerson presents dialogue as a mode of self-reflexive moral suasion, an intersubjective means of permitting an individual to achieve greater depth of self-understanding.

Emerson tells a parable that describes the ways in which the disruption of convention functions to enact a perfectionist and egalitarian conversation. Emerson explains: "You remember the story of the poor woman who importuned King Philip of Macedon to grant her justice, which Philip refused: the woman exclaimed, 'I appeal:' the king, astonished, asked to who she appealed: the woman replied, 'From Philip drunk to Philip sober.' The text will suit me very well. I believe not in two classes of men, but in man in two moods" (*CW* 3:159). In this parable, a supplicant entreats formal power to relate to her as a dialogic equal. When she is rejected by the king, she calls Philip into a new communicative relationship. In this changed context, Emerson imagines the king and the "poor woman" in an authentic and egalitarian conversation of justice rather than in a relation of supplication and condescension. This parable underscores the distinction Emerson makes between the mass polemics of parties and the intimate conversation of well-meaning citizens. The goal of reform discourse must be not to evangelize the masses through revivalistic rhetoric but to bring each individual to sober recognition of others by bringing him or her back to a sober recognition of self.

This development in Emerson's response to the reformers grew out of earlier proposals that love is the force that will overcome social ills. When Emerson describes dialogue with reformers in essays such as "Self-Reliance" and "Man the Reformer," he offers love as the alternative to participation in associations. In "Self-Reliance," he casts the "angry bigot" from his door and instructs him to love his infant and woodchopper. In "Man the Reformer," he contrasts the ascetic militancy of Islamic missionary-generals with the transformative power of love as a catalyst of social union: "There will dawn ere long on our politics, on our modes of living, a nobler morning than that Arabian faith, in the sentiment of love. This is the one remedy for all ills, the panacea of nature" (*CW* 1:158). In "New England Reformers," he recites a litany of reform causes and asks, "Do you complain of our Marriage? Our marriage is no worse than our education, our diet, our trade, our social customs." Focusing on property, Emerson offers love as a means of achieving economic justice. He continues: "Do you complain of the laws of Property? . . . Let into it the new and renewing principle of love, and property will be universality" (*CW* 3:155). In each of these instances, Emerson uses love in the sense of intimate friendship. It represents a dialogic force that compels individuals to do justice to one another.

But in "New England Reformers," Emerson exhorts the reformer not just to love but also to converse. The essay was part of the Amory Hall lecture series of 1844, which aimed to reinvigorate the connection between religious faith and social reform.[23] It serves as a pivot point between the transcendentalism of *Essays, Second Series* and the reform writings that began with "Address on Emancipation in the British West Indies," which he delivered at the end of that summer. When he addresses reformers in this essay, he accounts for the slow pace of moral suasion with a more or less sympathetic explanation of its failure rather than with the contemptuous dismissal of "Self-Reliance": "The reason why anyone refuses assent to your opinion, or his aid to your benevolent design, is in you: he refuses to accept you as a bringer of truth, because, though you think you have it, he feels that you have it not. You have not given him the authentic sign" (*CW* 3:164). Mass meetings and newspaper polemics will fail to represent the "authentic sign" and provoke genuine change because they represent an inauthentic mode of dialogue, a spectacle in which all participants are alienated by the conventions of mass communication. Authentic signs cannot be uttered by alienated individuals but must reflect the commitment and recognition of self-reliance.

Emerson goes on to argue in "New England Reformers" that once one steps outside the polemics of politics, religion, and radical reform and begins to engage in authentic dialogue, one learns that "disparities of power in men are superficial; and all frank and searching conversation, in which a man lays himself open to his brother, apprises each of their radical unity." Such conversation becomes a sacred act, bringing the discussants into shared communion with the Divine: "What is the operation we call Providence? . . . Every time we converse we seek to translate it into speech." This effort to translate providence into conversation equalizes even the most important differences. When "two persons sit and converse in a thoroughly good understanding," even the power of the eloquent man is democratized, and "the poet would confess that his creative imagination gave him no deep advantage, but only the superficial one that he could express himself and the other could not" (*CW* 3:164–65). In Emerson's canon of representatives, the poet ranks very high, largely because he or she is gifted with an eloquence that supercedes distinctions between public and private discourse. The merging of public and private and the sincere communication that it produces serves to harmonize self-reliance and community. In effect, it enables "actual individualism" to produce "actual union" without contradiction.

Stanley Cavell reaches a similar conclusion in analyzing the connection between sincere self-expression and the conventions of reform discourse. He links the angry bigot of "Self-Reliance" to Emerson's 1850 essay "Fate" by arguing that in "Fate" Emerson is preoccupied with the problem of participating in antislavery without lapsing into the rhetorical or psychological conventions of either the pro- or antislavery partisans. The self-reliant abolitionist, Cavell argues, must "take sides with the deity" rather than with either the proslavery or antislavery partisans. Cavell explains: "If 'taking sides with the Deity' does not, for Emerson, (just) mean taking the right side in the crowing about slavery, the side Daniel Webster failed to take as the armies were closing on the issue, how might it be taken? . . . taking sides with the Deity is a refusal to take sides in the human *crowing* over slavery. Emerson's turn to take sides with the Deity . . . is not exactly a call to revolution, but a claim to prophecy."[24] This means, Cavell holds, allowing the pain of slavery and of living in a slave society to drive communicative action. Cavell's Emerson seeks not to vent or proclaim pain as Garrison does but rather to write "every sentence in pain" as a truthful method of recognizing that pain is a fact of selfhood in a slaveholding nation. Poirier makes the same point more broadly, focusing not just on slavery but on the impossibility of repudiating one's participation in history: "Fate is always for Emerson the precondition of freedom, a notion which implies that every individual is to some degree responsible for the worst corporately done by all of us in history. There is no exoneration in Emerson; complicity is inevitable."[25]

The effort at truthfulness that Cavell finds in Emerson's antislavery ethic harmonizes an authentic recognition of the slave with Emerson's commitment to honest communication. Reading "Fate" as a "call for philosophy" underscores Emerson's effort to create self-reliant conversation as a means not just of legitimizing democratic publicity but of publicly taking a side against slavery without slipping into the rhetorical traps he had warned against since the 1830s. The call for philosophy that Cavell sees in "Fate" emerges out of Emerson's effort to mediate between a prayerful sincerity and a context of partisan rhetoric that represents strategic rather than critical discourse. Emerson's ambivalence about the emerging culture of reform revolves around his fear that the reformers were simply reproducing the conventions of partisan and sectarian publicity. Yet as the antislavery debate became more intense after passage of the Fugitive Slave Act in 1850, Emerson began to see the radical abolitionists in an increasingly sympathetic light. As the antislavery movement as a whole, and Frederick Douglass with them, was moving away from the Garrisonian perfectionists and toward political abolitionism, Emerson actually moved closer to the Garrisonians and embraced them as the only locus of uncompromising sincerity in a civil society profoundly threatened by dishonest and duplicitous rhetoric.

Slavery, Webster, and the Collapse of Sincerity

One thing that early essays such as "The American Scholar," the "Divinity School Address," and "Self-Reliance" share with later essays on slavery such as the 1844 address on emancipation in the British West Indies and Emerson's two addresses on the Fugitive Slave Act is that both groups of essays are deeply concerned with the problem of sincere communication. Whereas the earlier essays are paradigmatic in the sense that they address insincere public discourse in major social institutions such as church, government, reform discourse, and the academy, the later essays focus on a single issue, slavery, identifying it as the center of the forces that were working to undermine even the possibility of authentic selfhood and authentic public dialogue in the United States. As such, Emerson's thought about slavery is central to his theory of self-reliance. For my purpose, the antislavery writings are especially important because they dramatize tension between critical and strategic public discourse as the linchpin issue not only of debates over human rights but also of legitimate democracy and the honest, self-reliant thought that comprises autonomy within it.

Though he had been paying attention to the nuances of political and reform discourse since the Cherokee removals and the murder of Elijah Lovejoy in the 1830s, Emerson's concern about the implications of public insincerity found a focus in Daniel Webster's advocacy of the Fugitive Slave Act.[26] In Webster's effort to define support for the fugitive slave law as a constitutional obligation that virtuous citizens would feel compelled to embrace, Emerson saw a perfect corruption of sincerity. Webster's decision to support the "Union" at the expense of what Emerson viewed as the honor of Massachusetts, transformed him into a symbol of everything that was wrong with American politics. Emerson's outrage was exacerbated by his long-held conviction that Webster was the only person in American public life with the talents to integrate the sincerity of the poet with the practical skills of the politician. For twenty years Emerson believed that Webster had the potential to be the ultimate public man. But Webster's decision, as Emerson saw it, to accept strategic action as the standard for American politics drove Emerson to embrace the Anti-Slavery Society as a bastion of sincerity in a nation that was renouncing public honesty in order to avoid civil unrest.

In his March 9, 1850, speech "The Constitution and Slavery," Webster announced: "I propose to support [the Fugitive Slave Act] with all its provisions, to the fullest extent." Bringing his prestige behind the bill and creating political cover for others, Webster encouraged his northern colleagues to look at the law from a particular point of view: "I desire to call the attention of all sober-minded men at the North, of all conscientious men, of all men who are not carried away by some fanatical idea or some false impression, to their constitutional obligations. I put it to all the sober and sound minds at the North as a question of morals and a question of conscience" (*WSDW* 10:87). Webster then went on to denounce the abolitionists as obstacles to an orderly civil society. Remarking that in his view the abolition societies had "produced nothing good or valuable," Webster sought to cast the radicals out of the critical public sphere by characterizing them as people who had been "carried away by some fanatical idea" (*WSDW* 10:89, 87). Webster's refusal to take sides against slavery, a choice he followed by ridiculing Charles Sumner's speech on the higher law, had an instant effect on the way Emerson talked about civil society.[27]

As Stanley Cavell notices, a tone of contempt and bitterness is increasingly common in Emerson's writing from "Fate" through the outbreak of the war.[28] This new tone, in its way, is the counterpart of his earlier impulse to withdraw from institutions that threatened to compel conformity, an impulse characterizing essays such as "Self-Reliance" and "Circles." Like his response to Webster, however, this tone is carefully focused as a response to the distortion of ideals in the rhetoric of American democracy.[29] The distortion that Emerson saw in apologists for slavery worked against self-reliance as a foundation for community because it asked citizens to join a conspiracy in which they would willfully participate in censorship and misrepresentation. It implied a process tending toward a kind of anticonsensus in which hiding, hypocrisy, and denial displace mutual understanding and consent. With the passage of the Kansas-Nebraska Act, Emerson concluded that such a conspiracy was quickly consolidating its control over the nation.

Long before the uprisings of the 1850s, in a well-known journal entry on the murder of Elijah P. Lovejoy, Emerson ruminated on the tentativeness of public response to such a brutal and violent act of censorship. He remarked: "If the motto on all palace-gates is 'Hush,' the honorable ensign to our town-halls should be 'proclaim'" (*JMN* 12:151–52). In this sentence, Emerson revealed some of his basic assumptions about the role of dialogue in democratic society. The "palace" of a monarchy or empire is characterized by radical censorship. The town hall of a democracy, by contrast, is characterized by a call to unrestrained public utterance. As Emerson thought about Lovejoy's murder, he saw it quite explicitly in relation to contrast between free and totalitarian societies. For a society to face an issue as divisive as slavery through acts of repression and censorship represented a fundamental subversion of the procedures for democratic legitimation. Indeed, as both Len Gougeon and Albert von Frank note, Emerson entered reform discourse during the Lovejoy affair as a defender of free speech rather than as an opponent of slavery.[30]

Yet as threatening as efforts to blunt public dialogue through the intimidation of activists, the imposition of gag rules, and censorship of the mail were to Emerson's assumptions about the dialogues that legitimize democracy, overt censorship represented only the most obvious challenge Emerson saw to the integrity of the critical public sphere. In the aftermath of the Fugitive Slave Act, Emerson began to recognize that a corrupt rhetoric of civic virtue was an even more insidious threat than bald-faced suppression of civil discourse. The growth of systematic insincerity in public discourse, for Emerson, implied alienation both on the level of the self and on the level of the society. The lie of an insincere public virtue, in a way, must infect the soul before it can infect the public sphere. As early as *Nature*, Emerson articulates his fears regarding this form of dual alienation:

> The corruption of man is followed by the corruption of language. When simplicity of character and the sovereignty of ideas is broken up by the prevalence of secondary desires,—the desire of riches, of pleasure, of power, and of praise,—and duplicity and falsehood take the place of simplicity and truth, . . . old words are perverted to stand for things which are not. . . . In due time the fraud is manifest, and words lose all power to stimulate the understanding or the affections. (*CW*, 1:29–30)

In this passage Emerson describes a self corrupted by secondary desires. These desires stealthily colonize the imaginations of individuals and then work their way into the public realm of civil society by using words as Trojan horses. Looking at this passage from Cavell's perfectionist point of view, Emerson is describing a process of alienation in which words stop pointing toward the next perfect self. In the broader context of civil society, this alienation from individual perfectionism refers to a public discourse that fails even to aspire to a more perfect union. On the contrary, Emerson here describes a form of strategic action in which language is not just disconnected from the effort at sincere self-expression but on a more basic level is alienated as a vehicle of self-understanding. In the place of self-reliance as an aspiration to truthfulness, Emerson finds a corrosive duplicity that corrupts the self and thus makes critical conversation impossible.

As tenuous as the possibility of sincere self-expression seemed to Emerson when he wrote *Nature*, during the late 1840s the systematic distortion of terms of civic virtue emerged as a threat to his model of self-reliant community. In the debates over the annexation of Texas, the Mexican War, the Compromise of 1850, and the Kansas-Nebraska Act, Emerson watched proslavery forces struggle for control over the terms that describe political virtue and the obligations of citizenship. In a telling sentence in his first "Address on the Fugitive Slave Act," Emerson asks about abolition: "Is it possible to speak of it with reason and good nature?" (*AW* 69). This exasperated sentence sprang from a belief that the debate over slavery had worked consistently enough to the advantage of the slave states that the slave power no longer felt a need for authentic dialogue. Slavery, in Emerson's rapidly changing view, "is very industrious, [and] gives herself no holidays. No proclamations will put her down. She got Texas and now will have Cuba, and means to keep her majority" (*AW* 69). This conviction moved Emerson toward a belief that the possibility of critical conversation was quickly breaking down and that the public sphere was on the verge of being controlled by forces of strategic coercion rather than self-reliant communication.

Despite his concern over the changed nature of public dialogue, in the 1851 address Emerson still expresses faith in the power of public reason to reverse deteriorating standards of public discourse. The Thomas Simms affair, Emerson remarks, "has been like a university to the entire people. It has turned every dinner-table into a debating club, and made every citizen a student of natural law. When a moral quality comes into politics, when a right is invaded, the discussion draws on deeper sources; general principles are laid bare, which casts light on the whole frame of society" (*AW* 64). In an equally optimistic vein, he notes that the nature of American public culture still gravitated toward antislavery: "Unless you can suppress the newspaper, pass a law against bookshops, gag the English tongue in America, all short of this is futile. This dreadful English speech is saturated with songs, proverbs, and speeches that flatly contradict and defy every line" of the fugitive slave law (*AW* 61). Despite his disgust, Emerson saw the Simms episode as a kind of moral homeopathy that would inject poison into the nation's bloodstream and motivate the forces of liberty.

But as the decade progressed, Emerson grew more pessimistic and more convinced that a corrupted public dialogue was poisoning the nation. His sense that it was impossible to conduct a rational discussion of slavery achieved its most pointed expression in his speech at the Kansas relief meeting in 1856. Responding to newspaper reports on the guerilla war in Kansas, Emerson writes with disgust that

> language has lost its meaning in the universal cant. *Representative Government* is really misrepresentative: *Union* is a conspiracy against the Northern States . . . *the adding of Cuba and Central America* to the slave marts is *enlarging the area of freedom. Manifest*

Destiny, Democracy, Freedom, fine names for an ugly thing. They call it otto of rose and lavender,—I call it bilge water. . . .

But this is Union, and this is Democracy; and our poor people, led by the nose by these fine words, dance and sing, ring bells and fire cannon, with every new link of the chain which is forged for their limbs by the plotters in the Capitol. (*AW* 113–14)

Just as sincere speech and strategic speech always stand in dialectical tension, the danger that subtle "plotters" could turn civic virtue inside out was always hovering in the margins of Emerson's democratic idealism.[31] As Perry Miller frames this issue in his essay "Emersonian Genius and American Democracy," a "soliloquy" runs throughout the *Journals*: "It turns upon a triangle of counterstatements: democracy raises the problem of genius; genius the problem of Napoleon and the American politician; they in turn raise the problem of democracy and of America."[32] Miller emphasizes Emerson's fear that a demagogue such as Napoleon or Jackson would effectively simulate genius in order to bend democratic conversation away from the common weal and toward his own "partial" will. In effect, Miller expresses the same fear as Rousseau that private interests will corrupt the public sphere. Where Rousseau emphasizes differences between "general" and "particular" interests, Miller emphasizes the corrupting force of strategic discourse.

Cavell incorporates Miller's opposition between the egalitarian nature of democracy and the elitist qualities of leadership into a constantly evolving moral perfectionism. For Cavell rather than representing antidemocratic elitism, genius represents the aspiration toward moral perfection. It is the individualistic counterpart of the rhetoric of consensus that links social perfection, consensus, and divinity. In his revision of Miller, genius becomes "the capacity for self-reliance," a quality that "is universally distributed, as universally, at any rate, as the capacity to think."[33] Those who have genius are thus not so much a breed apart as they are an ideal type of everyman. They anticipate the perfection of the citizen in the same way that the rhetoric of consensus anticipates the perfection of democracy. Emerson's bitter denunciation of the corruption of the principles that underpin American democracy reflects a fear that Americans were renouncing this idealistic and perfectionist aspiration, which, for him, defined the highest virtue of liberal democratic society. Though there is little reason to doubt Emerson's elitism, there is also little reason to doubt his desire for a utopian democracy of poets.

The core of legitimate democracy for Emerson was a context in which people could discuss issues like slavery with "reason and good nature" rather than as strategic struggles for control over the ideological apparatus of the society. In the growth of the slave power, Emerson saw the balance tipping dramatically toward the duplicitous power struggles of strategic action.

Emerson's fear about the systematic distortion of public speech is expressed most vividly in his two lectures on Webster and the Fugitive Slave Act. In significant respects, Emerson's attack on Webster in the 1851 "Address to the Citizens of Concord" reiterates the dissatisfaction with small-minded partisanship that had been a standard theme in his journals and essays since the 1830s. The 1851 address shows Emerson raising the problem of public sincerity and beginning to recognize the implications of the systematic distortion of the rhetoric of civic virtue. In it the word "Union," so central to American patriotism in the 1850s, becomes a fulcrum on which rests the viability of the United States as a representation of anything more than possessive individualism. Emerson's flirtation with disunion in this essay is a new theme; and it is intrinsically connected to his sense that the rhetoric surrounding the constitutional Union and the value of northern compliance with the Compromise of 1850 was threatening to alienate language as a vehicle through which self and community could legitimately reinforce each other.[34]

Immediately after he characterizes the Fugitive Slave Act as a "powder magazine" laid "under the foundations of the capitol," Emerson remarks: "Nothing seems to me more hypocritical than the bluster about the Union." He describes the effect of the Fugitive Slave Act on his nationalism: "A year ago we were all lovers of the Union, and valued so dearly what seemed the immense destinies of this country. . . . But in the new attitude in which we find ourselves the personal dishonor which now rests on every family in Massachusetts, the sentiment is changed. No man can look his neighbor in the face. . . . The Union, such an Union, is intolerable" (*AW* 68). A society that once held out the promise of being the "home" of humankind, as he had termed it in "The Young American," seemed to have repudiated the foundational tenets of community by embracing a law that banned time-honored traditions of recognition and cooperation. Complicity in a union preserved by a corruption of its own liberal idealism, Emerson holds, is not just a moral revolution but also a personal disgrace to each citizen. To renew the national community after Webster's compromise would require a Garrison-style self-purification in which the citizen repudiated the old Union and began to reconstruct it on a new foundation.

Despite a sentence in which he clearly asserts, "I am a Unionist," Emerson's treatment of this issue was ambiguous enough to earn him the charge of being a Garrisonian come-outer.[35] In a sentence that syntactically writhes with the "ignominy" Emerson claims to wake up with every day, he actually refers to the Union in the past tense: "The Union,—I give you the sentiment of every decent citizen—The Union! O yes, I prized that, other things being equal; but what is the Union to a man self-condemned, with all the sense of self-respect and chance of fair fame cut off, with the names of conscience and religion become bitter ironies, and liberty the ghastly mockery which Mr. Webster means by that word" (*AW* 68). As civil dialogue became more and more hypocritical, the redefined terms of democratic self-representation threatened to infiltrate thought and undermine authentic selfhood. Self-respect was becoming impossible because the language that Emerson had always regarded as a pathway connecting the spirit, the individual, and the community had become a ghastly mockery as it was twisted to justify slavery. Thus, the citizen who accepts the Union on the terms Webster offered is "self-condemned"; he must in some sense either embrace slavery as a positive good, willingly recognize the hypocrisy as a necessary evil, or come out of the Union.

In post–Fugitive Slave Act America, loyalty to the Union required that the citizen accept the Websterian lexicon of terms and believe that the preservation of slavery was a moral and patriotic act. Given the redefinition of ideas such as "conscience," "religion," "liberty," and with Webster's equation of dissent with "treason" and of Boston antislavery with "prejudice," for an American citizen to be loyal to the Union required that he or she accept the realpolitik of the Compromise of 1850 over the perfectionist aspirations of the preamble to the Constitution and thus on some level embrace strategic action as the legitimate discourse of American morality. Rather than understanding the Union as both a set of democratic practices and a utopian aspiration for the harmonious fusion of self and society, the American Union is redefined to signify not just a conscious and willful insincerity but also a conspiracy to pretend that soul-crushing greed is a form of virtue. William Ellery Channing saw a similar problem but understood it basically in terms of moral suasion. The individual had to struggle against his inner slaveholder in order to draw out his likeness to God. Emerson saw the problem less in terms of an internal struggle and more in terms of fate or historical circumstance.

In the "Address on the Fugitive Slave Law," which Emerson wrote three years later, the problem of sincerity was so acute that Emerson attempted to rally a

small cadre of intellectuals to preserve an ideal of critical public discourse against
an overwhelming tide of forces that sought to simulate discursive democracy to
create false popular legitimations for slavery. Emerson identifies his audience as
"students and scholars" and explains: "It is only when the public event affects
them, that it very seriously affects me. And what I have to say is to them."
Defining his relation to an implied audience is important enough that Emerson
reiterates its boundaries: "It is to [scholars and students that] I am before hand
related and engaged,—in this audience or out of this audience,—to them and not
to others" (*AW* 73). Though Emerson also extends his audience by noting that
"the class of scholars and students . . . is a class which comprises in some sort
all mankind" (*AW* 74), in a letter he wrote a week after delivering the address,
Emerson described an audience that was simultaneously universal and extremely
narrow. Self-effacingly he wrote to Henry Furness that he hoped "to write a plea
for freedom addressed to *my set*."[36] By defining his audience narrowly, Emerson
shifted the locus of sincere discourse from a geographic site to a vocational site,
or from Massachusetts to the community of students and scholars. In the 1851
address, Emerson concludes by exhorting Massachusetts to become a "fastness"
against the corrupt rhetoric of civic virtue: "We must make a small State great,
by making every man in it true. . . . In this one fastness, let truth be spoken, and
right be done. Here let there be no confusion in our ideas. Let us not lie, nor
steal, nor help to steal; and let us not call stealing by any fine names, such as
'union' or 'patriotism'" (*AW* 71). If the Union could no longer be considered
an authentic community tied together by self-reliant conversation, perhaps the
narrower confines of his state could still maintain its integrity and hold out for
a better day.

In the 1854 address, he narrows his community of sincere speakers even more
carefully and connects rhetorical authenticity to particular vocations. Emerson
writes: "The one thing not to be forgiven to intellectual persons is not to know
their own task, or to take ideas from others and believe in the ideas of others.
From this want of manly rest in their own, and foolish acceptance of other
people's watchwords, comes the imbecility and fatigue of their conversation"
(*AW* 73). The 1854 address is a warning to a small class of people to preserve the
integrity of their public utterances. Emerson fears that if this group succumbs
to the corrupt standards of communication he has been denouncing in some
form or another since 1836, the vital tools for what Frederick Douglass called
"renovating the public mind" would be lost. Whereas the 1851 address deploys

a geographical metaphor to define a fastness against cant, the 1854 address is an appeal to people Emerson believed to hold an ethical relationship to the verbal process that mediates spirit, self, and publicity. It is an extended effort to draw the class of students and scholars away from the watchwords of Daniel Webster and back to the relationships between private experience and public expression that he describes in *Nature* and "The American Scholar."

In the 1854 address Emerson brings sincerity and critical conversation into the foreground of ethics as he makes a last-ditch attempt to convince his colleagues to maintain sincerity as a foundational value that can facilitate the combination of "actual individualism" and "actual union." Emerson sees the ideological leaders of society combining in "a general conspiracy" to justify the sentence "*Nothing is good but stealing.*" Uttering this sentence, as Emerson argues Americans were asked to do, is to embrace a corrupted model of selfhood and project it as a standard for public virtue. Indeed, this moment in the 1854 "Fugitive Slave Law" is paradigmatic of Emerson's fear of the simultaneous corruption of self and civil discourse. He imagines a conspiracy of ministers, scholars, judges, and other "official persons" combining to construct an inside-out virtue. This conspiracy, which Emerson felt closing in around him as even "intellectual persons" were drawn into the circle of proslavery rationalization, reflects a similar osmosis to that which he describes in *Nature*. Thinking of slavery and its effects on American public discourse, Emerson writes: "The habit of oppression cuts out the moral eyes, though the intellect goes on simulating the moral as before, its sanity is invaded and gradually destroyed" (*AW* 85).

Emerson returned to excoriate Daniel Webster such a long time after his fall because the danger posed by the Kansas-Nebraska Act brought Emerson back to Webster as the representative man of alienation from the spirit. Webster was a man who simulated morality and who eloquently asked his countrymen to simulate morality with him. Emerson had revered the great senator from Massachusetts because Webster represented the possibility of integrating the insight of the poet with the street smarts of the politician. Webster was part of the class of students and scholars to whom Emerson was speaking in 1854. But in relation to the vocational duties of this class, in Emerson's view, Webster not only exemplified personal failure and political betrayal; he also represented a permanent threat to liberal civil society. After Webster's speech of March 7, 1850, even after his death, Webster's watchwords continued to define a false rhetoric of virtue that enabled supporters and apologists for slavery to defend the Kansas-

Nebraska Act as a patriotic defense of the United States. As important as is Webster's substitution of "state reasons," as Emerson puts it, for higher law, his role in degrading a perfectionist rhetoric of virtue is equally threatening to authentic community. Webster's very poetic talent made him a perfect image of inauthenticity, a decoy marking the path to a society philosophically grounded in the principle that *"Nothing is good but stealing"* (*AW* 84).

Thus Emerson's criticism of the rhetoric that supported the Fugitive Slave Act is in a way a rearguard defense of the culture of reform, which, at its best, is a communal vision grounded in the idea of perfectionist civil dialogue. His political commentary of the 1850s is partly motivated by fear that in the defense of slavery, the creative energy of the society will be spent trying to legitimize evil rather than making "more perfect unions" in the transcendentalist sense. With the importance of public expression to his transcendentalism in mind, Emerson analyzes contemporary politics not in a way that represents either a "contradiction" to his philosophy, as John Carlos Rowe phrases it, or that is, to use George Kateb's term, "aberrant," but in a way that is attuned to preserving the flow of spirit from private truth to public expression and the critical conversation that public sincerity can provoke.[37] Gustaaf Van Cromphout has recently described the multiple affirmations that emerge from continuity in the path from private-to-public expression in terms of Hegelian recognition: "One cannot achieve real self-consciousness . . . without one's being recognized as a true self by others and without one's absorbing that recognition into one's self-reflection; moreover, the value of others as recognizers of one's true self depends upon one's granting them equal recognition as true selves."[38] This process of self-reflection and sincere expression that leads to intersubjective recognition is as vital as the private experience of transcendence. Far from steering away from the main current of his thought, by denouncing public hypocrisy and seeking stewards for public authenticity, Emerson is speaking in defense of the necessary conditions of selfhood and community.

Emerson's contribution to the culture of reform was thus to forge the link between reform as a mode of public dissent and reform as an expression of autonomous selfhood. In both his resistance to participation in reform associations and his focus on sincere public speech, Emerson articulated the importance of reform to liberal selfhood. In the Emersonian model, reformers are not antagonistic rebels but utopian individualists who compel their society toward a consensus in which free individuals are united in harmonious community. For Emerson the hallmarks of legitimate reform speech are that it must anticipate moral progress for the society and that it must reflect the authentic will of the individual speaker. Always suspicious of institutions that threaten to eclipse the ability of individuals to think, speak, and act freely, Emerson orients his thought about the public sphere toward an ideal of the transcendent equality of each citizen. But Emerson's liberal individualist cannot be a hermit; rather, he or she must speak in public and transparently represent his or her authentic sentiments.

Hence, Emerson responded to the culture of reform by neither validating nor repudiating it, but by analyzing the new phenomenon and imagining a better or an ideal model of reform. In some ways, Emerson saw practices of antebellum reform culture as the worst of all worlds. As the church was fragmenting into myriad denominations and the political parties were applying gag orders to suppress antislavery activism, reform organizations were popping up like mushrooms. But these movements were as likely to eclipse individuality and promote strategic discourse as they were to heal the ills of the public realm. The problem was not that the cure was worse than the disease but that it was the same as the disease.

In some respects, Emerson understood the interest-group pluralism that characterized contemporary society as an obstacle to the autonomy of the individual. Unity and truth were very similar concepts in Emerson's imagination. Just as his spiritual thought assumed a prelapsarian unity with the divine that inspiration reproduces, his social thought assumed an original consensus that genius or reform intends to reproduce. The pluralistic public sphere that was growing up around him was always in tension with the emphasis on unity that pervaded Emerson's spiritual and social thought. But it was only partly in tension—and it left plenty of room for Emerson to admire the reformers and participate in the culture they were creating. The interest-group pluralism founded by the organizers of antebellum reform movements produced a fragmented public sphere characterized by exactly the kind of partisanship and single-issue myopia that Emerson lamented. But contextualized within the rhetoric of liberal consensus, it also represents a form of critical conversation with strong similarities to Emerson's model of self-reliance. In its mutability, the voluntariness of association, the fluidity of borders between organizations, and the intense efforts at dialogue across ideological boundaries, the interest-group pluralism erected by the culture of reform represents a world of gaps across which individuals can constantly shoot as they seek self-reliant expression and mutual understanding. Emersonian perfectionism, and transcendentalism more generally, thus contributed to a rhetorical context that ironically positioned the antebellum culture of reform within a broader utopian rhetoric of consensus. It enabled the culture of reform to emerge as a progressive force and continues to legitimize it as a vehicle of social progress rather than as a threat to civil order.

Sincerity and Pluralism in Critical Conversation

The emphasis that early reformers placed on the right of access to public discourse also says much about ambiguities in the relationship of liberalism to discursive democracy. One reason that Frederick Douglass accepted the advantages of political antislavery and that the women's rights movement chose the path indicated by Angelina Grimké is that advocates of civil and equal rights sensed the role that access to critical public discourse had come to play in defining equality in American society. In the period between the Unitarian controversy and the beginning of the Civil War, women and African Americans, especially Grimké and Douglass, made the case that in order to have a public discourse grounded in the liberal ideals of individual autonomy, Americans must recognize the right of access very broadly. Grimké and Douglass explicitly understood such access as a necessary element of liberal equality. Even Catharine Beecher implicitly conceded that equality requires the right of access to political speech in the public sphere. Like Garrison, who paradoxically renounced political participation as a means of enhancing his authority in critical discourse, Beecher called on women to renounce legitimate claims to public equality as a means of authorizing domestic citizenship. As deeply embedded as the right to be left alone is in liberal constructions of autonomy, the right of access to public discourse is equally central because it alone allows individuals to participate in the legitimization of the norms under which all members of the society live.

In the magnetic pull that critical conversation exerted over this first generation of reformers, the emergence of the culture of reform signaled the working out of problems in the relationship between publicity and equality that are deeply embedded in Enlightenment thought. It explains the fate of Catharine Beecher's model of domestic citizenship and of the orthodox Congregationalists' effort to sustain the vigor of their doctrine. Orthodox Congregationalism could never recognize the autonomy of the individual in the way that liberalism requires. Ultimately, orthodoxy posed an epistemological challenge that pitted the obligation to obey against the right of self-representation in communal affairs. The idea of a critical public sphere where the minister's voice presents the will of God as one rational option in an egalitarian, pluralistic dialogue among several models of transcendence was incompatible with orthodox faith. At most, orthodoxy could frame the epistemological challenges of the Enlightenment as tests of self-control, tests of one's ability to remain faithful despite the enticements of new instruments of power. As the orthodox ministers discovered, their evangelical fervor and ability to call people to an orderly alternative world was well suited to partisan debate, but orthodoxy could never again expect the hegemony or superordinate status that is implicit in its world-view. Even today it stands in a position of permanent dissent against the very structure of critical discourse within which it operates.

Similar conclusions can be reached about Beecher's model of domestic citizenship and Garrisonian perfectionism. Beecher's and Garrison's argument that critical public discourse or political participation is incompatible with virtue is only valid if one accepts the proposition that politics is inherently strategic, insincere, and dishonest. Garrison never accepted this proposition. He repudiated the Constitution and the political system because it was implicated in slavery, not because it was inherently corrupt. Beecher also rejected the inherent corruption of political discourse. She argued that public political discourse that conforms to a set of "masculine" conventions would inherently emphasize domination over mutual understanding. She responded by trying to integrate politics and domesticity to create a new form of sincerity. Beecher's ideal described a domestication of discursive democracy grounded in the assumption of feminine sincerity. Emerson, in developing a theory of self-reliance grounded in a form of sincere conversation that obviates categories of private and public, also rejected the inherent corruption of political discourse.

Emerson, Grimké, and Douglass all implicitly argued that liberal selfhood could only be fully achieved through sincere self-representation in the public sphere. This is why Emerson's apocalyptic vision of a public sphere dominated by a conspiracy to sanctify the sentence *"nothing is good but stealing"* is so useful in describing the relationship between critical conversation and strategic discourse in antebellum America. In this statement, Emerson described not just the hypocritical slaveholders and their apologists but also the subversion of the realm of sincere dialogue that underpins self-reliance on an individual level and authentic community in the society as a whole. Since critical conversation is the source of self-reliance, self-reliance and the authentic community it comprises are impossible if conversation becomes corrupted to the point where sincerity is impossible. Indeed, the central importance of sincere public speech to Emerson's theory seems demonstrated by the fact that he became more rather than less politically active as public discourse deteriorated from bad to worse. Emerson saw passage of the Fugitive Slave Act as a kind of moral invasion of Massachusetts. But instead of withdrawing into a small circle of family and friends in order to maintain his integrity, Emerson responded by moving closer to the Garrisonians because their commitment to public sincerity had come to seem more important than their divisive partisanship.

The critical conversations that created the culture of reform in antebellum America thus ultimately have two fundamental components: sincerity and pluralism. The restructuring of the public sphere symbolically marked by the disestablishment of the church in New England indicates both a flattening out and an expansion of the critical public. As legitimization moved out of mutually reinforcing relationships between church and state and into an informal and extragovernmental sphere of critical public discourse, participation in that sphere became important as a material indication of equality—in the sense of full humanity rather than political citizenship—within the society. Even more than disenfranchisement from the official political sphere, exclusion from critical discourse indicated inferiority. This integration of access into equality as a necessary criterion has since become central to theories of discursive democracy and liberal publicity. As churches and political parties struggled to dominate the legitimization of norms and the civil offices that execute them, outsider groups claimed access to this sphere as a means of demonstrating equality and of voicing communal interests. Even as the culture of reform was compelled into being by changes in the nature of authority, the debates that it comprised influenced the transformation of the public sphere by insisting that the society recognize a plurality of perspectives, agendas, and identities.

Though the reformers who created the culture of reform never explicitly recognized it as such, this first generation of reformers laid the foundation for debates over the competing virtues of understanding American identity in pluralistic or homogeneous terms. As this structure has evolved, the critical public sphere has become less a Habermas-style site of discourse oriented toward achieving transparency and consensus and more a Rawlsian locus for mediating differences and achieving practical understanding among communities with fundamentally conflicting points of view. For example, the point of debates over sexual orientation is not to convince Christian fundamentalists of the beauty of same-sex love or to convince homosexuals that their love is evil but to negotiate the terms on which these communities can coexist in a just and harmonious society—even as the two groups try to evangelize each other.

High-stakes conversations about the diverse values and practices that comprise American society also, of course, must take place in a general atmosphere of confidence that people are talking honestly and that the outcome of critical conversations are not predetermined by coercive power. Americans have never had a critical conversation in which the stakes were higher than in the debate over slavery. In addition to arguing for Emerson's self-reliance as a theory of community and for its importance in contextualizing reform movements within a utopian and secular rhetoric of consensus, I have tried to emphasize the importance Emerson and other key reformers placed on sincerity. In some respects, public sincerity is both the perfection and the negation of liberalism. Through it, the individual acts as a perfectly private individual who articulates deeply held convictions. But it also denotes an individual who acts as a member of a community and holds nothing back for the self. It is both a kind of complete and unrestrained accomplishment of individuality and an unrestrained dedication of self to the public sphere. As Emerson's experiment with Margaret Fuller and Beecher's effort to domesticate political discourse indicate, the problem of sincerity is inextricably connected to the changing rhetoric of gender and the codification of antebellum gender-sphere ideology. But more importantly, the problem of sincerity is fundamental enough that it destabilized and continues to destabilize the personae through which members of free societies orient themselves to the world. The realm of critical conversation is thus finally represented by the unstable distinctions through which people understand private and public selfhood and the attributes that comprise equality in civil society. The central place that a permanent, freestanding, professional culture of reform plays in this ongoing dialogue is the result of the changing structure of public authority that produced the critical conversations of the antebellum period.

NOTES

INTRODUCTION
Discursive Democracy and the Culture of Reform

1. Walters, *American Reformers, 1815–1860*, 141; Mintz, *Moralists and Modernizers*, 72.

2. Gutmann provides a very useful analysis of the relation of interested and identity groups as a social form within democracy in *Identity in Democracy*, 8–30.

3. Taylor, "Politics of Recognition," 25–74; Rawls, *Political Liberalism*, xliv–xlix, 16–21.

4. Wiegman, *American Anatomies*, especially section 1, "Economics of Visibility," and section 3, "White Mythologies"; Fanuzzi, *Abolition's Public Sphere*. Fanuzzi draws extensively from Wiegman and applies her analysis of public embodiment to Frederick Douglass and, by contrast, William Lloyd Garrison. See also, by contrast, Isenberg, *Sex and Citizenship*.

5. The ebb and flow of the transcendentalists', especially Emerson's, relationship to reform culture has a long history. Fuller, though she is increasingly central as a founder of women's reform thought, kept out of the antislavery movement and was in Europe when the organized women's rights movement emerged in the late 1840s. Emerson's reputation as a reformer is thoroughly studied in Gougeon's chapter titled "Abolition and the Biographers" in *Virtue's Hero*. See also the introduction to *The Emerson Dilemma*, ed. T. Gregory Garvey, xi–xxviii; and Lopez's chapter, "The Anti-Emerson Tradition," in *Emerson and Power*. Particularly thoughtful recent arguments against Emerson's value as a progressive thinker are Newfield's *Emerson Effect* and Rowe's *At Emerson's Tomb*. Rowe, especially, has provoked response: Gougeon and von Frank react in "'Fortune of the Republic,'" and "Mrs. Brackett's Verdict," respectively.

6. Rousseau, *The Social Contract*, 150.

7. Ibid.

8. See Gutmann and Thompson, *Democracy and Disagreement*; Dryzek, *Discursive Democracy*; Benhabib, "Toward a Deliberative Model"; and Bohman, *Public Deliberation, Pluralism, Complexity*.

9. Habermas, *Theory of Communicative Action*. See also Fraser, "Rethinking the Public Sphere." This idea, though, is also very similar to that which Sennett describes in *Fall of Public Man*; see, for example, his chapter "Proof or Plausibility?" in the section titled "Roles," 28–45.

10. Honneth and Joas offer a very useful analysis of communicative action as both an epistemology and a critical theory. Their introduction to *Communicative Action* summarizes and contextualizes the theory. Taylor's essay in this collection, "Language and Society," situates communicative reason in debates about contemporary pluralism. Dux's essay "Communicative Reason and Interest" theorizes efforts of disenfranchised people to participate in norm-defining dialogues. The Dux essay serves as a bridge between Habermas's theory and the liberalism of Rawlsian communications theory. Barry lucidly

articulates the way Rawls's "original position" links liberalism and the Marxists' interest in capital: "Rawls's first principle of justice . . . articulated the classical ideal of liberal citizenship, while his second principle gave recognition to the demands of social and economic citizenship. [This] . . . second part made their justice of social and economic institutions depend on their making the worst-off socio-economic group in the society as well off as they could under any set of institutional arrangements" (*Culture and Equality*, 7).

11. See Rawls, *Political Liberalism*; Habermas, *Moral Consciousness*; and Habermas, *Justification and Application*.

12. Through "hermeneutic conversation," Warnke tries to integrate the idealism of Habermasian "discourse ethics" with the irreducible overlapping pluralism that Rawls addresses in *Political Liberalism*. By bringing these together, Warnke constructs a model of civil dialogue that retains pluralism as a virtue but also seeks the level of transparent mutual understanding that Habermas attributes to the ideal speech situation. Warnke writes: "The idea behind the notion of hermeneutic conversation is the idea that an interpretive pluralism can be educational for all parties involved. If we are to be educated by interpretations other than our own, however, we must both encourage the articulation of those alternative interpretations and help to make them as compelling as they can be. . . . Democracy thus turns out to be the condition for the possibility of an enriching exchange of insight. Democratic conditions act against the entrenchment of bigoted interpretations by offering others a fair fight as equals and hermeneutic conversation itself acts against the reduction of diversity by allowing that more than one rational interpretation might 'win.'" See Warnke, *Justice and Interpretation*, 157.

13. See Habermas, *Theory of Communicative Action*, 284–88. The major distinction of strategic action is that it is a form of purposive-rational, or goal-achieving, action that functions within social or communicative action. It thus hides a problem-solving form of action within a set of conventions that is normatively oriented toward achieving uncoerced mutual understanding. As such, it is a duplicitous and manipulative form of communication. It was and still is, of course, common to interpret public discourse that presents itself as civic-minded as a kind of open secret in which the real manipulative intent is barely disguised. See also McCarthy, *Critical Theory of Jürgen Habermas*, 23–25. McCarthy describes strategic action as a discursive tool "for the maximizing of the individual's own pleasure or advantage" in a dialogue that an auditor believes is oriented toward sympathetic understanding (25). See also Moon, "Practical Discourse and Communicative Ethics," 146.

14. Warner situates strategic action in the context of Revolutionary America by analyzing debate over rhetorical conventions of public discourse in monarchical and republican societies. The context of material dependence, Warner argues, creates an artificiality in conversation that makes authentic or republican selfhood impossible. Though the issue of material dependence would remain important in debates over

expanding the franchise, Warner usefully isolates the effect of dependence in distorting political dialogue. See Warner, *Letters of the Republic*, chapter 5, "Nationalism and the Problem of Republican Literature," especially 136–38.

15. Ibid., 144.

16. Ibid., li.

17. Ibid., xxvii.

18. The utopian perfectionism implicit in public discourse links Rawlsian and Habermasian theories of discursive democracy. Cavell also links Rawlsian perfectionism to Emersonian moral perfectionism. See Cavell's *Conditions Handsome and Unhandsome*. See especially his introduction and lecture 3, "The Conversation of Justice."

19. Two chapters in *Structural Transformation* are important here: chapter 3, "On the Genesis of the Bourgeois Public Sphere," and chapter 7, "The Public Sphere in the World of Letters in Relation to the Public Sphere in the Political Realm." These chapters describe the historical emergence of the public sphere and the way critical discourse works in it.

20. Warner, *Letters of the Republic*, 67.

21. Schudson, "Was There Ever a Public Sphere?" 144–45.

22. Ryan, "Gender and Public Access," 264.

23. Fanuzzi, *Abolition's Public Sphere*, xv–xvi.

24. Though a little indirect, an excellent articulation of this aspect of Habermasian neoclassicism is in Fraser's "Struggle over Needs." See also Benhabib's *Critique, Norm, and Utopia*.

25. Andrew Johnson, *Speeches of Andrew Johnson*, 65.

26. See Gutmann, *Identity in Democracy*, 42–43; and Honneth, "Integrity and Disrespect," in *Fragmented World of the Social*, 255–56.

27. Kateb, *Inner Ocean*, 36–43.

28. Evans, *Introductory Dictionary of Lacanian Psychoanalysis*, 95–96.

29. Kateb, *Inner Ocean*, 40.

30. Ibid., 38.

31. Lincoln, *Collected Works of Abraham Lincoln*, 2:320–21.

32. See Habermas, *Legitimation Crisis*; and McCarthy, *Critical Theory of Jürgen Habermas*. In applying Max Weber's typology of legitimate authority to advanced capitalist societies, Habermas explains that "Max Weber's concept of legitimate authority directs our attention to the connection between belief and the legitimacy of orders and their potential for justification on the one hand, and to their factual validity on the other"(96). Habermas points to the distinction between theory and practice and argues that challenges to the democratic nature of a theoretically democratic public sphere require the custodians of that sphere either to justify deviations from the principle of democratic universality or to redefine the foundations of legitimate authority. McCarthy, for example, describes

such a redefinition of legitimacy by citing Max Weber's argument that the process of demystification, which characterized the Enlightenment, undermined faith in the truth of traditional mythological systems and transferred the legitimating ideological force of a structure of social authority from its consistency with traditional practices to its consistency with a "mechanistic world view," such that "classical natural law was transformed into modern natural law, which provided the principles for a new form of legitimation" (37).

33. Fraser, "Rethinking the Public Sphere," 134–36.

34. Martineau, *Society in America*, 60.

35. Young, *Reconsidering American Liberalism*, 35. See also Williamson, *American Suffrage*.

36. Sir William Blackstone explains the reasoning behind connecting the ownership of property to the ability to think and act independently. The "true reason of requiring any qualification with regard to property in voters," Blackstone writes, "is to exclude such persons as are in so mean a situation as to be esteemed to have no will of their own." Blackstone thus justifies property requirements by linking them to an ability to exert free will. In his view, economic independence renders the individual free from coercion by employers or creditors and allows him to form opinions and to cast votes according to the dictates of his own will (*Commentaries on the Laws*, 1:171).

37. Webster, *Journal of Debates*, 306.

38. This quotation is from the memorial that Chief Justice John Marshall presented to the Virginia State Constitutional Convention on behalf of the nonfreeholders of Richmond, Virginia, in 1829 (in *Proceedings and Debates*, 27).

39. *Reports of the Proceedings and Debates of the Convention of 1821*, 225.

40. Fraser, "Rethinking the Public Sphere," 121–28.

CHAPTER ONE
Religious Pluralism and the Origins of the Culture of Reform

1. Warner argues that as Americans developed norms for democratic public dialogue in the period after the ratification of the U.S. Constitution, political, religious, and literary discourses were not clearly separated by discourse community or aesthetic conventions. All were, implicitly, masculine, though both the literary and the religious were tending toward feminization, at least in terms of audience. Isenberg, in *Sex and Citizenship*, underscores the instability in gendered identifications for all three of these discourses as the nation negotiated definitions of publicity, gender, and culture. See Warner's *Letters of the Republic*, especially his chapter on "Nationalism and the Problem of Republican Literature," 118–50. See Isenberg's chapters on "Citizenship Understood (and Misunderstood)," 15–40, and "Conscience, Custom, and Church Politics," 75–102.

2. Jerry Wayne Brown, *Rise of Biblical Criticism*, 10–60; Conrad E. Wright's *Beginnings of*

Unitarianism in America also views the tension between theology and philosophy as a basic source of Unitarian thought. See also Ahlstrom's essay "Theology in America," which emphasizes the pluralistic history of theological debate in American communities; and Douglas, *Feminization of American Culture*, 17–43, 121–64.

3. Hatch situates this within a larger process of the "individualization of conscience" in his book *The Democratization of American Christianity*, 41–46; Appleby also describes the crossover between political and religious consciousness in *Capitalism and the New Social Order*, 81–102.

4. Habermas, *Structural Transformation*, 11.

5. Rawls, *Political Liberalism*, xxvi, 158–60.

6. Robinson, *Unitarians and the Universalists*, 25.

7. Noll, *History of Christianity*, 227.

8. Conrad E. Wright, "Institutional Reconstruction," 25.

9. In *Feminization of American Culture* Douglas makes an argument that is remarkably similar to that which Michael Warner makes regarding the novel in the early republic. In her chapter "The Loss of Theology: From Dogma to Fiction," 121–65, Douglas argues that in part the growth of religious pluralism compelled a movement toward narrative in the culture wars of Jacksonian America. Also see Moberg, *Church as a Social Institution*, chapter 5, "The Rise and Growth of Churches," 100–126, and part 4, "Social Functions and Dysfunctions of the Church," 127–240; Smith, *Revivalism and Social Reform*, 95–102; Hutchinson, *Transcendentalist Ministers*, 1–22; Wilbur, *History of Unitarianism*; Cayton, *Emerson's Emergence*, 84–109.

10. Noll refers to this period between the Second Great Awakening and the Civil War as the "Protestant Century," marked as it is by the growth of evangelism and the expansion of "outsider" religious communities (*History of Christianity*, 227); also see Hatch, *Democratization of American Christianity*, 163–208.

11. May, *Enlightenment in America*.

12. Wineapple, *Hawthorne: A Life*, 17.

13. Bentley, *Diary of William Bentley*, 3:61.

14. Describing the way the faithful in seventeenth-century New England responded to social change, Bercovitch concludes that Puritan faith was "a composite of social challenge and imaginative response. . . . Appearances meant nothing without the spirit, and since the spirit yielded a significance that was transcendent and immutable, [the minister's task] was not to invent new interpretations, but to devise strategies which would sustain the discovered meaning" (*Puritan Origins*, 124–25).

15. Thompson, *Address to the Society*, 34.

16. Chapin, "Sermon," 3.

17. Ibid., 3, 4, 19.

18. Ibid., 3.

19. Ibid., 7.

20. Conrad E. Wright gives an extensive account of the Dorchester episode as a case study in the reorganization of Massachusetts's Congregationalist churches. See his "Institutional Reconstruction in the Unitarian Controversy." See also William Allen, *Memoir of John Codman D. D.*; and an essay probably written by Jeremiah Evarts for the orthodox journal he edited, "Review of the Dorchester Controversy."

21. John Codman, "Proceedings of the Second Church and Parish in Dorchester" (Boston, 1812), 9–10.

22. In the recent article "Who Were the Evangelicals?" Cayton neatly sums up the way this issue relates to the assumptions of orthodox and liberal Christianity: "Religion for the Conservatives was based on uniformity of belief and was exclusive; Unitarianism was a pluralistic belief system premised on toleration, the maintenance of a social ethic of maximum inclusiveness and self-culture" (101).

23. Miller to Codman, 1809, quoted in William Allen, *Memoir of John Codman D. D.*, 102–3.

24. Rawls, *Law of Peoples*, 151.

25. Jackson, "Jedidiah Morse," 13. See also Schantz, "Religious Tracts."

26. See also Conrad E. Wright, *Beginnings of Unitarianism in America*, 244; Phillips, *Jedidiah Morse*, 78–99; and Moss, *Life of Jedidiah Morse*, 68–87.

27. Moss, *Life of Jedidiah Morse*, 69.

28. Morse, *Sermon Exhibiting the Present Dangers*, 13.

29. Ibid., 21, 17.

30. Ibid., 15–16.

31. Ibid., 24.

32. Ibid., 27, 119, 174–75.

33. The stakes of the propaganda debate, Handlin argues, were "between [liberal] supporters of 'a scheme' and [conservative] supporters of 'a revelation,' for a new definition of 'personal holiness.' Whoever determined this definition would control the future of the republic, for warfare waged between the party of the past and the party of the future had cosmic ramifications." In summing up her argument for Andrew Norton's role in the Unitarian controversy, Handlin unequivocally gives the upper hand to the orthodox: "The earlier clash about the definitions of personal holiness . . . aimed to extirpate orthodoxy, not modify it. Hopkinsians, Taylorites, and Beecherites, might compete for the prize of having dealt liberalism a death blow," but by the 1830s, liberalism was clearly an embattled rather than a rising spirituality ("Babylon est Delenda," 65, 76).

34. Ruttenburg, *Democratic Personality*, 85.

35. Noll, *History of Christianity*, 174–78.

36. Story, in "Harvard and the Boston Brahmins," describes the decline of interest in theological matters as Harvard College came increasingly to represent the interests

of "the wealthiest, most enterprising, most [politically] conservative families of post-Revolutionary New England" (99). As this class solidified its control over the culture of Boston, theological debates were consciously avoided.

37. Joseph Henry Allen, *Our Liberal Movement in Theology*, 116. See also Hutchinson, *Transcendentalist Ministers*.

38. Clarke, "Christian Church," 294.

39. Ibid., 296.

40. See Conrad E. Wright's chapter titled "Rationalism: 1755–1780" in *Beginnings of Unitarianism in America*, 135–60; Howe, *Unitarian Conscience*, 61–76; and Cayton, "Who Were the Evangelicals?"

41. Masur, *1831*, 81–88. Masur quotes from the *Working Man's Advocate* on p. 76. The quotation is from the edition for Nov. 5, 1831.

42. Masur, *1831*, 88.

43. Rawls, *Political Liberalism*, 9–10.

44. Levy, *Blasphemy in Massachusetts*, 293–306; see also Burkholder, "Emerson, Kneeland." Collison also provides an interesting review of the response of Harvard Divinity School to the Kneeland episode in "Harvard Divinity School Students," 222–23.

45. Levy, *Blasphemy in Massachusetts*, 293–306.

46. William Ellery Channing to Joseph Tuckerman, July 1, 1838, in W. H. Channing, *Memoir*, 3:101–8. Also quoted in Rice, *Federal Street Pastor*, 203.

47. Chapin, "Sermon," 15.

48. Ibid., 19.

49. Stuart, *Letters to the Rev. Wm. E. Channing*, 11.

50. Samuel Miller, *Letters on Unitarianism*, 30, 232, 243.

51. Buell, *Literary Transcendentalism*, 34.

52. Cayton, "Who Were the Evangelicals?" 101.

53. "Review of the Rev. Dr. Channing's Discourse," 3–13.

54. Pease and Pease, "Whose Right Hand of Fellowship?"

55. Howard Sunday School, revised constitution, as quoted in Pease and Pease, "Whose Right Hand of Fellowship?" 191.

56. West Boston Sunday School, Records of Teachers Meetings, Minutes of Oct. 16, 1837, Harvard Divinity School, quoted in Pease and Pease, "Whose Right Hand of Fellowship?" 191–92.

57. Robinson, *Unitarians and the Universalists*, 46; Stange, *Patterns of Antislavery*, especially the chapter "Antislavery as Philosophy: The Prudent Party," 74–100.

58. Douglas, *Feminization of American Culture*, 33–34. Also see Conrad E. Wright's chapter "The Minister as Reformer: Profiles on Unitarian Ministers in the Antislavery Reform," in *Liberal Christians*, 62–80; also see Wach, "Unitarian Philanthropy and Cultural Hegemony."

59. Gary L. Collison concludes that "a virtual taboo banned the subject of slavery from many Boston pulpits. It was not that Unitarians loved slavery; most abhorred it. But many loved order and stability more" ("'Harvard Divinity Students and Unitarianism," 215).

60. Stange, *Patterns of Antislavery*, 173.

61. Elizur Wright, "Slavery and Its Ecclesiastical Defenders," 341.

62. Delbanco, *William Ellery Channing*, 134.

63. Ibid., 136.

CHAPTER TWO

Sincerity and Publicity in the Grimké-Beecher Debate

1. Douglas emphasizes the parallel nature of feminine and clerical disestablishment throughout her chapter titled "Feminine Disestablishment." Using Sarah Hale of *Godey's Lady's Book* as a representative example, Douglas explains that Hale's reprinting of clerical "injunctions" on women's behavior suggests that Hale and her readers "were engaged in a struggle for identity and esteem as real and complex as the one which absorbed the liberal ministry in the same period" (*Feminization of American Culture*, 45–48).

2. Much of the best work on women's emergence as public actors has focused on reform movements. See Ginzberg, *Women and the Work of Benevolence*; Boylan, "Women in Groups" and "Timid Girls"; Hewitt, *Women's Activism and Social Change*; Freedman, *Their Sister's Keepers*; and Hobson, *Uneasy Virtue*.

3. Ginzberg, *Women and the Work of Benevolence*, 18; see the conclusion of Cott, *Bonds of Womanhood*, 197–206; Berg, *Remembered Gate*; Ryan, "Femininity and Capitalism."

4. Browne offers a rich and thorough analysis of the speech Grimké gave at Pennsylvania Hall on May 16, 1838; see *Angelina Grimké*, 139–66. See also Lerner, *Grimké Sisters of South Carolina*, 243–51. Mayer has a vivid description of the riot at Pennsylvania Hall in his biography of Garrison, *All on Fire*, 244–47.

5. Lerner, *Grimké Sisters of South Carolina*, 98.

6. Ibid., 97–100; Lumpkin, *Emancipation of Angelina Grimké*, 62–66; Hedrick, *Harriet Beecher Stowe*, 64–66; Sklar, *Catharine Beecher*, 98–100.

7. Sklar reads Beecher's response to Sedgwick's Unitarianism and subsequent criticism of Calvinism as a form of class-based betrayal, noting that Beecher's "horror was fully aroused by Catharine Sedgwick's betrayal of her social leadership and religious heritage" (*Catharine Beecher*, 45). This incident also reveals Beecher's early sense of the broad cultural authority of women's voices. She complained to her brother: "I believe she has done more injury to the cause of truth, than Dr. [Henry] Ware or Professor [Andrews] Norton," who, with Channing, led the Unitarian critique of orthodoxy. In ranking Sedgwick's novel with the works of the most prominent Unitarian ministers of the day, Beecher

projected an extraordinary level of influence onto Sedgwick's voice (Catharine Beecher to Edward Beecher, Oct. 22, 1822, Beecher-Stowe Collection, Beinecke Library, Yale University). However, Beecher also recognized Sedgwick's cultural capital and shared interest in a form of femininity that combined domesticity with public authority. In 1852 Beecher invited Sedgwick along with Lydia Sigourney and Sarah Josepha Hale to serve on the board of the American Woman's Education Association (Sklar, *Catharine Beecher*, 45–48).

8. Sklar, *Catharine Beecher*, 28–50; Hedrick, *Harriet Beecher Stowe*, 32–40, 89.

9. Beecher's work at the Hartford Female Seminary is a key starting point for theoretical approaches to women's role in American society. Sklar concludes her chapter on Beecher's early career with a sentence noting that Beecher "began to teach a course in moral philosophy" (*Catharine Beecher*, 77). Sklar implies that the introduction of this course masks a turning point between Beecher's development of a career and her development of a theory of women's citizenship. In the opening essay of a volume on American women reformers, Berkeley refers to the Hartford School as "Beecher's educational laboratory" in which she refined and developed the foundational assumptions of her career ("Catharine Beecher and Domestic Relations," 7).

10. Lerner treats this transition as one of the key formative periods in Grimké's life; see *Grimké Sisters of South Carolina*, 68–91. See also Lumpkin, *Emancipation of Angelina Grimké*, 11–26.

11. The article that provoked Grimké's letter was written by Garrison in response to heightening violence against antislavery activists. It appeared as "Appeal to Our Fellow Citizens" (*Lib.*, Aug. 22, 1835).

12. This point in Grimké's movement toward activism has been represented in various ways. Lerner emphasizes Garrison's recognition of the potential importance of the text, noting that "he dared not suppress it," and stresses Grimké's recognition that the letter might find its way into print (*Grimké Sisters of South Carolina*, 123–25). Lumpkin emphasizes the role this letter played in disrupting Angelina's relationship with the Friends and in driving her into a crucible-like social exile (*Emancipation of Angelina Grimké*, 83–85). Along with Lerner, Browne assumes that the letter was essentially a public document, referring to it as "Grimké's abolitionist debut" that "creates for the author an identity of sufficient strength to allow her to enter and help determine the course of public life" (*Angelina Grimké*, 41–42). Henry emphasizes the intersection of private and public discourses: "Garrison clearly saw an advantage to identifying the author of the letter as the daughter of a prominent slave-holding family. . . . [He] draws on a publicity of exposure whose source and ground is ostensibly personal" ("Angelina Grimké's Rhetoric of Exposure," 343). Wiegman also articulates the disciplinary nature of visibility for the feminine; see *American Anatomies*, 36–41.

13. Angelina Grimké, letter to Jane Smith, Mar. 22, 1837, quoted in Lumpkin, *Emancipation of Angelina Grimké*, 102.

14. Antislavery appeals that set precedents and created preliminary tradition for Grimké's *Appeal to the Christian Women of the South* include Elizabeth Heyrick's *Immediate, Not Gradual Emancipation* (1826); David Walker's *Appeal in Four Articles* (1829); and Lydia Maria Child's *Appeal on Behalf of That Class of American Called Africans* (1833).

15. Browne, *Angelina Grimké*, 62.

16. Lerner, *Grimké Sisters of South Carolina*, 141.

17. This paradoxical deployment of transgression to confirm rhetorical sincerity is at the center of Henry's analysis of Grimké's method of asserting sincerity. Henry specifically addresses the implications of the example of Esther in "Angelina Grimké's Rhetoric of Exposure," 340–41.

18. Browne, *Angelina Grimké*, 62–63.

19. As debates between Habermas and Nancy Fraser, among others, indicate, this discussion continues in ways that underscore the equality-making value of the right to self-representation. One recent critic sums up this argument by emphasizing the historical positionalities that shape people's access to the public sphere: "The largest gap in Habermas work is his failure to consider the generalized character of roles of worker and citizen" that emerged along with industrialization. "Feminist historians have documented the parallel construction of the roles of housewife and mother and the restriction of women to these roles" as a response to the growth of critical public discourse as a mode of legitimization for civil authority (Arato and Cohen, *Civil Society and Political Theory*, 543). See also Fraser, "What's Critical about Critical Theory," 21–56; and *Unruly Practices*, 161–82.

20. Fraser, *Unruly Practices*, 166.

21. Angelina Grimké to Sarah Grimké, July 19, 1836, quoted in Browne, *Angelina Grimké*, 61.

22. Grimké wrote at a time when assumptions about women's education and intellectual equality were especially unstable. Beecher's ability to gain prominence as an education reformer derived from the same instability that underpinned Grimké's plan for the reformation of women's political consciousness. See Preston, "Domestic Ideology"; Kelley, "Vindicating the Equality"; and Zschoche, "Dr. Clark Revisited."

23. Wiegman offers an analysis of *Uncle Tom's Cabin* that contrasts usefully with Grimké's strategy. Wiegman argues that Stowe works to simultaneously humanize and neutralize blackness by linking blackness to femininity; see *American Anatomies*, 193–99.

24. In a letter to Angelina in 1838, George Bancroft focuses on this issue as he criticizes her method in the *Appeal*: "Will Angelina Grimké place the question of the divinity of slavery at issue on the interpretation of a Hebrew word? . . . If you put your faith at the

mercy of Hebrew scholars, you will so far stray from the blessed regions of that kingdom which is within. Respect conscience and not professors" (*WGL* 1:525–26).

25. See Steele, "Limits of Political Sympathy," 115–38.

26. Davidson, *Revolution and the Word*, especially chapters 3 and 4. See also Clinton, *Plantation Mistress*, 173–74.

27. Isenberg, *Sex and Citizenship*, 77.

28. Quoted in Browne, *Angelina Grimké*, 61.

29. Ibid., 69.

30. Ibid., 73.

31. See Elshtain, "Moral Man and Immoral Woman," 453–73; and Sen, "Equality of What?" 195–220.

32. Adams's letter is reprinted in several anthologies; see, for example, Moynihan, Russert, and Crumpacker, *Second to None*, 1:251–52.

33. Sarah M. Grimké, *Letters on Equality*, 10.

34. Wiegman, *American Anatomies*, especially the chapter "Sexing the Difference," 43–80.

35. Ryan, *Women in Public*, 8.

36. In *Feminization of American Culture*, Douglas makes what has become the paradigmatic case for the complicity of antebellum domesticity in the construction of Jacksonian individualism (244–56). This position was rebutted by Tompkins, who argues in *Sensational Designs* that domesticity represents an oppositional counterdiscourse of moral sympathy. Baym analyzes the debate between these two models for understanding domestic discourse in the introduction to the second edition of her book *Women's Fiction*. Gillian Brown does much to break down the opposition between domestic femininity and masculine individualism in her book *Domestic Individualism*.

37. Ruttenburg, *Democratic Personality*, 17.

38. Gillian Brown extends this structuralist mode of Beecher's imagination to include her careful integration of domestic labor and the ideological integration of domesticity and possessive individualism; see *Domestic Individualism*, 18–34. See also Boydston, Kelley, and Margolis, *Limits of Sisterhood*, 142–47.

39. Boydston, Kelley, and Margolis, *Limits of Sisterhood*, 19, 121; Sklar, *Catharine Beecher*, 93–94.

40. Sklar emphasizes the role of common-sense philosophy in this aspect of American liberal thought. Yet rather than emphasizing the shared public rationalism that leads to social harmony, Beecher adapted it to the terms of antebellum feminine authority. Sklar writes that Beecher "saw the weak spot in the system whereby women could assert their own claim" to leadership by emphasizing "submission of the self to the general good . . . into signs of moral superiority and leadership" (*Catharine Beecher*, 82–83).

41. Ibid., 174, 203.

42. Ibid., 114.

43. For Beecher's opposition to suffrage, see Sklar, *Catharine Beecher*, 266–67; and Boydston, Kelley, and Margolis, *Limits of Sisterhood*, 250–57.

44. Boydston, Kelley, and Margolis, *Limits of Sisterhood*, 117.

45. Tocqueville, *Democracy in America*, 11.

46. Matthews deftly contrasts the ideological apparatus of Beecher's *Treatise* with Lydia Maria Child's *American Frugal Housewife*, published twelve years earlier. Whereas Child "had given common-sense advice in a matter-of-fact tone with only a modicum of philosophizing," Beecher deployed Tocqueville "as the starting point for her own program for American women, a program that was both domestic and political from the first page" (*Just a Housewife*, 47–48).

47. Tocqueville, *Democracy in America*, 9.

48. Ibid., 603.

49. Ibid., 531.

50. Ibid., 591–93.

CHAPTER THREE

Garrison, Douglass, and the Problem of Politics

1. See Kirkland, "Enslavement, Moral Suasion, and Struggles," especially 279–99. Contemporary theories of recognition have roots in early liberalism. Kant and later Hegel both analyzed problems of intersubjective recognition with regard to master-slave relationships. This analysis has been the foundation for contemporary theories of recognition, which follow two lines of thought; one integrates recognition into post linguistic turn philosophy and asks questions about the dialogic nature of selfhood; the other integrates recognition into ethnicity-multiculturalism studies and asks questions about intersubjective relationships across ideological chasms. See Westphal, *Hegel, Freedom and Modernity*, 82–85 on recognition, and also chapter 3, "Hegel's Radical Idealism: Family and State as Ethical Communities," 37–54. For recognition in poststructuralist philosophy, see Honneth, *Fragmented World of the Social*. Two chapters in this book are influential in the argument I make about Douglass's move from moral suasion into the political structure: chapter nine, "The Struggle for Recognition: On Sartre's Theory of Intersubjectivity," 158–67; and chapter 15, "Integrity and Disrespect: Principles of a Conception of Morality Based on a Theory of Recognition," 247–60. Taylor analyzes recognition in a pluralist society in "Politics of Recognition," 25–74. Stewart applies this theory to Douglass in "Claims of Frederick Douglass," 145–72.

2. Levine's theory of Douglass as a "temperate revolutionary" fighting against processes of "imbrutification" is important as a counterargument to this moment in Douglass's biography. For my purpose, Levine's argument is most relevant as a demonstration of

Douglass's effort to position himself within rational critical discourse. As a voice of "temperance," Douglass emphasized self-control and even socialization according to public norms. See Levine's *Martin Delany, Frederick Douglass*, 126–33.

3. *Lib.* Jan. 8, 1831; Jan. 12, 1838; and June 11, 1847. See also Goodman, *Of One Blood*, 43; Mayer, *All on Fire*, 433–34; and Pole, *Pursuit of Equality*, chapter 6, "Equal Rights, Unequal Conditions, and the Emergence of Equality of Opportunity," 132–73.

4. Lowell, *Complete Poetical Works*, 102–3.

5. Analysis of the simultaneously communal and individualistic aspects of Garrisonian reform is fairly common in histories of abolitionism. Friedman expresses it succinctly as he sums up the culture of the Boston Clique: "Although Clique insurgents had longed for a stable and perfect balance between harmonious collective efficiency and unrestrained pious individuality, they never secured it except as a vague ideological construct. . . . The persistent tension between cooperative collectivity and free individuality was actually the Clique's most fundamental strength, despite the desires of its members to reconcile the two permanently somehow" (*Gregarious Saint*, 67). Perry addresses this tension in chapter 7 of *Radical Abolitionism*, "Law and Love: The Problem of Authority," 188–230. In *Of One Blood*, Goodman credits Garrison's involvement in the free black community for much of the egalitarian communalism of his ethics. See Goodman's chapter titled "The Conversion of William Lloyd Garrison," 36–44.

6. Mintz, *Moralists and Modernizers*. Mintz emphasizes the Christian origins of reform and describes the breadth of the movement, focusing especially on the agendas of voluntary associations.

7. This conclusion is where I differ most from Fanuzzi's analysis of Garrisonian culture. Fanuzzi emphasizes, to the literal exclusion of Garrison's spirituality, the radicals' effort to create a public sphere similar in its openness to that which preceded the Revolution. Fanuzzi emphasizes important links between Garrison and Thomas Paine, and Garrison certainly believed that the right kind of publicity would galvanize the nation against slavery. In my view, though, Garrison was not motivated by anything truly grounded in secular civil society. On the contrary, he sought to live a perfectly Christian life, and it is that desire that drove his participation in reform. See Fanuzzi's *Abolition's Public Sphere*, especially chapter 1, "The Sedition of Nonresistance," and chapter 2, "Garrisonism and the Public Sphere."

8. See Mayer's chapter "A New Race of Editors" in *All on Fire*, 33–44; see also Merrill, *Against Wind and Tide*, 13–25.

9. Davis contextualizes immediatist antislavery in "The Emergence of Immediatism," 209–30. Mayer situates this transition for Garrison in the 1829–30 period, especially when he was working with Benjamin Lundy in Baltimore. See Mayer, *All on Fire*, 70–75.

10. Bercovitch, *American Jeremiad*, 62.

11. Crane, *Race, Citizenship, and Law*, 28.

12. Perry, *Radical Abolitionism*, 58.

13. Leo Tolstoi, "What I Owe to Garrison," 49. See also Perry's chapter "Tolstoy's Discovery" in *Radical Abolitionism* on the importance of nonresistance as a foundational principle in the human rights philosophy of Garrison and the radical abolitionists.

14. Tolstoi, "What I Owe to Garrison," 48.

15. Leverenz, *Manhood and the American Renaissance*, 18–20; Rotundo, "Learning about Manhood," 35–51; Dixon "True Manly Life," 213–36.

16. Disunion became important in Garrison's thought in 1842 but became urgent with the annexation of Texas and the Fugitive Slave Act. Garrison began advocating women's rights in 1832. See Mayer, *All on Fire*, 313–16, 339–43. Von Frank's chapter on Garrison and the Fourth of July in 1854 describes the catalyzing of disunion sentiment as proslavery forces gained power over policy and wealth even in New England; see *Trials of Anthony Burns*, 276–85.

17. Mayer, *All on Fire*, 250–62; Thomas, *Liberator, William Lloyd Garrison*, 258–63; Merrill, *Against Wind and Tide*, 177.

18. Thoreau, "Resistance to Civil Government," in *Reform Papers*, 75. See also Linck C. Johnson, "Emerson, Thoreau's Arrest," 35–66.

19. Fanuzzi, "Organ of an Individual"; Friedman, *Gregarious Saints*.

20. Lowell, *Letters*, 1:125.

21. *National Anti-Slavery Standard*, Oct. 25, 1856. See also James B. Stewart. "Aims of Garrisonian Abolitionism," 197– 209.

22. See Amy Gutmann's chapter "The Values of Voluntary Groups" in *Identity in Democracy*, 86–116.

23. Ericson, *Debate over Slavery*.

24. Martin does not situate this in a kind of continuum, but clearly distinguishes between Garrison's Christian perfectionism and Douglass's liberal humanism: "Frederick Douglass's view of the self-made man drew upon the religious, economic, and combined personal and social aspects of self-improvement and success in America. He stressed, in order of relative importance: First, the personal and social aspect; second; the economic; and third, the religious. Reflecting his belief in human will and action as against divine providence and religious faith as the primary agent of social change, his interpretation of the self-made man was intensely secular" (*Mind of Frederick Douglass*, 255).

25. Rawls, *Political Liberalism*, 218.

26. *New York Herald*, May 12, 1848.

27. In his analysis of Douglass's liberal humanism, Martin describes the complex tension between Douglass's desire to think in terms of universal human rights and his equally deeply grounded impulse to understand equality in pluralistic rather than

hegemonic terms. See Martin's chapter "Humanism, Race, and Leadership" in *Mind of Frederick Douglass*, 92–108.

28. Fishkin and Peterson analyze Douglass's response to proslavery rhetoric in "'We Hold These Truths to be Self-Evident,'" 193–95.

29. Luria, "Racial Equality Begins at Home," 25–43.

30. Fanuzzi, *Abolition's Public Sphere*, 61–64.

31. By reconstructing African American cultural life as a model for self-recognition as the aesthetic and cultural equals of their white oppressors, Gates articulates a struggle for recognition in the realm of culture and the arts that parallels the struggle Douglass sought to initiate in the more explicitly political realm. In a way, my argument replicates Gates's in the realm of critical discourse. Just as Gates argues that African Americans defined themselves as equals through participation in artistic and literary dialogues, I think that Douglass defined ex-slaves as equals of their former masters through participation in reform dialogue. Of course, in the case of the slave narrative, artistic self-representation and political self-presentation coincide. Stepto's presentation of Douglass's writings as a form of "authorization" is also closely related to my effort to define Douglass's claims to legitimacy as a presence in a public sphere that he is fundamentally important in redefining. See Gates, *Figures in Black*, 10–21; and Stepto, *From Behind the Veil*, 18–25. Sundquist develops this line of thought in relation to Douglass's quest for fatherly recognition, which perhaps can be understood as a form of seeking integration that allows both familial homogeneity and generational heterogeneity. His story, Sundquist argues, is a mode of self-representation that offered "a self-authoring authority that was in its own right a signal of patrimony and freedom" (*To Wake the Nations*, 100). Gates, Stepto, and Sundquist all describe Douglass's motivations partly in terms of quests for recognition. See Sundquist, *To Wake the Nations*, 83–93.

32. Hoganson, "Garrisonian Abolitionists," 558–95. See also Sanchez-Eppler, *Touching Liberty*, 133–42. Sanchez-Eppler's reading of Douglass's tears are especially revealing of the relation of his testimonial voice to modes of discourse associated with femininity. Unlike white female authors whose "liberating tears prove her whiteness and link her to her wet-eyed readers," Douglass's tears mark not the "emancipatory effect" of his prose but the instantiation of a specific subject-object relationship to publicity. My argument for the change Douglass makes is tied to his effort to construct a critical voice that gets away from the feminized implications of the "confessional or testimonial genre" (Ibid., 135–36). Sundquist also discusses this intersection. Along the razor's edge between slavery's totalizing elision of the self and democracy's plenitude of self, Sundquist argues, "lay the key to Douglass's literary formulation of African American identity, as the discourse of political democracy and the discourse of sentimental domesticity were likewise pried open to include slave culture and black America" (*To Wake the Nations*, 101).

33. See Wiegman's chapter on "Visual Modernity" and 71–76 in *American Anatomies*.

34. Wardrop, "'While I Am Writing,'" 649–60.

35. See Martin, *Mind of Frederick Douglass*, 56.

36. Douglass's recognition of ideological multiplicity resembles that which Bakhtin attributes to an ignorant peasant who discovers himself in a discursively complex world. Bakhtin writes: "As soon as a critical interanimation of languages began to occur in the consciousness of our peasant, as soon as it became clear that these were not only various different languages, but even internally variegated languages, that the ideological approaches to the world that were indissolubly connected with these languages contradicted each other and in no way could live in peace and harmony with one another—then the inviolability and predetermined quality of these languages came to an end, and the necessity of actively choosing one's orientation among them began" ("Discourse in the Novel," in *Dialogic Imagination*, 296).

37. Wiegman, *American Anatomies*, 70.

38. Dorsey, "Becoming the Other," 435–50.

39. See Giles, "Narrative Reversals," 779–810; Levine, *Martin Delany, Frederick Douglass*, 20–32. Giles and Levine have recently offered important reconsiderations of Douglass's motive for breaking away from the Garrisonians and founding a competing newspaper, the *North Star*. Both of these analyses underscore the way this episode in Douglass's career represents an effort to redefine his relationship to the public sphere: Giles by arguing that his two-year lecture and fundraising tour in Britain shows Douglass adopting a "transnational" perspective; Levine by emphasizing the competing models of African American advancement that Douglass and Delany constructed between 1847 and 1849.

40. Foner, *LWFD*, 1:93. Foner quotes from *Howard University Review 1*. See also Jasinski, "Rearticulating History," 71–89.

41. Sundquist, *To Wake the Nations*, 104.

42. Selby has dealt with this most recently; see "Limits of Accommodation," 52–66.

43. Sundquist, *To Wake the Nations*, 110–12.

44. Ibid., 83–93.

45. McFeely, *Frederick Douglass*, 150–62.

46. Levine, *Martin Delany, Frederick Douglass*, 19–22.

47. Ibid., 31–32.

48. Ibid., 27–32.

49. Levine comes to a similar conclusion, trying to head off simple Douglass/assimilation, Delany/separatism interpretations: "We need to resist a binary interpretation of the eventual split between Delany and Douglass as that between the militant black separatist and the 'color-blind' assimilationist. An increasing conflict over claims to

representative leadership, rather than any stark ideological differences, may have been the principal reason for the consequential parting of the ways of the *North Star*'s coeditors" (Ibid., 22).

50. Wiegman, *American Anatomies*, 67. See also Sundquist, *To Wake the Nations*, 97–100.

51. McKivigan, "Frederick Douglass–Gerrit Smith Friendship," 212–13.

52. Mills, "Whose Fourth of July?" 109–16. See also Wiecek, *Sources of Antislavery Constitutionalism*, 75–76.

53. McFeely, *Frederick Douglass*, 176; and Mayer, *All on Fire*, 428–30.

CHAPTER FOUR
Emerson's Self-Reliance as a Theory of Community

1. Zwarg, *Feminist Conversations*; see chapter 1, "Falling without Speed: The Feminist Frame of Emerson's Letters to Fuller," 32–58.

2. In the mid-1830s the passage of the gag rule in the House of Representatives was only a symptom of a trend toward the censorship of antislavery speech. As Strong explains, churches also began to restrict speech by implementing gag rules at church meetings and at meetings of the benevolent associations they sponsored; see *Perfectionist Politics*, 49–51.

3. Zwarg, *Feminist Conversations*, 51.

4. Ibid., 55.

5. Emerson, "Editors to the Reader," 2–3.

6. Cavell, *Philosophical Passages*, especially "Emerson's Constitutional Amending: Reading 'Fate,'" 12–41.

7. Rowe, *At Emerson's Tomb*, 22.

8. Ibid., 22.

9. In his study of literature and constitutional thought, Crane also treats this impulse of Emerson's as the weaker of several responses. Crane emphasizes a form of "cosmopolitanism" that he associates with both Emerson and Douglass. Quoting "The Poet," he imagines Emerson imagining a creative jurist who, like the poet, has "a great imaginative soul, a broad cosmopolitan mind" (*Race, Citizenship, and Law*, 103).

10. In *The Emerson Effect*, Newfield develops this submissive or passive dimension of Emersonian thought into a broad theory of Emerson's cultural influence. In contrast to transcendentalist ideals of the creative power of the individual, Newfield reasserts a type of Puritan origin theory that stresses submission to overwhelming supernatural-like powers. For my purpose, what is important about this passive or submissive strain is that it is in dialectical tension with the Emersonian will to power and is related to listening or attentiveness to context. For a fundamentally different reading, one that emphasizes listening as a mode of defining autonomy rather than provoking submission,

see Esquith, *Intimacy and Spectacle,* especially the section titled "Power's Laws" in the chapter titled "Emerson Reconsidered," 250–61.

11. Buell, *Literary Transcendentalism,* 106–7.

12. Van Cromphout offers an intensive study of the self-community problem in Emerson's early writings in his chapter "Others" in *Emerson's Ethics,* 90–114. This chapter is a kind of counterpart to Kateb's chapter titled "Friendship and Love" in *Emerson and Self-Reliance.*

13. Poirier, *Poetry and Pragmatism,* 67–68.

14. Levin begins his book, *The Poetics of Transition,* by citing this passage from "Self-Reliance" to frame his extended analysis of "transition" as a structuring metaphor in American culture (22).

15. In this regard Cavell sees Emerson in somewhat Kantian terms by viewing his thought as "a kind of conversation with itself" (*Conditions Handsome and Unhandsome,* 8). Much of Cavell's commentary on Emerson concentrates on defining Emerson's effort to individuate the self from institutional structures that threaten to undermine autonomy. Kateb also develops this line of criticism but is less interested in Emerson as a critic of his society than in Emerson as a theorist of liberal identity; see Kateb, *Emerson and Self-Reliance.*

16. Derrida, "Structure, Sign, and Play in the Discourse of the Human Sciences," in *Writing and Difference,* 278–94.

17. Richardson, *Emerson,* 258; von Frank, *Emerson Chronology,* 120, 133.

18. Bercovitch, *Rites of Assent,* 320–21.

19. Ibid., 342–43.

20. Emersonian moral perfectionism, while not actually anticipating utopia, is oriented toward constant moral reinvention in both individual and social terms. Cavell's theory is especially useful for my purpose of emphasizing the conversational nature of Emersonian self-reliance because it works through an ongoing critical dialogue between self and society. While his interpretation is much more historically rooted, Bercovitch sees Emerson's "utopian consciousness" epitomizing the combination of critical antagonism and utopian idealism that characterized reform culture in the decades leading up to the Civil War. Bercovitch writes: "Emersonian individualism . . . is a form of utopian consciousness developed within the premises of liberal culture. It carries with it the profoundly unsettling energies released by that culture in its formative phase—well designated 'the era of boundlessness'" (*Rites of Assent,* 345).

21. Gougeon, *Virtue's Hero,* 60–67; and von Frank, *Trials of Anthony Burns,* 94–97.

22. Buell, *Emerson,* 255.

23. Linck C. Johnson, "Reforming the Reformers."

24. Cavell, *Philosophical Passages,* 21.

25. Poirier, *Poetry and Pragmatism*, 39.

26. Gougeon, *Virtue's Hero*, 37–38.

27. Crane, *Race, Citizenship, and Law*, 96–99; and von Frank, *Trials of Anthony Burns*, 145–49.

28. Cavell, *Philosophical Passages*, 15–17.

29. See also Cadava's chapter "The Rhetoric of Slavery and War" in his book *Emerson and the Climates of History*, 148–201.

30. Gougeon, *Virtue's Hero*, 37–38; *AW*, xv, xxxvii; and Richardson, *Emerson*, 268–69.

31. See Cadava, *Emerson and the Climates of History*, 145–50.

32. Perry Miller, *Nature's Nation*, 168.

33. Cavell, *Conditions Handsome and Unhandsome*, 26.

34. Buell pushes Emerson's treatment of disunion back to the 1844 "New England Reformers" address at Amory Hall and attributes Emerson's use of this theme directly to Garrison. Buell writes: "Garrisonianism was probably the source of Emerson's and Thoreau's frequent pronouncements, starting with the 1 August address, that the union was effectively dead because of its corruption by pro-slavery interests" (*Emerson*, 255).

35. Gougeon, *Virtue's Hero*, 169–70.

36. Quoted in Gougeon, *Virtue's Hero*, 198. Gougeon cites Furness, ed., *Records of a Lifelong Friendship*, 92–93.

37. Rowe, *At Emerson's Tomb*, 22–25, 40–41; Kateb, *Emerson and Self-Reliance*, 175.

38. Van Cromphout, *Emerson's Ethics*, 91.

BIBLIOGRAPHY

Ahlstrom, Sydney E. "Theology in America: A Historical Survey." In *The Shaping of American Religion*, edited by Leland A. Jamison and James Ward Smith, 232–321. Princeton, N.J.: Princeton University Press, 1961.

Allen, Joseph Henry. *Our Liberal Movement in Theology*. 1882. Reprint, New York: Arno Press, 1972.

Allen, William. *Memoir of John Codman D. D.* Boston, 1853.

Appleby, Joyce. *Capitalism and the New Social Order: The Republican Vision of the 1790s*. New York: New York University Press, 1984.

Arato, Andrew, and Jean L. Cohen. *Civil Society and Political Theory*. Cambridge, Mass.: MIT Press, 1994.

Bakhtin, Mikhail M. *The Dialogic Imagination: Four Essays by M. M. Bakhtin*. Edited by Michael Holquist. Translated by Caryl Emerson. Austin: University of Texas Press, 1981.

Bancroft, George. "The Office of the People in Art, Government and Religion, 1835." In *Literary and Historical Miscellanies*. New York: Harper & Brothers, 1855.

Barry, Brian. *Culture and Equality: An Egalitarian Critique of Multiculturalism*. Cambridge, Mass.: Harvard University Press, 2001.

Baym, Nina. *Woman's Fiction: A Guide to Novels by and about Women in America, 1820–1870*. 2nd ed. Urbana: University of Illinois Press, 1993.

Beecher, Catharine E. *An Essay on Slavery and Abolitionism with Reference to the Duty of American Females*. Philadelphia: Henry Perkins, 1837.

———. *An Essay on the Education of Female Teachers*. New York: Van Nostrand & Dwight, 1835.

Beecher, Lyman. *Autobiography of Lyman Beecher*. Edited by Barbara Cross. 2 vols. Cambridge, Mass.: Harvard University Press, 1961.

———. *The Works of Lyman Beecher*. 3 vols. Boston: John P. Jewett, 1852–53.

Benhabib, Seyla. *Critique, Norm, and Utopia: A Study for the Foundation of Critical Theory*. New York: Columbia University Press, 1986.

———. "Toward a Deliberative Model of Democratic Legitimacy." In *Democracy and Difference: Contesting the Boundaries of the Political*, edited by Seyla Benhabib, 67–95. Princeton, N.J.: Princeton University Press, 1996.

Bentley, William. *Diary of William Bentley, D. D., Pastor of the East Church Salem, Massachusetts*. 1914. 4 vols. Gloucester, Mass: Peter Smith, 1962.

Bercovitch, Sacvan. *The American Jeremiad*. Madison: University of Wisconsin Press, 1978.

———. *The Puritan Origins of the American Self*. New Haven, Conn.: Yale University Press, 1975.

————. *The Rites of Assent: Transformations in the Symbolic Construction of America*. New York: Routledge, 1993.

Berg, Barbara J. *The Remembered Gate: Origins of American Feminism: The Woman and the City, 1800–1860*. New York: Oxford University Press, 1978.

Berkeley, Kathleen C. "Catharine Beecher and Domestic Relations." In *Against the Tide: Women Reformers and Domestic Relations*, edited by P. A. Cimbala and R. M. Miller, 1–18. London: Praeger, 1997.

Blackstone, Sir William. *Commentaries on the Laws of England*. 4 vols. Philadelphia: Robert Bell, 1771–73.

Bohman, James. *Public Deliberation, Pluralism, Complexity and Democracy*. Cambridge, Mass.: MIT Press, 1996.

Boydston, Jeanne, Mary Kelley, and Anne Margolis. *The Limits of Sisterhood: The Beecher Sisters on Women's Rights and Women's Sphere*. Chapel Hill: University of North Carolina Press, 1988.

Boylan, Anne M. "Timid Girls, Venerable Widows and Dignified Matrons: Life Cycle Patterns among Organized Women in New York and Boston, 1797–1840." *American Quarterly* 38 (1986): 779–97.

————. "Women in Groups: An Analysis of Women's Benevolent Organizations in New York and Boston, 1797–1840." *Journal of American History* 71 (1984): 497–523.

Brown, Gillian. *Domestic Individualism: Imagining Self in Nineteenth-Century America*. Berkeley: University of California Press, 1990.

Brown, Jerry Wayne. *The Rise of Biblical Criticism in America, 1800–1870: The New England Scholars*. Middleton, Conn.: Wesleyan University Press, 1969.

Browne, Stephen Howard. *Angelina Grimké: Rhetoric, Identity, and the Radical Imagination*. East Lansing: Michigan State University Press, 1999.

Buell, Lawrence. *Emerson*. Cambridge, Mass.: Harvard University Press, 2003.

————. *Literary Transcendentalism: Style and Vision in the American Renaissance*. Ithaca, N.Y.: Cornell University Press, 1973.

Burkholder, Robert E. "Emerson, Kneeland, and the Divinity School Address." *American Literature* 58 (1986): 1–14.

Cadava, Eduardo. *Emerson and the Climates of History*. Stanford, Calif.: Stanford University Press, 1997.

Cavell, Stanley. *Conditions Handsome and Unhandsome: The Constitution of Emersonian Perfectionism*. Chicago: University of Chicago Press, 1988.

————. *Philosophical Passages: Wittgenstein, Emerson, Austin, Derrida*. Cambridge: Blackwell, 1995.

Cayton, Mary Kupiec. *Emerson's Emergence: Self and Society in the Transformation of New England, 1800–1845*. Chapel Hill: University of North Carolina Press, 1989.

————. "Toward a Democratic Politics of Meaning Making: The Transcendentalist

Controversy and the Rise of Pluralist Discourse in Jacksonian Boston." *Prospects* 25 (2000): 35–68.

———. "Who Were the Evangelicals? Conservative and Liberal Identity in the Unitarian Controversy in Boston, 1804–1833." *Journal of Social History* (Fall 1997): 85–107.

Channing, William Ellery. *Memoir of William Ellery Channing, with Extracts from His Correspondence and Manuscripts.* Edited by William Henry Channing. 3 vols. Boston: W. Crosby & H. P. Nichols, 1848.

———. *The Works of William Ellery Channing, D.D.* 6 vols. Boston: James Monroe, 1843.

Chapin, Horace B. "A Sermon, Delivered before the Congregational Church and Society in Hempster N.H." Concord, N.H.: Henry E. Moore, 1828.

Child, Lydia Maria. *Appeal in Favor of That Class of American Called Africans.* Boston: Allen & Ticknor, 1833.

Clarke, James Freeman. "The Christian Church." In *An American Reformation: A Documentary History of Unitarian Christianity*, edited by Sydney E. Ahlstrom and Jonathan S. Carey. Middletown, Conn.: Wesleyan University Press, 1985.

Clinton, Catharine. *The Plantation Mistress: Women's World in the Old South.* New York: Pantheon Books, 1982.

Collison, Gary L. "Harvard Divinity School Students and Unitarianism." In *American Unitarianism: 1805–1865*, edited by Conrad E. Wright, 209–240. Boston: Massachusetts Historical Society and Northeastern University Press, 1989.

Cott, Nancy. *The Bonds of Womanhood: "Woman's Sphere" in New England, 1780–1835.* 2nd ed. New Haven, Conn.: Yale University Press, 1997.

Crane, Gregg D. *Race, Citizenship, and Law in American Literature.* New York: Cambridge University Press, 2002.

Davidson, Cathy N. *Revolution and the Word: The Rise of the Novel in America.* New York: Oxford University Press, 1986.

Davis, David Brion. "The Emergence of Immediatism in British and American Anti-slavery Thought." *Mississippi Valley Historical Review* 49 (1962): 209–30.

Delbanco, Andrew. *William Ellery Channing: An Essay on the Liberal Spirit in America.* Cambridge, Mass.: Harvard University Press, 1981.

Derrida, Jacques. *Writing and Difference.* Translated by Alan Bass. Chicago: University of Chicago Press, 1978.

Dixon, Christopher. "A True Manly Life: Abolitionism and the Masculine Ideal." *Mid-America* 77 (1995): 213–36.

Dorsey, Peter A. "Becoming the Other: The Mimesis of Metaphor in Douglass's *My Bondage and My Freedom*." *PMLA* 111, no. 3 (1996): 435–50.

Douglas, Ann. *The Feminization of American Culture.* New York: Alfred A. Knopf, 1977.

Douglass, Frederick. *The Frederick Douglass Papers.* Edited by John Blassingame and John R. McGivigan. 6 vols. New Haven, Conn.: Yale University Press, 1979–92.

————. *The Life and Writings of Frederick Douglass.* Edited by Philip S. Foner. 5 vols. New York: International Publishers, 1950–75.

————. *My Bondage and My Freedom.* 1855. Edited by William L. Andrews. Urbana: University of Illinois Press, 1987.

————. *Narrative of the Life of Frederick Douglass, An American Slave.* 1845. Reprint, Boston: Bedford Books, 1993.

Dryzek, John. *Discursive Democracy.* Cambridge: Cambridge University Press, 1990.

Dux, Gunter. "Communicative Reason and Interest: On the Reconstruction of the Normative Order in Societies Structured by Egalitarianism or Domination." In *Communicative Action: Essays on Jürgen Habermas's Theory of Communicative Action,* edited by Axel Honneth and Hans Joas, 74–96. Cambridge, Mass.: MIT Press, 1991.

Elshtaine, Jean Bethke. "Moral Man and Immoral Woman: A Consideration of the Public-Private Split and Its Political Ramifications." *Politics and Society* 4 (1974): 453–73.

Emerson, Ralph Waldo. *Collected Works of Ralph Waldo Emerson.* Edited by Alfred R. Ferguson, Jean Ferguson Carr, et al. 6 vols. to date. Cambridge, Mass.: Harvard University Press, 1971–.

————. *The Complete Works of Ralph Waldo Emerson.* Edited by E. W. Emerson. Centenary edition. 12 vols. Boston: Houghton Mifflin, 1903–4.

————. "The Editors to the Reader." *The Dial,* July 1, 1840, 2–3.

————. *Emerson's Antislavery Writings.* Edited by Len Gougeon and Joel Myerson. New Haven, Conn.: Yale University Press, 1995.

————. *The Journals and Miscellaneous Notebooks of Ralph Waldo Emerson.* Edited by William H. Gilman et al. 16 vols. Cambridge, Mass.: Harvard University Press, 1960–82.

————. *The Letters of Ralph Waldo Emerson.* Edited by Ralph Rusk and Eleanor Tilton. 10 vols. New York: Columbia University Press, 1939–95.

Ericson, David F. *The Debate over Slavery: Antislavery and Proslavery Liberalism in Antebellum America.* New York: New York University Press, 2000.

Esquith, Stephen L. *Intimacy and Spectacle: Liberal Theory as Political Education.* Ithaca, N.Y.: Cornell University Press, 1994.

Evans, Dylan. *An Introductory Dictionary of Lacanian Psychoanalysis.* New York: Routledge, 1996.

Evarts, Jeremiah (attributed). "Review of the Dorchester Controversy." *Panoplist and Missionary Magazine* 10 (1814): 256–81, 289–307.

Fanuzzi, Robert. *Abolition's Public Sphere.* Minneapolis: University of Minnesota Press, 2003.

————. "The Organ of an Individual: William Lloyd Garrison and the *Liberator.*" *Prospects* 23 (June 2000): 107–27.

Festenstein, Matthew, and Simon Thompson, eds. *Richard Rorty: Critical Dialogues*. Cambridge: Polity, 2001.

Fishkin, Shelley Fisher, and Carla L. Peterson. "'We Hold These Truths to Be Self-Evident': The Rhetoric of Frederick Douglass's Journalism." In *The Black Press: New Literary and Historical Essays*, edited by Todd Vogel, 71–89. New Brunswick, N.J.: Rutgers University Press, 2001.

Fraser, Nancy. "Rethinking the Public Sphere: A Contribution to the Critique of Actually Existing Democracy." In *Habermas and the Public Sphere*, edited by Craig Calhoun, 109–42. Cambridge, Mass.: MIT Press, 1992.

———. "Struggle over Needs: Outline of a Socialist-Feminist Critical Theory of Late-Capitalist Political Culture." In *Women, the State, and Welfare*, edited by Linda Gordon, 199–225. Madison: University of Wisconsin Press, 1990.

———. *Unruly Practices: Discourse and Gender in Contemporary Social Theory*. Minneapolis: University of Minnesota Press, 1989.

———. "What's Critical about Critical Theory." In *Feminists Read Habermas: Gendering the Subject of Discourse*, edited by Johanna A. Meehan, 21–56. New York: Routledge, 1995.

Freedman, Estelle B. *Their Sister's Keepers: Women's Prison Reform in America, 1830–1930*. Ann Arbor: University of Michigan Press, 1981.

Friedman, Lawrence J. *Gregarious Saints: Self and Community in American Abolitionism, 1830–1870*. New York: Cambridge University Press, 1982.

Fuller, Margaret. *Memoirs of Margaret Fuller Ossoli*. Edited by James Freeman Clarke and Ralph Waldo Emerson. 2 vols. Boston: Phillips, Sampson, 1851.

Furness, Henry, ed. *Records of a Lifelong Friendship: Ralph Waldo Emerson and William Henry Furness*. Boston: Houghton Mifflin, 1910.

Garrison, William Lloyd. *The Letters of William Lloyd Garrison*. Edited by Walter M. Merrill and Louis Ruchames. 6 vols. Cambridge, Mass.: Harvard University Press, 1971–81.

———. *The Liberator*. Boston, 1831–65.

Garvey, T. Gregory. "Introduction: The Emerson Dilemma." In *The Emerson Dilemma: Essays on Emerson and Social Reform*, edited by T. Gregory Garvey, xi–xxvii. Athens: University of Georgia Press, 2001.

Gates, Henry Louis, Jr. *Figures in Black: Words, Signs, and the "Racial" Self*. New York: Oxford University Press, 1987.

Giles, Paul. "Narrative Reversals and Power Exchange: Frederick Douglass and British Culture." *American Literature* 73, no. 4 (2001): 779–810.

Ginzberg, Lori D. *Women and the Work of Benevolence: Morality, Politics, and Class in the Nineteenth-Century United States*. New Haven, Conn.: Yale University Press, 1990.

Goodman, Paul. *Of One Blood: Abolitionism and the Origins of Racial Equality*. Berkeley: University of California Press, 1998.

Gougeon, Len. "'Fortune of the Republic': Emerson, Lincoln, and Transcendental Warfare." *ESQ: A Journal of the American Renaissance* 45, no. 2–3 (1999): 259–324.

———. *Virtue's Hero: Emerson, Antislavery, and Reform.* Athens: University of Georgia Press,
1990.

Grimké, Angelina. *Letters to Catherine E. Beecher, in Reply to an Essay on Slavery and Abolitionism.*
Boston: I. Knapp, 1838.

Grimké, Angelina, and Sarah Grimké. *Letters of Theodore Weld, Angelina Grimké Weld, and Sarah
Grimké.* Edited by Gilbert H. Barnes and Dwight L. Dumond. 2 vols. New York:
D. Appleton–Century, 1938.

———. *Public Years of Sarah and Angelina Grimké: Selected Writings, 1835–1839.* Edited by Larry
Ceplair. New York: Columbia University Press, 1989.

Grimké, Sarah M. *Letters on the Equality of the Sexes and the Condition of Woman: Addressed to
Mary S. Parker, President of the Boston Female Anti-Slavery Society.* Boston: I. Knapp, 1838.

Gutmann, Amy. *Identity in Democracy.* Princeton, N.J.: Princeton University Press, 2003.

Gutmann, Amy, and Dennis Thompson. *Democracy and Disagreement.* Cambridge, Mass.:
Harvard University Press, 1996.

Habermas, Jürgen. *Justification and Application: Remarks on Discourse Ethics.* Translated by Ciaran
Cronin. Cambridge, Mass.: MIT Press, 1990.

———. *Legitimation Crisis.* Translated by Thomas McCarthy. Boston: Beacon Press, 1973.

———. *Moral Consciousness and Communicative Action.* Translated by Christian Lenhardt
and Shierry Weber Nicholsen. Cambridge, Mass.: MIT Press, 1990.

———. *The Structural Transformation of the Public Sphere: An Inquiry into a Category of Bourgeois
Society.* 1962. Translated by Thomas Burger. Cambridge, Mass.: MIT Press, 1989.

———. *Theory of Communicative Action.* Translated by Thomas McCarthy. 2 vols. Boston:
Beacon Press, 1987.

Hale, Sarah Josepha. *The Lecturess, or Woman's Sphere.* Boston: Whipple & Damrell, 1839.

Handlin, Lilian. "Babylon est Delenda—The Young Andrews Norton." In *American
Unitarianism: 1805–1865,* edited by Conrad E. Wright, 63–76. Boston: Massachusetts
Historical Society and Northeastern University Press, 1989.

Hatch, Nathan O. *The Democratization of American Christianity.* New Haven, Conn.: Yale
University Press, 1989.

Hedrick, Joan D. *Harriet Beecher Stowe: A Life.* New York: Oxford University Press, 1994.

Henry, Katherine. "Angelina Grimké's Rhetoric of Exposure." *American Quarterly* 49, no.
2 (1997): 328–55.

Hewitt, Nancy. *Women's Activism and Social Change: Rochester, New York, 1822–1872.* Ithaca,
N.Y.: Cornell University Press, 1984.

Heyrick, Elizabeth. *Immediate, Not Gradual Abolition.* Manchester: Henry Smith, 1826.

Hobson, Barbara Meil. *Uneasy Virtue: The Politics of Prostitution and the American Reform Tradition.*
New York: Basic Books, 1987.

Hofstadter, Richard. *The Paranoid Style in American Politics and Other Essays.* New York: Knopf, 1965.

Hoganson, Kristin. "Garrisonian Abolitionists and the Rhetoric of Gender, 1850–1860." *American Quarterly* 45, no. 4 (Dec. 1993): 558–95.

Honneth, Axel. *The Fragmented World of the Social: Essays on Social and Political Philosophy.* Albany: State University of New York Press, 1995.

Honneth, Axel, and Hans Joas. Introduction to *Communicative Action: Essays on Jürgen Habermas's Theory of Communicative Action,* edited by Axel Honneth and Hans Joas. Cambridge, Mass.: MIT Press, 1991.

Howe, Daniel Walker. *The Unitarian Conscience: Harvard Moral Philosophy, 1805–1861.* Cambridge, Mass.: Harvard University Press, 1970.

Hutchinson, William R. *The Transcendentalist Ministers: Church Reform in the New England Renaissance.* New Haven, Conn.: Yale University Press, 1959.

Isenberg, Nancy. *Sex and Citizenship in Antebellum America.* Chapel Hill: University of North Carolina Press, 1998.

Jackson, Leon. "Jedidiah Morse and the Transformation of Print Culture in New England, 1784–1826." *Early American Literature* 34, no. 1 (1999): 2–31.

Jasinski, James. "Rearticulating History in Epideictic Discourse: Frederick Douglass's 'The Meaning of the Fourth of July to the Negro.'" In *Rhetoric and Political Culture in Nineteenth-Century America,* edited by Thomas W. Benson, 71–89. East Lansing: Michigan State University Press, 1997.

Johnson, Andrew. *Speeches of Andrew Johnson, President of the United States.* Edited by Frank Moore. Boston: Little, Brown, 1865.

Johnson, Linck C. "Emerson, Thoreau's Arrest, and the Trials of American Manhood." In *The Emerson Dilemma: Essays on Emerson and Social Reform,* edited by T. Gregory Garvey, 35–66. Athens: University of Georgia Press, 2001.

———. "Reforming the Reformers: Emerson, Thoreau, and the Sunday Lectures at Amory Hall, Boston." *ESQ: A Journal of the American Renaissance* 37 (1991): 241–54.

Kateb, George. *Emerson and Self-Reliance.* Thousand Oaks, Calif.: Sage Publications, 1995.

———. *The Inner Ocean: Individualism and Democratic Culture.* Ithaca, N.Y.: Cornell University Press, 1992.

Kelley, Mary. "Vindicating the Equality of Female Intellect: Women and Authority in the Early Republic." *Prospects: An Annual of American Cultural Studies* 17 (1992): 1–27.

Kirkland, Frank M. "Enslavement, Moral Suasion, and Struggles for Recognition: Frederick Douglass's Answer to the Question—'What Is Enlightenment?'" In *Frederick Douglass: A Critical Reader,* edited by Bill E. Lawson and Frank M. Kirkland, 243–310. Malden, Mass.: Blackwell, 1999.

Lerner, Gerda. *The Grimké Sisters of South Carolina: Rebels against Slavery.* Boston: Houghton Mifflin, 1967.

Leverenz, David. *Manhood and the American Renaissance*. Ithaca, N.Y.: Cornell University Press, 1989.

Levin, Jonathan. *The Poetics of Transition: Emerson, Pragmatism, and American Literary Modernism*. Durham, N.C.: Duke University Press, 1999.

Levine, Robert. *Martin Delany, Frederick Douglass and the Politics of Representative Identity*. Chapel Hill: University of North Carolina Press, 1997.

Levy, Leonard W. Editor. *Blasphemy in Massachusetts, Freedom of Conscience, and the Abner Kneeland Case: A Documentary Record*. New York: Da Capo Press, 1973.

Lincoln, Abraham. *The Collected Works of Abraham Lincoln*. Edited by Roy P. Basler et al. 8 vols. New Brunswick, N.J.: Rutgers University Press, 1953–55.

Lopez, Michael. *Emerson and Power: Creative Antagonism in the Nineteenth Century*. Dekalb: Northern Illinois University Press, 1996.

Lowell, James Russell. *The Complete Poetical Works of James Russell Lowell*. Boston: Houghton Mifflin, 1896.

———. *Letters of James Russell Lowell*. Edited by Charles Eliot Norton. 2 vols. New York: Harper, 1894.

Lumpkin, Katharine DuPre. *The Emancipation of Angelina Grimké*. Chapel Hill: University of North Carolina Press, 1974.

Luria, Sarah. "Racial Equality Begins at Home: Frederick Douglass's Challenge to American Domesticity." In *The American Home: Material Culture, Domestic Space, and Family Life*, edited by Eleanor Thompson, 25–43. Hanover, N.H.: University Press of New England, 1998.

Marshall, John. "Memorial on Behalf of the Nonfreeholders of Richmond, Virginia." In *Proceedings and Debates of the Virginia State Convention of 1829–1830*, 27. Richmond: Ritchie & Cooke, 1830.

Martin, Waldo E., Jr. *The Mind of Frederick Douglass*. Chapel Hill: University of North Carolina Press, 1984.

Martineau, Harriet. *Society in America*. Edited by Peter Smith. New York: Doubleday, 1962.

Masur, Louis P. *1831: Year of Eclipse*. New York: Hill & Wang, 2001.

Matthews, Glenna. *Just a Housewife: The Rise and Fall of Domesticity in America*. New York: Oxford University Press, 1987.

May, Henry. *The Enlightenment in America*. New York: Oxford University Press, 1976.

Mayer, Henry. *All on Fire: William Lloyd Garrison and the Abolition of Slavery*. New York: St. Martin's Press, 1998.

McCarthy, Thomas. *The Critical Theory of Jürgen Habermas*. Cambridge, Mass.: MIT Press, 1978.

McFeely, William S. *Frederick Douglass*. New York: W. W. Norton, 1991.

McKivigan, John R. "The Frederick Douglass–Gerrit Smith Friendship." In *Frederick

Douglass: New Literary and Historical Essays, edited by Eric Sundquist, 205–32. Cambridge: Cambridge University Press, 1991.

Merrill, Walter McIntosh. *Against Wind and Tide: A Biography of William Lloyd Garrison.* Cambridge, Mass.: Harvard University Press, 1963.

Miller, Perry. *Nature's Nation.* Cambridge, Mass.: Belknap Press, 1967.

Miller, Samuel. *Letters on Unitarianism.* Trenton, N.J.: G. Sherman, 1821.

Mills, Charles W. "Whose Fourth of July? Frederick Douglass and 'Original Intent.'" In *Frederick Douglass: A Critical Reader*, edited by Bill E. Lawson and Frank M. Kirkland, 109–16. Malden, Mass.: Blackwell, 1999.

Mintz, Steven. *Moralists and Modernizers: America's Pre–Civil War Reformers.* Baltimore: Johns Hopkins University Press, 1995.

Moberg, David O. *The Church as a Social Institution: The Sociology of American Religion.* Englewood Cliffs, N.J.: Prentice Hall, 1962.

Moon, J. Donald. "Practical Discourse and Communicative Ethics." In *The Cambridge Companion to Habermas*, edited by Stephen K. White, 143–66. New York: Cambridge University Press, 1995.

Morse, Jedidiah. *A Sermon Exhibiting the Present Dangers, and Consequent Duties of the Citizens of the United States of America: Delivered at Charlestown, April 25, 1799, the Day of the National Fast.* Charlestown, Mass: Printed and sold by Samuel Ethridge, 1799.

Moss, Richard J. *The Life of Jedidiah Morse: A Station of Peculiar Exposure.* Knoxville: University of Tennessee Press, 1995.

Moynihan, Ruth Barnes, Cynthia Russert, and Laurie Crumpacker, eds. *Second to None: A Documentary History of American Women.* Lincoln: University of Nebraska Press, 1993.

Newfield, Christopher. *The Emerson Effect: Individualism and Submission in America.* Chicago: University of Chicago Press, 1996.

Noll, Mark A. *A History of Christianity in the United States and Canada.* Grand Rapids, Mich.: W. B. Eerdmans, 1992.

Pease, Jane H., and William H. Pease. "Whose Right Hand of Fellowship? Pew and Pulpit in Shaping Church Practice." In *American Unitarianism: 1805–1865*, edited by Conrad E. Wright, 181–206. Boston: Massachusetts Historical Society and Northeastern University Press, 1989.

Perry, Lewis. *Radical Abolitionism: Anarchy and the Government of a God in Antislavery Thought.* Ithaca, N.Y.: Cornell University Press, 1973.

Phillips, Joseph W. *Jedidiah Morse and New England Congregationalism.* New Brunswick, N.J.: Rutgers University Press, 1983.

Poirier, Richard. *Poetry and Pragmatism.* Cambridge, Mass.: Harvard University Press, 1992.

Pole, R. J. *The Pursuit of Equality in American History.* Rev. ed. Berkeley: University of California Press, 1993.

Potter, David M. *The Impending Crisis: 1848–1861*. New York: Harper Collins, 1976.

Preston, Jo Anne. "Domestic Ideology, School Reformers, and Female Teachers: School Teaching Becomes Women's Work in Nineteenth-Century New England." *New England Quarterly* 66, no. 4 (1993): 531–51.

Rawls, John. *The Law of Peoples*. Cambridge, Mass.: Harvard University Press, 1999.

———. *Political Liberalism*. New York: Columbia University Press, 1993.

Reports of the Proceedings and Debates of the Convention of 1821, Assembled for the Purpose of Amending the Constitution of the State of New York. Albany, 1821.

"A Review of the Rev. Dr. Channing's Discourse, Preached at the Dedication of the Second Congregationalist Unitarian Church, New York, December 7, 1826." Boston, 1827.

Rice, Madeleine Hooke. *Federal Street Pastor: The Life of William Ellery Channing*. New York: Bookman Associates, 1961.

Richardson, Robert D., Jr. *Emerson: The Mind on Fire*. Los Angeles: University of California Press, 1995.

Robinson, David. *The Unitarians and the Universalists*. Westport, Conn.: Greenwood Press, 1985.

Rorty, Richard. *Philosophy and the Mirror of Nature*. Princeton, N.J.: Princeton University Press, 1979.

———. *Philosophy and Social Hope*. New York: Penguin, 1999.

Rotundo, E. Anthony. "Learning about Manhood: Gender Ideals and the Middle-Class Family in Nineteenth-Century America." In *Manliness and Morality: Middle-Class Masculinity in Britain and America, 1800–1940*, edited by J. A. Morgan and James Walvin, 35–51. New York: St. Martin's Press, 1987.

Rousseau, Jean-Jacques. *The Social Contract*. 1762. Translated by Maurice Cranston. New York: Penguin Books, 1968.

Rowe, John Carlos. *At Emerson's Tomb: The Politics of Classic American Literature*. New York: Columbia University Press, 1997.

Ruttenburg, Nancy. *Democratic Personality: Popular Voice and the Trial of American Authorship*. Stanford, Calif.: Stanford University Press, 1998.

Ryan, Mary P. "Femininity and Capitalism in Antebellum America." In *Capitalist Patriarchy and the Case for Socialist Feminism*, edited by Zillah Einstein, 67–91. New York: Monthly Review Press, 1979.

———. "Gender and Public Access: Women's Politics in Nineteenth-Century America." In *Habermas and the Public Sphere*, edited by Craig Calhoun, 259–88. Cambridge, Mass.: MIT Press, 1992.

———. *Women in Public: Between Banners and Ballots 1825–1880*. Baltimore: Johns Hopkins University Press, 1990.

Sanchez-Eppler, Karen. *Touching Liberty: Abolition, Feminism, and the Politics of the Body*. Berkeley: University of California Press, 1993.

Schantz, Mark. "Religious Tracts, Evangelical Reform, and the Market Revolution in Antebellum America." *Journal of the Early Republic* 17 (Fall 1997): 425–66.

Schrader, David E. "Natural Law in the Constitutional Thought of Frederick Douglass." In *Frederick Douglass: A Critical Reader*, edited by Bill E. Lawson and Frank M. Kirkland, 85–99. Oxford: Blackwell, 1999.

Schudson, Michael. "Was There Ever a Public Sphere? If So, When? Reflections on the American Case." In *Habermas and the Public Sphere*, edited by Craig Calhoun, 143–63. Cambridge, Mass.: MIT Press, 1992.

Selby, Gary S. "The Limits of Accommodation: Frederick Douglass and the Garrisonian Abolitionists." *The Southern Communication Journal* 66, no. 1 (2000): 52–66.

Sen, Amartya. "Equality of What?" In *The Tanner Lectures on Human Values*, edited by S. M. McMurrin, 195–220. New York: Cambridge University Press, 1980.

Sennett, Richard. *The Fall of Public Man.* New York: Alfred A. Knopf, 1977.

Sklar, Kathryn Kish. *Catharine Beecher: A Study in American Domesticity.* New Haven, Conn.: Yale University Press, 1973.

Smith, Timothy L. *Revivalism and Social Reform in Mid-Nineteenth-Century America.* New York: Abingdon Press, 1957.

Stange, Douglas C. *Patterns of Antislavery among American Unitarians, 1831–1860.* Teaneck, N.J.: Fairleigh Dickinson University Press, 1977.

Steele, Jeffrey A. "The Limits of Political Sympathy: Emerson, Margaret Fuller, and Woman's Rights." In *The Emerson Dilemma: Essays on Emerson and Social Reform*, edited by T. Gregory Garvey, 115–38. Athens: University of Georgia Press, 2001.

Stepto, Robert B. *From Behind the Veil: A Study of Afro-American Narrative.* 2nd ed. Chicago: University of Illinois Press, 1991.

Stewart, James B. "The Aims and Impact of Garrisonian Abolitionism, 1840–1860." *Civil War History* 15 (1969): 197–209.

Stewart, Roderick M. "The Claims of Frederick Douglass Philosophically Considered." In *Frederick Douglass: A Critical Reader*, edited by Bill E. Lawson and Frank M. Kirkland, 145–72. Malden, Mass.: Blackwell, 1999.

Story, Ronald. "Harvard and the Boston Brahmins: A Study in Institutional and Class Development, 1800–1865." *Journal of Social History* (Spring 1975): 99–104.

Strong, Douglas M. *Perfectionist Politics: Abolitionism and the Religious Tensions of American Democracy.* Syracuse, N.Y.: Syracuse University Press, 1999.

Stuart, Moses. *Letters to the Rev. Wm. E. Channing, Containing Remarks on His Sermon Recently Preached and Published at Baltimore.* Andover, Mass.: Flagg & Gould, 1819.

Sundquist, Eric J. *To Wake the Nations: Race in the Making of American Literature.* Cambridge, Mass.: Belknap Press, 1993.

Taylor, Charles. "Language and Society." In *Communicative Action: Essays on Jürgen Habermas's Theory of Communicative Action*, edited by Axel Honneth and Hans Joas, 23–35. Cambridge, Mass.: MIT Press, 1991.

————. "The Politics of Recognition." In *Multiculturalism and "The Politics of Recognition,"* edited by Amy Gutmann, 25–74. Princeton, N.J.: Princeton University Press, 1992.

Thomas, John L. *The Liberator, William Lloyd Garrison, a Biography.* Boston: Little, Brown, 1965.

Thompson, James W. *Address to the Society.* Concord, Mass.: Henry E. Moore, 1828.

Thoreau, Henry David. *Reform Papers.* Princeton, N.J.: Princeton University Press, 1973.

Tocqueville, Alexis de. *Democracy in America.* Translated by George Lawrence. New York: Harper & Row, 1966.

Tolstoi, Leo. "What I Owe to Garrison." In *William Lloyd Garrison on Non-Resistance,* edited by Fanny Garrison Villard, 3–12. New York: Nation Press, 1924.

Tompkins, Jane. *Sensational Designs: The Cultural Work of American Fiction, 1790–1860.* New York: Oxford University Press, 1985.

Van Cromphout, Gustaaf. *Emerson's Ethics.* Columbia: University of Missouri Press, 1999.

von Frank, Albert J. *An Emerson Chronology.* New York: G. K. Hall, 1994.

————. "Mrs. Brackett's Verdict: Magic and Means in Transcendental Antislavery Work." In *The Transcendentalist Movement and Its Contexts,* edited by Charles Capper and Conrad Edick Wright, 385–406. Boston: Massachusetts Historical Society, 1999.

————. *The Trials of Anthony Burns: Freedom and Slavery in Emerson's Boston.* Cambridge, Mass.: Harvard University Press, 1998.

Wach, Howard M. "Unitarian Philanthropy and Cultural Hegemony in Comparative Perspective: Manchester and Boston, 1827–1848." *Journal of Social History* (Spring 1993): 539–59.

Walker, David. *David Walker's Appeal in Four Articles, Together with a Preamble to the Coloured Citizens of the World, but in particular and very expressly to those of the United States of America.* 1829. Reprint, New York: Hill & Wang, 1995.

Walters, Ronald G. *American Reformers, 1815–1860.* New York: Hill & Wang, 1978.

Wardrop, Daneen. "'While I Am Writing': Webster's 1825 *Spelling Book,* the Ell, and Frederick Douglass's Positioning of Language." *African American Review* 32, no. 4 (1998): 649–60.

Warner, Michael. *The Letters of the Republic: Publication and the Public Sphere in Eighteenth Century America.* Cambridge, Mass.: Harvard University Press, 1990.

Warnke, Georgia. *Justice and Interpretation.* Cambridge, Mass.: MIT Press, 1993.

Webster, Daniel. *Journal of Debates and Proceedings in the Convention of Delegates Chosen to Revise the Constitution of Massachusetts.* New edition, revised and corrected. Boston, 1853.

————. *The Writings and Speeches of Daniel Webster.* 18 vols. Boston: Little, Brown, 1903.

Westphal, Merold. *Hegel, Freedom and Modernity.* Albany: State University of New York Press, 1992.

Wiecek, William M. *The Sources of Antislavery Constitutionalism in America, 1760–1848.* Ithaca, N.Y.: Cornell University Press, 1977.

Wiegman, Robyn. *American Anatomies: Theorizing Race and Gender*. Durham, N.C.: Duke University Press, 1995.

Wilbur, Earl Morris. *A History of Unitarianism*. Cambridge, Mass.: Harvard University Press, 1945–52.

Williamson, Chilton. *American Suffrage: From Property to Democracy, 1760–1860*. Princeton, N.J.: Princeton University Press, 1960.

Wineapple, Brenda. *Hawthorne: A Life*. New York: Alfred A. Knopf, 2003.

Wright, Conrad E. *The Beginnings of Unitarianism in America*. Boston: Beacon Press, 1955.

———. "Institutional Reconstruction in the Unitarian Controversy." In *American Unitarianism: 1805–1865*, edited by Conrad E. Wright, 3–30. Boston: Massachusetts Historical Society and Northeastern University Press, 1989.

———. *The Liberal Christians: Essays on American Unitarian History*. Boston: Beacon Press, 1970.

Wright, Elizur. "Slavery and Its Ecclesiastical Defenders." *Quarterly Antislavery Magazine* 1 (1836): 341.

Young, James P. *Reconsidering American Liberalism: The Troubled Odyssey of the Liberal Idea*. Boulder, Colo.: Westview Press, 1996.

Zschoche, Sue. "Dr. Clark Revisited: Science, True Womanhood, and Female Collegiate Education." *History of Education Quarterly* 29, no. 4 (1989): 545–69.

Zwarg, Christina. *Feminist Conversations: Fuller, Emerson, and the Play of Reading*. Ithaca, N.Y.: Cornell University Press, 1995.

INDEX

and antislavery movement, 81–82; appropriation of religious discourse by, 95; compared with Catharine Beecher, 78–79, 106, 107, 114, 119–20, 212n22; compared with Douglass, 22–23, 121–22, 123–24, 141–42, 145–47; compared with Emerson, 200; compared with Garrison, 127, 130; compared with the Pilgrims, 83; feminism of, 90, 96; four-step program of, 102; and justice, 92; letter of, to Garrison, 81, 84, 87, 211n10; ministry's attempt to suppress, 97–100; and public sphere, 80–81, 85–86, 211n12; and Quakerism, 81–82; rebuttal of, to Catharine Beecher's argument for women's deference, 91–92; and restructuring of public discourse, 88; and revision of the critical public, 95; and sincerity, 212n17; transgression of, 85–86; and treatment of publicity, 90; and universal equality, 90; on women's rights to political speech, 95

Grimké, Angelina, works of: *Appeal to the Christian Women of the South*, 78–108 passim, 163, 212n24; "Human Rights Not Founded on Sex," 90

Grimké, Sarah, 75, 78, 81, 98; compared with Pilgrims, 83

Grimké, Sarah, works of: *Epistle to the Clergy of the Southern States*, 82–83; *Letters on the Equality of the Sexes and the Condition of Women*, 83

Grimké-Beecher debate, 6–7, 25, 146, 164, 166

Habermas, Jürgen, 13, 87, 179, 202, 212n19; on authority, 33, 109–10, 205n32; on bourgeois public sphere,

15, 18; on critical public discourse, 14–20; on democracy, 179; on ideal speech situation, 15–16, 204nn12–13; on sincerity, 15; on strategic action, 15, 204n13; on truthfulness, 16

Hale, Sarah Josepha, 75, 210–11n7; *Lectruess*, 95

Hall of Science, 54

Hartford Female Academy, 78, 80, 211n9

Harvard College, 41; growth of liberal Christianity at, 45

Hatch, Nathan, 33–34, 36; *Democratization of American Religion*, 33

Hawthorne, Nathaniel, 38; *Scarlet Letter*, 116

Hegel, Georg Wilhelm Friedrich, 214n1

Henry, Catherine, 85–86

Higginson, Thomas W., 68

Hofstadter, Richard, 16

Hoganson, Kristin, 143

home, 120, 179, 182; and church, 103; as new kind of church, 118; professionalization of, 104; as public institution, 104, 118–19

Homestead Bill, 22

homogeneity, 24, 29, 77, 101

Hooker, Asahel, 45

Hopkins, Daniel, 38–39, 44, 45

Hopkins, Samuel, 38

Horkheimer, Max, 37

House of Representatives, 25, 219n2; 1835 gag rule, 25

Howard Sunday School, 68

humanism, 46; and Christianity, 60; civic, 72; of Declaration of Independence, 89; discourse of, 60; liberal, 216n24

humanity's "likeness to God," 55, 59, 62–63, 71

women, 17; access for, 19, 75, 83, 90, 123,
199; activism of, 74–76, 95, 102, 109;
and antislavery movement, 83, 87,
90, 93, 94, 119; and authority, 74–78,
88, 103, 106–8, 111–19, 210n7; and
the church, 97–101; and citizenship,
99, 211n9; civic obligations of, 94,
96; and civil society, 97–102; and
critical discourse, 74, 83, 84, 118; as
cultural mediators, 118; deference
of, to masculine political authority,
91–92; disenfranchisement of, 75,
90, 107, 115, 116, 118; disestablishment
of, 100; education of, 79, 90, 104–5,
212n22; entrance of, into the public
sphere, 210n2; equality of, 75, 77,
83, 88, 91, 94; in evangelical reform,
91; and "female politician," 77, 79;
femininity of, 6; identity of, 106;
influence of, 120; intellectual lives of,
89; as mediators of virtue, 106, 118;
and ministry, 75, 91, 103, 105, 118; moral
nature of, 90; and partisanship, 7;
and political consciousness, 212n22;
political speech of, 85, 94, 95, 98–99;
power of, 103, 115; professional status
of, 104, 106; and public discourse,
83, 100; as public intellectuals,
77; and publicity, 80, 97–102; as
reformers, 74, 75, 76; rights of (see
women's rights); role of, in American
society, 115, 211n9; self-education
of, 90; and slavery, 94; southern,
78, 84, 85, 89, 93, 95; subjectivity
of, 88, 102; and sympathy, 114; as

teachers, 106–7; Tocqueville on,
115
women's associations, 108
women's education, 79, 90, 104–5, 212n22
women's reform movements, 76, 98, 112,
203n5
women's rights, 1–5 passim, 23, 25;
Angelina Grimké on, 96–97, 101,
119–20; and antislavery, 73, 82; as
divisive issue among reformers, 132; to
free speech, 75; and Garrison, 131, 132,
216n16; and publicity, 66; and Unitarian
controversy, 76–77. *See also* feminism;
women's rights movement
women's rights convention at Seneca Falls,
84, 132
women's rights movement, 199, 203n5;
Emerson's criticism of, 161
women's suffrage, 107
women teachers, 117
working-class movement, 54
Working Man's Advocate, 54
Workingmen's party, 54
World Anti-Slavery Meeting, 132
worship: collective, 168–69; individual,
168; secularization of, 63
Wright, Conrad, 41
Wright, Elizur, 70, 82
Wright, Frances, 54, 75
Wright, Henry C., 132, 138

Young, James P., 27

Zwarg, Christina, 164–65